DWELLING, SEEING, AND DESIGNING

SUNY Series in Environmental and Architectural Phenomenology

David Seamon, Editor

DWELLING, SEEING, AND DESIGNING

TOWARD A
PHENOMENOLOGICAL ECOLOGY

Edited by

David Seamon

1993

State University of New York Press

Published by
State University of New York Press, Albany

© 1993 State University of New York

For information, address State University of New York
Press, State University Plaza, Albany, N.Y., 12246

Production by Diane Ganeles
Marketing by Lynne Lekakis

Library of Congress Cataloging-in-Publication Data

Dwelling, seeing, and designing : toward a phenomenological ecology /
    edited by David Seamon.
        p.   cm. — (SUNY series in environmental and architectural
    phenomenology)
    Includes bibliographical references.
    ISBN (invalid) 0–7914–0277–6 (acid-free). — ISBN (invalid)
    0–7914–0278–4 (pbk. : acid-free)
        1. Architecture—Environmental aspects.   2. Phenomenology.
    I. Seamon, David.   II. Series.
    NA2542.35.D88   1993
    720'.1—dc20   91–43854
                                                                    CIP

10 9 8 7 6 5 4 3 2 1

Contents

Part III. Living, Understanding, and Designing

Illustrations

Tables

Acknowledgments

In the preparation of this collection, I would like to thank Kansas State University for faculty research grants in 1988, 1989, and 1990. I am also grateful for two Design Arts grants from the National Endowment for the Arts. These grants provided me a practical context for pondering conceptual ways whereby theory and practice in regard to the natural and built environments might be better brought together in harmony.

I also wish to thank the many individuals who have contributed to this collection in various ways. First, I would like to thank Claire Waffle and Renée Frasier, who have helped with many of the practical needs required by this collection, especially relaying messages between the contributors and me. I am particularly grateful to Peggie Armour, who typed and retyped most of the manuscript. Without her interest, competence, and speed, this volume would have required many more months of work.

I would also like to thank graduate students Lee Schriever, Anne Vittoria, Alma Hubbard, Murali Ramaswami, Louise Million, and Yuan Lin, who talked through various stages of this project with me and read drafts of articles. I am also grateful to the following colleagues, who encouraged my work on this collection either directly or indirectly: Mark Lapping, Bob Burnham, William Miller, Gary Coates, Susanne Siepl-Coates, George Tunstall, David Rothenberg, Warwick Fox, Saul Kuchinsky, Anne Buttimer, David Saile, Fran Violich, Joe Grange, Karen Franck, Luna Carne-Ross, David Appelbaum, Pat Condon, Kim Dovey, Cathy Alington, Ray Streeter, Carola Sautter, and Diane Ganeles. I express particular thanks to Margaret Boschetti, who struggles with the same philosophical and methodological questions that I do. She has been a sounding board and critic, and I am very much appreciative.

I would also like to thank colleague Robert Mugerauer, with whom I collaborated on an earlier phenomenological collection, *Dwelling, Place, and Environment*. Bob realized my need to edit a collection on my own and has continued to offer invaluable advice and encouragement. When I have felt disheartened or dubious about my devotion to phenomenological work, Bob has always been there to return me to my aim. Finally, I express my deep gratitude to Jim Ryan, who in the last five years has helped me see aspects of the world to which I was oblivious before.

To all these people, as well as the many others who have voiced support for the kind of phenomenological research presented in this collection, I am sincerely grateful. May the essays of this volume help the world to become a better place by helping us to imagine better environments and to become better people.

David Seamon

Chapter 1

Dwelling, Seeing, and Designing:
An Introduction

◻

David Seamon

In the last several years, I have come to believe firmly that phenomenology provides an important intellectual means for healing the rifts between art and science, seeing and understanding, knowledge and action, and design and building. As an environment-behavior researcher working with architects and landscape architects, I have sought to communicate with scholars and designers who use a phenomenological perspective, either explicitly or implicitly, and to synthesize their work in review articles and edited collections.[1] *Dwelling, Seeing and Designing* is one step toward this aim and in many ways can be seen as a companion to *Dwelling, Place, and Environment,* an earlier volume of phenomenological essays that I edited with philosopher Robert Mugerauer (Seamon and Mugerauer, 1985).

The greatest contrast between these two books is that this new collection represents fewer disciplines and gives more attention to environmental design and the built environment. Of the thirteen contributors, seven are environmental designers—four architects, two landscape architects and one planner; and six are in the sciences and humanities—three geographers, two philosophers, and one ecologist. In requesting essays, I suggested in my letter of invitation that contributors might focus on such themes as environmental awareness, environmental aesthetics, architectural experience, architectural meaning, and environmental design as place making. I was particularly interested in design and scholarly work that illustrates the reciprocal relationship between human livability and the built environment. I hoped for real-world examples of environmental design nurtured by phenomenological and related understandings.

1

Eventually, I received the thirteen articles presented here, which I have arranged around three major themes: First, modernity and the built environment; second, architectural and landscape meaning; and, third, relationships among living, understanding and designing. This introduction overviews these three themes and considers underlying commonalities. My hope is that the essays of this collection illustrate how phenomenological and similar qualitative approaches can lead to environmental understanding and design more in tune with our experiences and lives as human beings in the everyday world.

Part I. Modernity and the Built Environment: Problems and Possibilities

The three articles in part I of the collection are by geographer Edward Relph, philosopher Karsten Harries, and landscape architect Catherine Howett. These authors suggest that current Western environments are too often determined by economic, technological or aesthetic concerns alone and do not always relate to the full range of human experience, particularly a sense of place and dwelling. In various ways, the three authors argue that the built environment contributes to who we are as human beings and partly establishes how we see, understand and live in the world.

In "Modernity and the Reclamation of Place," Edward Relph emphasizes that a sense of place is not a romantic anachronism as some modern thinkers, particularly post-structuralists and deconstructivists, claim. Rather, places are an integral part of psychological and social well-being. Relph points out that a sense of place cannot be designed and created in all its details, since by its very nature, place is largely ineffable and indeterminate. Yet Relph suggests that an explicit understanding of place might contribute to political, economic and design decisions that would support and enhance particular places.

A key need is the involvement and commitment of people who live and work in these places, which must be made "from the inside out." In this sense, designers and policy-makers are no longer environmental manipulators but, rather, environmental midwives who provide "direction and advice based on their special skills and breadth of experience that allow them to resolve specific technical matters, overcome parochialism, and see the broad effects and implications of local actions." Relph concludes that an understanding of place might help to facilitate locally committed development that is self-consciously aware of wider contextual issues and relationships.[2]

Karsten Harries, in his "Thoughts on a Non-Arbitrary Architecture," speaks of modern architecture in much the same way that Relph speaks of modern places: Neither buildings nor planned environments do full justice to the needs of human dwelling because they have been made arbitrarily rather than allowed to arise spontaneously out of the requirements and concerns of particular people and landscapes. Harries begins by criticizing postmodernist approaches to design, which are valuable in that they are creative and free, but troublesome in that they are eclectic and without conviction. The modern Western world is fortunate in that people are no longer constrained geographically or historically and can borrow freely from buildings and design styles of any time or place. The result too often, however, is architecture that is arbitrary in the sense that it could readily be other than what it is formally and stylistically.

Harries argues that the dilemma of arbitrariness cannot be solved by aesthetic, functional, or historical solutions because meaning cannot finally be made or invented. Instead, meaning can only be discovered through the lives and worlds that a building is meant to support and reflect. Harries suggests that the thinking of German philosopher Martin Heidegger (1890–1976), especially his notion of *dwelling* (Heidegger, 1971), provides one conceptual means for considering building as it might sustain and mirror the worlds of particular persons, groups and environments. Harries is not the first scholar to suggest the value of Heidegger's philosophy to architecture (cf. Mugerauer, 1988; Norberg-Schulz, 1980, 1985). What is innovative about Harries's presentation is its call for a language of *natural symbols*—essential meanings that provide identity and orientation in human life, for example, up/down, heavy/light, inside/outside, vertical/horizontal, front/back, left/right, natural/human-made, and so forth.

A key question with which Harries concludes is how architectural elements such as column, lintel, door, and window might be understood as physical expressions of natural symbols and thereby provide one kind of tacit order to particular worlds and places (also see Harries, 1988). Several essays in part II of the collection illustrate how architectural elements like roof and porch can by their very nature express and sustain essential qualities of human experience like insideness, outsideness, threshold and betweenness. In this sense, these articles provide concrete examples of what Harries identifies as the key task of environmental design: "Interpreting the world as a meaningful order in which the individual can find his or her place in the midst of nature and community."[3]

If architecture, from a phenomenological perspective, deals largely with buildings as they support a sense of place and dwelling, then one aim of landscape architecture is to place people in a harmonious way with the world of nature. But as Catherine Howett explains in her essay, " 'If the Doors of Perception Were Cleansed': Toward an Experiential Aesthetics for the Designed Landscape," landscape architecture has often ignored the full range of environmental experience by reducing the landscape to a set of views that satisfy various aesthetic and visual design criteria. Howett summarizes the intellectual history of this "scenographic" approach to landscape architecture and calls for a more comprehensive perspective that would create places where "we are invited to experience nature—and ourselves in community with nature and with each other—more profoundly, more intimately, more physically, than is possible when conventional scenographic values are enforced."

Practically, Howett suggests that a more holistic experience of nature and landscape might be helped if designers gave attention to three themes. First, she advocates an emphasis on *genius loci,* or spirit of place. She believes that a deeper understanding of a place's essential qualities would better attune the landscape architect to the ways that the natural environment contributes to a particular sense of place. Second, Howett suggests that landscape architects should continually be aware of their taken-for-granted design definitions and preferences. How, for example, does one think of "the beautiful," "the tasteful," or "the pleasing"? Through such directed attention, landscape architects might be better able to bypass unself-conscious biases and predilections and open themselves to other design possibilities. Third, Howett suggests that it might be useful to consider landscape design as a living process rather than a static product. In this way, the designer might be better able to create a more holistic environmental experience that would incorporate other senses besides sight and give people the opportunity to participate with landscapes more thoroughly, particularly in terms of bodily and emotional encounter.

As a group, the three essays of Part I suggest that current environmental design and policy are often arbitrary and incomplete.

Environmental scholars and professionals need to find ways whereby places, buildings and landscapes can say for themselves what they are rather than being constricted by a language and interpretation that is imposed from without. The three essays suggest that if academic and professional descriptions of the built environment can be more accurate and thorough, then this deepened understanding might provide the foundation for more humane and harmonious environmental design.[4]

Part II. Interpreting Architecture and Landscape

The essays of Part II illustrate ways in which deepened understanding might be had in regard to particular architectural elements, buildings and landscapes. In "The First Roof: Interpreting a Spatial Pattern," architect Murray Silverstein explores the roof in implicit phenomenological fashion. He suggests that the roof is an essential architectural element because it expresses three polarities that are an integral part of human living: inside/outside, self/world, and practical/ideal. Silverstein examines each of these polarities as they simultaneously shape and are shaped by the roof. Next, he illustrates their practical application in a house designed by Jacobson Silverstein Winslow Architects, the Berkeley architectural firm in which he is a partner.

In Karsten Harries's terms, the polarities described by Silverstein are natural symbols, and his explication of the roof demonstrates how they can be supported, mirrored and drawn together through built form. For example, the roof expresses the inside-outside polarity because it naturally divides the world into two spaces—one that contains and the other that excludes. The automatic, accompanying result is the two distinct experiences of insideness and outsideness. Silverstein also explains how the roof helps to establish the two related existential polarities of self/world and practicality/idealism. *Just by being what it is,* the roof allows particular human meanings to unfold and thereby helps to define and support a human world that is one way rather than another.[5]

This tacit reciprocity between the built environment and human experience is a central phenomenological insight, and philosopher Robert Mugerauer's "Toward an Architectural Vocabulary: The Porch as a Between," draws on Martin Heidegger's interpretation of dwelling and building to clarify this reciprocity further, using Midwestern and Texan porches as an example. In agreement with Harries and Silverstein, Mugerauer suggests that a building element such as *porch* best joins people and world when, through its very nature, it provides particular situations and meanings that are present automatically and require no direct action or attention to happen.

Mugerauer demonstrates in his essay that the porch, like the roof, naturally expresses meaning and directs experience just by being what it is, though the specific nature of these meanings and experiences is considerably different from the roof's. If the latter relates to such essential human qualities as centeredness and selfness, the former relates to *betweenness,* in the sense that the porch makes itself into a place by providing a threshold between inside and outside, people and nature, and individual and society. Mugerauer explains that there are many modes of betweenness and no doubt each is evoked by specific architectural elements such as door, window, foyer and stair. The need he says, echoing Harries, is a phenomenology of architectural elements as they support particular human experiences, situations and events.[6]

A start toward such an architectural phenomenology is suggested by architect Ronald Walkey's "A Lesson in Continuity: The Legacy of the Builders' Guild in Northern Greece," which identifies the special architectural qualities of one particular building type— the multi-story, guild-built houses of mountainous northern Greece, western Turkey, and the adjoining Balkan states. Built from the fifteenth to the late nineteenth centuries, these houses and their communities had a powerful sense of order and place. Walkey examines the building process responsible for these houses and then identifies eight architectural qualities that mark the buildings' essential character. These qualities include seasonal activities, sense of front and back, protection versus openness, ascending lightness, centeredness, and so forth.

Walkey emphasizes that these qualities do not involve imposed, arbitrary rules that the guild builders were forced to incorporate in their construction as, say, a contractor must in building suburban tract houses today. Rather, these qualities resided intuitively in the builders' imaginations and were automatically called forth when a particular dwelling was built. *Iconic house* is the term that Walkey gives to this architectural image arising naturally in the builder's imagination. A major question that Walkey's article suggests is whether such iconic images might be cultivated in a modern design context. One significant tool may be the kind of qualitative explication illustrated in Walkey's study. His work is an important complement to the approaches of Harries, Silverstein, and Mugerauer because he integrates a series of relationships among various natural symbols and architectural forms and demonstrates how they come together as a whole to create a specific building type that is effective both practically and aesthetically.

In "Toward a Phenomenology of Landscape and Landscape Experience: An Example from Catalonia," geographer Joan Nogué i Font moves from the built to the natural environment. He seeks to describe the essential landscape character of *Garrotxa,* a region in Spain's Pyrenees foothills north of Barcelona. Nogué i Font's aim is a phenomenology of region, and to carry out this aim practically, he involves himself in extended discussions with two groups of people at home in the Garrotxa landscape—farmers and landscape painters. Nogué i Font's study is innovative methodologically because it uses the descriptions of insiders to Garrotxa to discover its underlying regional qualities. The study is also important conceptually because it addresses a crucial ontological question that a phenomenology of environment must sooner or later face: Can there be a phenomenology of landscape in its own right, or does there exist only a phenomenology of that landscape as particular individuals and groups experience it?

Nogué i Font answers this question by concluding that both phenomenologies exist and one does not exclude the other. In exploring the Garrotxa experience for the farmers and landscape painters separately, he points out that in some ways the environment has significantly different meanings for the two groups. The farmers, for example, know the landscape most thoroughly at a sensual, bodily level, since practical success provides the farmers' means of livelihood. In contrast, the painters first interpret Garrotxa aesthetically in terms of mass, form and color; they strive to touch the landscape intuitively and discover its underlying character and atmosphere. Yet, in spite of the differences in the way the two groups speak about Garrotxa, there are certain physical elements and experienced qualities that mark the uniqueness of Garrotxa as a "thing in itself." Perhaps most striking is the environmental characteristic marked by the meaning of *Garrotxa*—a wild, tangled landscape of gorges, precipices and forests that, because of their harshness and difficult access, inspire a sense of respect and endurance.

The last essay of Part II, ecologist Mark Riegner's "Toward a Holistic Understanding of Place: Reading Landscape Through Its Flora and Fauna," also provides an innovative way to interpret the natural environment phenomenologically. Unlike Nogué i Font, however, who seeks to discover the landscape through people's environmental experiences, Riegner draws on a way of science developed by Johann Wolfgang von Goethe (1749–1832), who believed that thoughtful, dedicated looking at a particular phenomenon would eventually lead to a vivid moment of seeing in which the phenomenon and its various aspects are understood in a deeper, more holistic way (Amrine, Zucker and Wheeler, 1987; Bortoft, 1985, 1986).

Goethe's own descriptive investigations included studies of plant form and shape—that is, plant morphology (Goethe, 1988). In turn, the zoologist Wolfgang Schad (1971) drew on Goethe's approach to plants as a way to study animal morphology descriptively. Riegner uses the work of Goethe and Schad as a base from which to read the character of landscape. He argues that there is an intimate relationship between a landscape and its living forms; thus, a deeper understanding of a landscape's plants and animals should foster a deeper understanding of the landscape, and vice versa.

Riegner first explains that there is a relationship between a plant's morphology and specific environmental qualities, such as degrees of light and moisture. Plants with leaf silhouettes more rounded, for example, generally are associated with darker and moister environments, while plants with leaf silhouettes more incised generally are associated with lighter and drier environments. Similarly an animal's form and shape says much about its environment—for example, whether it lives underground or in the water, or whether it is active by day or by night. In one sense, Riegner's work suggests that a landscape and its living forms comprise a kind of language, and that through a Goethean way of science, they can be "read" in terms of underlying patterns and interconnections. His research illustrates how landscape and its living forms are part and parcel. He suggests that creatures are *immersed* in their world and that to look carefully at one can provide insights into the other.

Of all the essays in the collection, Riegner's work is perhaps the most provocative because it describes an intimacy between living form and world that is profoundly different from conventional biological and ecological perspectives that tacitly divide environment and organisms into parts and flows of energy. In his essay, Riegner provides no detailed reading of a particular landscape or its living forms because he is marking out a research terrain—what he calls *phenomenological ecology*—that has barely been explored.

In spite of its preliminary quality, however, Riegner's work is important because it points toward certain relationships—for example, roundness/wetness/darkness/flatness versus angularity/dryness/lightness/ undulation—that would seem to serve as directives for further Goethean research in regard to landscapes and their living forms. Riegner notes, for instance, that a prairie landscape expresses uniformity, both in its own appearance and through its living forms. What would a detailed exploration of prairie landscapes from this perspective lead to, and would one find parallel descriptive patterns if one conducted a complementary study of people who live on prairies, through an approach like Nogué i Font's? And what if the living forms of different prairies suggested differences as well as commonalities? Could such differences perhaps point toward other environmental qualities—geology, relative location and so forth—that define the differences among the prairies more precisely?

In addition, Riegner's approach would seem to have potential value for architectural phenomenology. For instance, do the vernacular architectures found in particular landscapes like prairies, forests or river plains reflect and highlight qualities of the landscapes themselves? Consider Walkey's guild-built houses. Does their form or organization say anything about the rugged, mountainous landscape in which they were built? And are there commonalities with other vernacular buildings in similar mountainous terrains? In short, Riegner's use of the Goethean approach suggests creative possibilities for qualitatively exploring the relationship between worlds and the things and living forms that reside in those worlds.

Considering the essays of Part II as a whole, one can say that they illustrate a crucial aspect of architectural and landscape meaning: It is not added on cognitively but arises directly through immediate unself-conscious experience of what the natural and built environments offer. For example, the meaning of the roof is first of all *existential* in the sense that it spontaneously establishes such basic experienced qualities as inside/outside, self/world and so forth, *simply by being present and being what it is* (Seamon, 1990; Thiis-Evensen, 1987). Similarly, the meanings of Walkey's guild-built houses, Nogué i Font's Garrotxa landscape, or Riegner's plants and animals in their natural environment are *always already present*. Landscapes, objects, buildings, creatures and people all have particular ways of being in their worlds. The essays of Part II illustrate approaches whereby these ways of being-in-the-world can be studied empathetically and critically.

Part III. Living, Understanding, and Designing

The essays of Part III move away from material entities—architectural elements, buildings, and landscapes—and move toward less visible processes that exist in time as well as space—designing, learning, understanding, living, and creating community. All of the essays deal with *relationship,* whether between teaching and learning, designing and building, building and using, individual and group, or client and designer.

My essay, "Different Worlds Coming Together: A Phenomenology of Relationship as Portrayed in Doris Lessing's *Diaries of Jane Somers,*" directly explores relationship, which I define as the coming together of two separate worlds in a widening sphere of interaction, experience and concern. I argue that all relationships involve a cyclic process that can be described by seven progressive stages that begin with dissatisfaction and search and move toward understanding and deeper involvement. I call this temporal process the "relationship cycle," which I explicate through British-African writer Doris Lessing's *Diaries of Jane Somers,* a novel that describes the growing friendship between two unlikely people—an indigent old woman and a stylish London editor of a fashionable women's magazine.

By using Lessing's novel as a descriptive base from which to extract more general characteristics of these two different worlds coming together, I argue that the development of relationship involves hazard and offers no guarantee that any growth or understanding will occur. In contrast to relationship is what I call *connection*—an arbitrary linkage between worlds that is susceptible to failure when changed or stressed in any way. I argue that social policy and environmental design often fail today because they are founded on the superficiality and forced contact of connection rather than on the depth and genuine contact of relationship. In the last part of the essay, I attempt to illustrate the generalizing value of the relationship cycle by using it to examine the student-teacher and client-architect relationships.

In "Putting Geometry in Its Place: Toward a Phenomenology of the Design Process," architect Kimberly Dovey explores the client-architect relationship directly by drawing on the phenomenological notion of *lived-space*—everyday environments and places as people live in and use them. He examines design translations between lived-space and *geometric space*—space as objective measurement. He points out potential disjunctions that cause confusion between architect and client and lead to a poorly conceived design that does not work well for its users.

Dovey describes the design process in terms of a "cycle of lived-space." In this cycle, the designer, first, must understand clients' everyday environmental needs—their lived-space, in other words; second, he or she must translate those needs into geometric expression—distances, heights, spaces, and so forth. In turn, this built environment becomes the context for human actions and, thus, another lived-space. Dovey examines two phases of the lived-space cycle—sketch planning and working drawings. He shows how in each phase there can be a failure in translation from experience and lived-space to measured expression and geometric space. Dovey ends by suggesting changes in the design process that might overcome breakdowns in the lived-space cycle. These changes include experiential simulation, a design process that involves piecemeal change, and phenomenological evaluations of environments already built.

Landscape architect Randolph T. Hester, Jr.'s "Sacred Structures and Everyday Life: A Return to Manteo, North Carolina," echoes Dovey's lived-space cycle in that Hester returns to evaluate a community design that he did in 1983 for the Outer Banks town of Manteo, North Carolina (Hester 1986). Hester's aim is to overview the design process that led to the Manteo plan and determine its various successes and failures in the five years since it was implemented.

Hester's work is important because it is an effort to develop community planning that arises from the everyday lives and needs of the insiders of place—one of Edward Relph's key emphases in his opening essay. Hester discovers that the elements of place important for Manteo residents were often difficult to identify and to articulate because these elements were seemingly mundane and not striking visually or aesthetically. Through the use of behavior mapping, surveys, and interviews, Hester and his team eventually identified Manteo's "Sacred Structure"—a set of settings, situations, and events that marked the heart of Manteo as a place for its residents. This Sacred Structure was then used as the basis for Manteo's community design.

In returning to Manteo, Hester informally evaluates how successful the Sacred Structure design has been in maintaining

Manteo's traditional sense of place while at the same time helping to stimulate the town's economy. Overall, he finds that the master design has helped strengthen Manteo's small-town quality, though some new commercial development is overscaled and, therefore, out of place. He also traces the politics of the town design and finds that some residents' opposition to the design has slowed and changed its development. He concludes that, as a design tool, the Sacred Structure provides one way to reduce differences between insiders and outsiders. In Relph's terms, Hester illustrates one way in which the environmental designer can become a midwife who helps insiders articulate local needs and then translates those needs into design incorporating wider contextual concerns—in the case of Manteo, a secure economic base.

The relationship between community and design is also a central theme in Clare Cooper Marcus's "Designing for a Commitment to Place: Lessons from the Alternative Community *Findhorn*." Cooper Marcus, a community planner, examines how the physical environment has contributed to a sense of community at Findhorn, a small alternative community founded in 1962 on the coast of northeastern Scotland. Like nineteenth century utopian experiments such as Oneida, Harmony, and Shaker settlements, Findhorn is important because it is an intentional effort to establish a sense of group and community. In a modern era when designers, planners and policy-makers seek to create a sense of place self-consciously, Cooper Marcus believes that Findhorn might offer some useful design and policy lessons.

To organize her study conceptually, Cooper Marcus draws on Rosabeth Moss Kanter's *Commitment and Community* (Kanter, 1973), a sociological study of nineteenth century utopian communities. In this work, Kanter identified six "commitment mechanisms"—sacrifice, investment, renunciation, communion, mortification and transcendence—that fostered community loyalty and strength. Drawing on descriptive accounts, surveys, and her own experience of living at Findhorn for a year and visiting several times since, Cooper Marcus uses Kanter's six commitment mechanisms as an organizational framework to examine qualitatively the social patterns and structures that have led to a sense of togetherness at Findhorn. Next, Cooper Marcus considers the contribution that the physical environment makes to Findhorn's sense of community and, last, points to lessons for the design and policy of more typical residential settings.

Cooper Marcus's conclusions are important because, like Hester's, they indicate that the creation of community and place takes time and involves a developmental process that is grounded in commitment. One crucial point she makes is that a community involves some degree of shared human values which, if not present in a planned residential setting, may immediately mean failure. In the case of Hester's Manteo, shared values grow historically out of many people living in the same place for generations; at Findhorn, those values arise from a shared world view and way of living. One question with which Cooper Marcus concludes is whether a sense of community can be guided and designed to happen self-consciously, particularly the promotion of shared values. She highlights such potential design and policy tools as residents' having a stake in community management and maintenance; pedestrian-scaled environments that facilitate informal social interaction; and beautiful settings, which are more likely to foster residents' affection and pride. She concludes that physical design alone cannot create a sense of community, but it can make important contributions.

The last article in Part III, architect Gary Coates and my "Promoting a Foundational Ecology Practically Through Christopher Alexander's Pattern Language: The Example of Meadowcreek," focuses on the relationship between understanding and designing in upper-level architectural design studios. We speak of design education that fosters what philosopher Joseph Grange (1977) calls a *foundational ecology*—that is, a respect for natural environments and places that arises out of care and concern. We argue that architect Christopher Alexander's "Pattern Language"—an effort to identify design qualities that support and evoke a sense of place—is one way in which design students might gain a practical sense of foundational ecology (Alexander et al., 1977, Alexander, 1979; Coates, Siepl and Seamon, 1987).

The design focus in our article is *Meadowcreek,* a center for environmental education in the Ozark mountains of Arkansas. Meadowcreek aims to provide an educational program that emphasizes an intellectual understanding of ecology and the environment as well as practical skills like forestry, farming and land conservation. Coates and I examine the efforts of a studio of upper-level architectural students to understand the environmental needs of Meadowcreek and to translate those needs into a master design. Our major learning and design tool in the studio is Pattern Language, and the essay summarizes the studio's results in terms of the master design itself as well as students' evaluation of the studio process and their resulting understandings.

Dichotomies, Healing and a Phenomenological Ecology

There are many commonalities that link the thirteen essays of this collection: An interest in accurate seeing and thoughtful description, a concern for creative design that evokes a sense of place, and a focus on experiential patterns and processes that mark the foundation of our lives as human beings immersed in a natural and built world. Beneath these interrelated topics, however, might there be some deeper theme that marks the center of a vortex flowing outward toward these other issues?

As I have worked with this collection for over three years, one theme that continually returns to mind is *dichotomies, healing and a phenomenological ecology.* Our world is injured in many ways, the essays seem to say. How can scholarship soothe the wounds of the world and speak to a sense of use, wholeness and harmony? How can design, planning, and policy be a midwife to the world and nurture buildings, places, and communities that are livable and life-enhancing?

A major wound that the thirteen essays seek to heal is the modern Western tendency to divide and isolate, both intellectually and practically. Conventional Western philosophy assumes a division between person and world, between body and mind, between feeling and knowing, between subject and object, between theory and practice, between nature and culture. These Cartesian-Kantian dichotomies emphasize isolation over togetherness, specialization over generalization, things over processes, matter over spirit, and secondhand cerebral knowledge over firsthand lived-experience. The wholeness of the world and human experience is fractured. At the same time, this ethos of separation affects practical life, thus the design professions debate such divisions as beauty versus practicality, form versus function, art versus life, designing versus building, and understanding versus designing.

But what if these divisions are not the most accurate way of marking out our situation as human beings? This, I believe, is the central question suggested by the essays of this collection. If we split the world into a series of parts that may not really be in touch with what the world is, how can any real understanding or change happen, either intellectually or practically? Might one be able to bypass these taken-for-granted dichotomies and to find new ways to differentiate the parts without isolating them or converting them into things they may not be?

In various ways, the following essays take on this task to return to human experience afresh and to look at the world anew. A first way the essays attempt this aim is through *method:* there is an effort to approach the subject kindly and thoughtfully so that it can say who and what it is. For example, Silverstein and Mugerauer seek to elucidate the essential nature of roof and porch, while Hester and Cooper Marcus look for central qualities of community and sense of place. Yet again, Nogué i Font and Riegner hope to get landscapes to speak for themselves, and Dovey and I strive to highlight general patterns of human relationships. It is true, of course, that each author's specific research method varies, thus Nogué i Font, Hester, and Cooper Marcus make varying use of interviews, while Relph, Walkey, and Riegner rely on careful observation and interpretation. In spite of procedural differences, however, the shared aim is a practical method that minimizes the distance between student and subject studied so that the student has the freedom to see, and the subject has the freedom to speak. The aim is "an imaginative sympathy [that is] receptive without ceasing to be critical" (Harvey, 1958, p. x).

A second way that the essays work for openness and fairness is *epistemologically.* How, in other words, can we as human beings come to know the world? How can the human and environmental disciplines come to know the world? Conventional scientific research generally relies on empirical information that can be identified and correlated mathematically. A thing does not exist if it cannot be measured. Knowledge becomes factual and material. In contrast, ways of knowing represented by the essays in this collection are wider-ranging and incorporate qualitative description, intuitive insight, and thoughtful interpretation. The suggestion is that human beings, including scholars, "know" in many different ways—intellectually, emotionally, intuitively, viscerally, bodily, and so forth. A full understanding of any phenomenon requires that all these modes of knowing belong and have a place.

Perhaps the most striking example of a multi-dimensioned knowing is Riegner's Goethean approach to landscape and living forms. Goethe's way of knowledge is grounded in sincere interest, heartfelt dedication and growing sensitivity. The student's knowledge of the phenomenon changes and deepens as he or she becomes more intimate with it. In a similar way, Harries argues that a study

of natural symbols requires openness and patience. He says that
any language of natural symbols must first be understood emotionally rather than intellectually: "If we can speak of a language at all,
this is a language addressed, first, to sense and imagination. Before
attempts are made to articulate it in words, it needs to be felt."
The possibility of such a language is illustrated by Silverstein,
Mugerauer and Walkey, who make use of careful looking, thoughtful
seeing, and inspired interpretation in their perceptive explications
of architectural elements and buildings.

Overall, the essays in this collection, as well as those in the earlier *Dwelling, Place, and Environment,* point toward a new discipline and profession whose substantive focus is *environment and
place,* whose methodological thrust is *openness and fairness,* and
whose ontological vision is *togetherness, belonging and wholeness.*
There are several labels that might describe this discipline—for example, "phenomenology of place," "architectural phenomenology," or
"phenomenological geography." Perhaps the designation that Riegner coins in his essay—*phenomenological ecology*—provides the
best description. Phenomenological ecology is an interdisciplinary
field that explores and describes the ways that things, living forms,
people, events, situations and worlds come together environmentally. A key focus is how all these entities *belong* together in place,
why they might not belong, and how they might better belong
through more sensitive understanding, design and policy-making.

Phenomenological ecology supposes that beneath the seeming
disorder and chaos of our world and daily life are a series of underlying patterns, structures, relationships and processes that can be
described qualitatively through heartfelt concern, sustained effort,
and moments of inspired seeing and interpretation. Phenomenological ecology, therefore, not only widens and deepens our knowledge
of the world *outside* ourselves but also facilitates our *own* growth as
individuals whose abilities to see and understand can become
keener and more refined. We become more awake to the world, and
see things in a more perceptive, multi-dimensioned way.

More than likely, the world cannot be healed only by technological solutions provided by a materialist science. Nor is the hope only
in political and cultural changes that restructure the world economically and socially. We must also change ourselves as individual persons—the ways we understand, feel, decide and act. Especially, we
must discover ways to be less self-centered and to put other human
beings, living forms and things *first* before our own selves. On one
hand, we must find ways to celebrate difference, complexity, unique-

ness, freedom, disorder, chaos, and flux.[7] On the other hand, we must believe that—beneath this diversity, entropy, and continuous change—there may lie an existential order and commonality that help to reconfigure and to transform such traditional divisions as theory/practice, unity/plurality, stability/mobility, nature/culture, animals/people, Western/non-Western, black/white, male/female, straight/gay, and so forth.

In seeking this intellectual and applied transfiguration, a phenomenological ecology is central because it seeks to allow the person, group, place or thing to speak in an appropriate language, yet also realizes that this speaking may hold points of commonality with the languages of other people, groups, places, and things. Phenomenological ecology works to foster a sympathetic and systematic contact between student and thing studied, between particular real-world instance and wider conceptual pattern, and between specific individuals and the larger natural and human worlds of which those individuals are a part. In this sense, phenomenological ecology opens our feelings outward and evokes a sense of positive obligation toward nature, toward our own immediate worlds, and toward worlds that, at least on the surface, are greatly different from our own. Where there was an *either/or*, a phenomenological ecology nourishes a *both/and*.

Notes

1. See Seamon, 1982, 1986, 1987, 1989, 1990. At the start, the reader should realize that there is not one phenomenology but many (Spiegelberg 1982). The phenomenological approach represented by the essays in this volume, either explicitly or indirectly, relates to the tradition of *existential phenomenology,* fathered by philosophers Martin Heidegger (1962) and Maurice Merleau-Ponty (1962) and transcribed into use for the human sciences, especially, by the Duquesne School of Phenomenological Psychology (Giorgi, Barton, and Maes, 1983). A central aim of existential phenomenology is a generalized description and understanding of human experience, behavior, meaning and awareness *as they are lived by real people in real times and places.* The reality of these concrete experiences and situations are not an end in themselves, however, but a field of descriptive evidence out of which can be drawn underlying patterns and structures that mark the essential core of humanness.

Though many authors in the present volume would not call themselves phenomenologists or their work phenomenological, I feel their studies are significant phenomenologically because there is a search for general

experiential patterns that arise from real-world situations and circumstances. Just as quantitative, aggregate studies have the larger conceptual
framework of "positivist science" around which to organize their evidence
and claims, so qualitative descriptive research also requires such an over-
arching conceptual structure, which I believe is best provided by existential
phenomenology, or *phenomenology*, as I call it for convenience here. For one
discussion that opposes this interpretation, particularly as it has been
used in the environmental disciplines, see Pickles, 1985. For a rebuttal, see
Seamon, 1987. Also see Cloke, Philo, and Sadler, 1991, chap. 3.

2. Much of Relph's other writings work to explore in depth the broad
themes of this article. See, for example, Relph, 1976, 1981, 1987, 1989, 1991.

3. Other works by Harries that explore these issues in various ways
include: Harries, 1978, 1982, 1984a, 1984b, 1985a, 1985b, 1987, 1988a,
1988b. On the relationship of natural symbols to architecture, see Thiis-
Evensen, 1987.

4. For another thoughtful philosophical discussion of these issues, see
Corner, 1990.

5. For further discussion of the way that experienced polarities can be
used in the design process, see Jacobson, Silverstein, and Winslow, 1990;
Thiis-Evensen, 1987.

6. For a discussion of what this phenomenological argument means for
deconstructionist architecture, see Mugerauer, 1988.

7. On the contrasts between phenomenological and post-structural-
deconstructionist approaches to diversity and difference, see Cheney, 1989,
1990; Cloke, Philo and Sadler, 1991; Mugerauer, 1988; Relph, 1991; Seamon, 1990; Stefanovic, 1991; and Zimmerman, 1990.

References

Alexander, C. (1979). *The Timeless Way of Building*. New York: Oxford University Press.

Alexander, C., Ishikawa, S., and Silverstein, M. (1977). *A Pattern Language*.
New York: Oxford University Press.

Amrine, F., Zucker, F. J. and Wheeler, H. (eds.) (1987). *Goethe and the Sciences: A Reappraisal*. Dordrecht, the Netherlands: D. Reidel.

Bortoft, H. (1985). Counterfeit and Authentic Wholes: Finding a Means for
Dwelling in Nature. In D. Seamon and R. Mugerauer (Eds.), *Dwell-
ing, Place and Environment: Toward a Phenomenology of Person and
World* (pp. 281–302). Dordrecht, the Netherlands: Martinus Nijhoff.

————. (1986). *Goethe's Scientific Consciousness*. London: Institute for Cultural Research Monograph Series No. 22, Octagon Press.

Cheney, R. (1989). Postmodern Environmental Ethics: Ethics as Bioregional Narrative. *Environmental Ethics, 11*, 117–134.

————. (1990). Review Essay. *Phenomenology and the Human Sciences Newsletter, 15* (September), 6–24.

Cloke, P., Philo, C. and Sadler, D. (1991). *Approaching Human Geography*. New York: Guildford Press.

Coates, G., Siepl, S. and Seamon, D. (1987). Christopher Alexander and the Nature of Architecture. *Orion Nature Quarterly, 6* (spring), 20–33.

Corner, J. (1990). A Discourse on Theory I: "Sounding the Depths"— Origins, Theory, and Representation. *Landscape Journal, 9*, 61–77.

Giorgi, A., Barton, A. and Maes, C. (eds.) (1983). *Duquesne Studies in Phenomenological Psychology*, Vol. 4. Pittsburgh: Duquesne University Press.

Goethe, J. W. von (1988). *Goethe: Scientific Studies*. D. Miller (ed. and trans.). New York: Suhrkamp Publishers.

Grange, J. (1977). Towards a Foundational Ecology. In *Soundings, 60*, 135–149.

Harries, K. (1978). Fundamental Ontology and the Search for Man's Place. In M. Murray (Ed.). *Heidegger and Modern Philosophy* (pp. 65–78). New Haven: Yale University Press.

————. (1982). Building and the Terror of Time. *Perspecta, 19*, 58–69.

————. (1984a). On Truth and Lie in Architecture, *Via, 7*, 47–57.

————. (1984b). Space, Place, and Ethos, *artibus et historiae, 9*, 159–165.

————. (1985a). The Ethical Function of Architecture. In D. Ihde and H. J. Silverman (eds.), *Descriptions*. Albany: State University of New York Press.

————. (1985b). Modernity's Bad Conscience, *AA Files, 10* (autumn), 53–60.

————. (1987). Philosophy and the Task of Architecture. *Journal of Architectural Education, 40*, 29–30.

————. (1988a). Representation and Re-presentation in Architecture, *Via, 9*, 12–25.

————. (1988b). The Voices of Space. In M. Benedikt (ed.), *Buildings and Reality* [vol. 4 of *Center: A Journal for Architecture in America*], pp. 34–49. New York: Rizzoli.

Harvey, J. W. (1958). Translator's Preface. In R. Otto, *The Idea of the Holy*. New York: Oxford University Press.

Heidegger, M. (1962). *Being and Time*. J. Macquarrie and E. Robinson (trans.). New York: Harper and Row.

———. (1971). *Poetry, Language, Thought*. A. Hofstadter (trans.). New York: Harper and Row.

Hester, Jr., R. (1986). Subconscious Landscapes of the Heart, *Places, 2*, 10–22.

Jacobson, M., Silverstein, M., and Winslow, B. (1990). *The Good House: Contrast as a Design Tool*. Newtown, CT: Taunton Press.

Kanter, R. M. (1973). *Commitment and Community*. Cambridge, Massachusetts: Harvard University Press.

Merleau-Ponty, M. (1962). *A Phenomenology of Perception*. New York: Humanities Press.

Mugerauer, R. (1988). Derrida and Beyond. In M. Benedikt (ed.), *Buildings and Reality* [vol. 4 of *Center: A Journal for Architecture in America*], pp. 66–75. New York: Rizzoli.

Norberg-Schulz, C. (1980). *Genius Loci: Toward a Phenomenology of Architecture*. New York: Rizzoli.

———. (1985). *The Concept of Dwelling: On the Way to a Figurative Architecture*. New York: Rizzoli.

Pickles, J. (1985). *Phenomenology, Science and Geography: Spatiality and the Human Sciences*. Cambridge: Cambridge University Press.

Relph, E. (1976). *Place and Placelessness*. London: Pion, 1976.

———. (1981). *Rational Landscapes and Humanistic Geography*. Totowa, NJ: Barnes & Noble.

———. (1987). *The Modern Urban Landscape*. Baltimore: Johns Hopkins Press.

———. (1989). Responsive Methods, Geographical Imagination and the Study of Landscapes. In A. Kobayashi & S. MacKenzie, eds. *Remaking Human Geography* (149–163). Boston: Unwin Hyman.

———. (1991). Post-Modern Geography, *Canadian Geographer, 35*, 98–105.

Schad, W. (1977). *Man and Mammals: Toward a Biology of Form*. Garden City, New York: Waldorf Press.

Seamon, D. (1982). The Phenomenological Contribution to Environmental Psychology. *Journal of Environmental Psychology, 2*, 119–140.

————. (1986). Phenomenology and Vernacular Lifeworlds. In D. G. Saile (ed.), *Architecture in Cultural Change* (pp. 17–24). Lawrence, Kansas: School of Architecture, University of Kansas.

————. (1987). Phenomenology and Environment-Behavior Research. In G. T. Moore and E. H. Zube (eds.), *Advances in Environment, Behavior, and Design,* vol. 1 (pp. 3–27). New York: Plenum.

————. (1989). Humanistic and Phenomenological Advances in Environmental Design. *The Humanistic Psychologist, 17,* 280–293.

————. (1990). Architecture, Experience, and Phenomenology: Toward Reconciling Order and Freedom, paper no. 2, *Person-Environment Theory Series,* edited by R. Ellis. Berkeley: Center for Environmental Design Research, University of California, Berkeley.

Seamon, D. and Mugerauer, R. (eds.) (1985). *Dwelling, Place, and Environment: Toward a Phenomenology of Person and World.* New York: Columbia University Press.

Spiegelberg, H. (1982). *The Phenomenological Movement.* The Hague: Martinus Nijhoff.

Stefanovic, I. L. (1991). Evolving Sustainability: A Re-thinking of Ontological Foundations. *Trumpeter, 8,* 194–200.

Thiis-Evensen, T. (1987). *Archetypes in Architecture.* Oslo: Norwegian University Press; New York: Oxford University Press, 1989.

Zimmerman, M. (1990). *Heidegger's Confrontation with Modernity: Technology, Politics, Art.* Bloomington: Indiana University Press.

Part I

Modernity and the Built Environment:
Problems and Possibilities

Chapter 2

Modernity and the Reclamation of Place

◻

Edward Relph

Somewhere behind most discussions about place and sense of place lies an image of quiet, simple landscapes where there are no great cities, no suburban tracts, no ugly factories, no money-based economies, and no authoritarian political systems.[1] In this landscape, people know their neighbors, who share traditions and social rituals. People have an intimate familiarity with the local geography, and they feel a responsibility for maintaining the nameless qualities of their place with its intricate townscape and regionally distinctive architectural styles.

This may be an impossibly romantic vision both of the past and for the future, but it persists nonetheless. It can be recognized in Gordon Cullen's writing on townscape (Cullen, 1961), in Christian Norberg-Schulz' account of *genius loci* (Norberg-Schulz, 1980), in Christopher Alexander's "Pattern Language" (Alexander, 1977, 1979), and in Kevin Lynch's place utopia (Lynch, 1981). These ideals and images are valuable for a modern world rapidly being overwhelmed by the renitent landscapes of rationalism. Unfortunately, the skills and social contexts for making such places no longer exist. Indeed, in a world of multi-national corporations, universal planning practices and instantaneous global communications, we have to take seriously the argument that sense of place is just another form of nostalgia and that places are obsolete.

I have thought about place and sense of place for more than a decade (Relph, 1976, 1981, 1987), and it is my conviction that they are not obsolete. On the contrary, I believe that distinctive places are necessary for a reasonable quality of communal life and psychological well-being. Furthermore, a serious concern for the qualities of specific places is an important element in finding an antidote to the abstract and generalized knowledge that leads otherwise intelligent people to talk, for example, of targeted sites and mega-deaths instead of devastated towns and human agony. Attending to places means attending directly to one of the immediate realities of everyday life. This understanding is not as easy as it might seem. First, one must develop a sensitivity to the spirit of place. Then, one must circumvent the grand delusions of technology, ideology and obscure theory that beset the late-twentieth century and that cause environments to be made and processed like sliced bread. Finally, one must strive for an understanding of the vital qualities that are essential for all distinctive and significant places.

Haunted Houses and Sacred Places

In a talk to architects, the Canadian novelist Robertson Davies chose the topic, "How to Design a Haunted House" (Davies, 1978). His purpose, at least half-serious, was to point out the lack of personality in most modern buildings—no hidden tunnels, no priest-holes, not even plush Victorian draperies to hide behind. In effect, modern buildings deny the possibility of being haunted. But Davies also wanted to emphasize that there are limits to what can and ought to be designed. There are still things in the world over which we have no rational control. A self-consciously designed haunted house can never be more than a fairground mockup, and architects have neither the skill nor the right to create ghosts.

In making places in our modern world, the problems involved in designing haunted houses are greatly magnified. Architects conventionally focus their attention on buildings as visible, substantial entities considered in isolation. Places, however, are impalpable territories of social activities and meanings projected into entire assemblages of buildings and spaces (Relph, 1976). They are, in other words, indeterminate wholes. It is impossible to draw precise boundaries around them or to break them down into their components without losing touch with them as places. Moreover, while it is safe to assume that most individual buildings are not possessed by ghosts, it is a defining characteristic of any worthwhile place that it have its own spirit—its own *genius loci*. In this sense, all places are sacred, and it is most unlikely that they can be designed using the same techniques as those employed for single buildings. Indeed, how can mere mortals dare to design places, for is such an effort not to try to make gods and spirits? If religion has any meaning at all, the very idea of making *genius loci* borders on sacrilege.

This is a difficult problem. If any credence is give to *genius loci*, then it seems that we must either regard places in an attitude of contrite awe and do nothing to them, or assume that we have the power and authority to make gods and goddesses, albeit local ones. Fortunately there is a middle route between these two extremes, one that was carefully thought through in antiquity by Stoic philosophers and geographers such as Strabo (1959). Their argument was that divine providence, the gods, had filled the earth with an animating presence and had endowed many locations with attributes or virtues, such as an attractive site or an abundance of resources. Human beings, to take advantage of these positive qualities, must exercise their foresight and their ability to perceive the virtues of places. For some people, this understanding of place is an innate ability; for others it has to be learned through deliberate efforts of observation and thought. In either case, foresight is the means to attain the good life that is lived in harmony with the provisions of the gods. There is, in other words, the possibility of a mutual relationship between the use of human reason and foresight, and divine providence as it is revealed in places. This relationship is manifest in sound farming practices, the building of cities well adapted to their sites, or the making of temples which explicitly call the spirits of place into presence and propitiate them. The virtues of place could also be ignored, but the Stoics had only contempt for such people, who were seen to be out of harmony with the gods and incapable of attaining excellence.

We, however, live in an age when it is unfashionable to talk in such terms. Nietzsche long ago announced the "God is dead," and Max Weber referred to the "disenchantment of the world." Without wishing to promote an anachronistic sense of environmental piety, I nevertheless think it is important always to bear in mind the original meanings of *genius loci* and of the virtue of places. Place, even stripped of its spiritual dimension, is a powerful concept and an invaluable component of human experience that should not be reduced to abstract generalizations and measures of profitability. Places should be approached with due humility and openness to their intrinsic merits and disadvantages. Above all, places should be viewed with the clear understanding that it is not possible to design everything about them. Unfortunately, this approach to place seems all too rarely what is done nowadays.

The Instant Environment Machine

"The perfection of Art in an American's eyes," wrote James Fergusson in 1862, "would be attained by the invention of a

self-acting machine which should produce plans of cities and designs
for Gothic churches or Classic municipal buildings at so much per
foot super, and so save all further trouble and thought" (Fergusson
1873, p. 499). It took most of a century to achieve Fergusson's invention, and the effort was as much European as American. But
the twentieth century has created just such a self-acting machine,
which can level places and mix histories in any way desired. Capable now of making or destroying environments of almost any type or
scale, from sensory deprivation chambers to entire cities, modern
builders have at their disposal an "instant environment machine."

This machine is big but subtle. It is, in Lewis Mumford's term,
a mega-machine and comprised of the interacting components of
ideologies, economic linkages, institutions and corporations, meth-
odologies for planning and design, huge organizations and communications systems, and a veritable panoply of technologies. It is
fueled by money and lubricated by the personal gratifications that
come with increasing levels of comfort and leisure. It is steered by
an unswerving conviction in growth and progress. Places, landscapes, buildings, and cities seem largely incidental to its purpose;
new or old, distinctive or ordinary, they are treated like other economic resources. They are commodities to be exploited, managed,
preserved or otherwise manipulated in whatever ways promote the
self-maintenance and profitability of the machine. Here, I want to
illustrate this instant environment machine by discussing two aspects of its mechanism: *corporatisation* and *telecommunications*.

Corporatisation

Since 1945, especially with the growth of multinational corporations, the commodification of landscape has become common-
place. Corporations, banks and contracting firms are the primary
players because they can mobilize enormous financial and material
resources to develop suburban tracts or to redevelop city blocks.
These institutions construct theme parks like Canada's Wonder-
land or Florida's Disneyworld with their fake mountains and real
security forces; they build huge shopping malls, such as Alberta's
West Edmonton Mall, which includes theme parks, skating rinks
and wave pools; they develop entire corporate new towns, such as
Columbia, Maryland.

Much of this building is done in concert with municipal planning departments, which have also greatly expanded their powers
since World War II. The central aim, apparently, is to create ratio-

nal and efficient developments by controlling change and eliminating chance. Batteries of standardized regulations and models of
development are applied to almost every aspect of the built environment so that unpredicted events either will not occur or will be of
no consequence. The result is a sort of planning-by-numbers that
appears in uniform street standards that are in no way adapted to
existing settlements, in the segregation of land uses, and in the
trim neatness of suburbs where almost everything—grades, setbacks, building materials, illumination levels, curb shapes, road
width—is governed by some regulation, by-law, property standard,
or building code.

In a somewhat different way, corporations try to eliminate uncertainty by using whatever marketing strategies prove to be effective, but it is always the corporation and its profitability to which
everything else is subsumed. In these strategies, national identi-
ties, let alone local histories and geographies, are reduced to little
more than a street name here and there, or perhaps some token like
the miniature maple leaf that McDonald's graciously puts on the
golden arches at its Canadian outlets. The intrinsic qualities of
places serve merely to make money, either by packaging them as a
tourist attraction, or by detaching built-forms from all other place
aspects and shipping them elsewhere to use as a background for
selling something.

This commodification of place qualities permits commercial designers to employ an eclectic selection of whatever is best from any
time or place. The West Edmonton Mall, for example, has a nine-
hole version of the Pebble Beach golf course on the Monterey peninsula, albeit miniaturized. With marginally more sensitivity to
locality, the Barnyard, a chic postmodern shopping center near
Monterey in California, consists of replicas of eight Californian
barns-as-stores selling Cinzano and Scottish woolens, needlepoint
and pewter, all grouped around a landscaped pedestrian courtyard
and maintained by a janitorial staff suitably attired in blue cover-
alls and straw hats.

Large areas of Monterey itself have also been commodified,
chiefly because the town was the setting for John Steinbeck's *Cannery Row*. The tourist guide explains the "Vacationers follow the
footsteps of departed ghosts: John Steinbeck's characters. Yes—on
Cannery Row—the very place that Steinbeck struck life into the
Row's wonderful figures . . . the rotting buildings were remodelled
into stores and shops, and former brothels became restaurants."
Cannery Row has been turned into a strange parody of itself, with

condominium apartment buildings designed to look like canning plants and a "Steinbeck's Lady" boutique. None of this is unpleasant. The buildings are interesting, many of them restored or carefully integrated with the old fabric of the town; the streets are good to walk and to look at. Yet in such contexts, the very term "place" takes on an entirely new set of meanings: fiction and reality, location and imagination, history and invention are blurred beyond recognition.

Telecommunications

In its most recent phase, the instant environment machine has become more subtle. It has created a world in which images, elusive and commercial though they may be, are often accorded more substance than material realities. For example, the romantic and bucolic images of Hallmark greeting cards are created and mass-produced in a barren factory situated next to a twelve-lane highway in the suburban fringe of Toronto. This inconsistency amounts to the promotion of landscape blindness, an insensitivity to the actual qualities of real places while delighting in their imaginary qualities.

There are many sources of this insensitivity, but none is perhaps more important than telecommunications, especially television. The impact of electronic technologies on landscapes and places is by no means clearly understood. This impact is worth considering carefully because these technologies are now so important. In 1981 almost sixty percent of the American labor force was involved in processing and manipulating information in some way. In addition, these electronic technologies have significant social consequences as Joshua Meyrowitz has provocatively argued in *No Sense of Place* (Meyrowitz, 1984). He proposes that the "electronic media affect us primarily not through their content but by changing the 'situational geography' of social life" (p. 6).

These technologies reprocess traditional social and physical environments by turning them into information settings that can be left anonymous, changed or glorified depending on the producer's inclination and camera angles. Television series supposedly about Minneapolis, Cincinnati, or Atlanta are produced in Hollywood. Toronto and Vancouver are frequently used as New York or Los Angeles because they have lower production costs and can be easily disguised on screen. Telecommunications reproduce and then change many of the social processes once found only in close-knit communities—for instance, most spoken language is now heard from radio or television; and for many people, television is the primary source of what they know about the world. Furthermore, telecommunications provide vicarious access to all landscapes and places, no matter how remote, and they put geographically isolated places into "direct" contact with the centers of electronic influence.

Telecommunications flow indiscriminately and almost invisibly through all regions; their only marks are aerials, microwave towers and satellite dishes. Neither in their transmission nor their reception do they adapt to locality. Meyrowitz writes that "electronic media bring information and experience to everyplace from everyplace" (ibid., p. 118). By this process, they change everything while appearing to change nothing, for they continue the separation of community from location that was begun by the telegraph and the railway, and they override all distinctions among places that were based on geographical isolation. A flexible and elusive vagueness is thereby conferred on everyday experience. Meyrowitz suggests cautiously that the resulting homogenisation is a matter of degree; places are still different from one another, but the differences are much less than they once were. Meyrowitz's chief argument is that the traditional sense of place, and by this he means both the logic and perception of place, has been deeply undermined. He concludes that "our world may seem senseless to many people because, for the first time in modern history, it is relatively placeless" (p. 308).

The Disassembly of Place

Arguments for place making that fail to consider the scale, momentum and subtlety of the environmental mega-machine are ill founded, for the history of our modern era is also the history of the decline of place. Perhaps even when Fergusson speculated about self-acting machines in the 1860s there was still a geography of clearly defined places that had been made largely by craftsmen working within local or regional traditions, and which were maintained by neighborly communities. A place then comprised a specific landscape, a set of social activities, and webs of meanings and rituals, all inseparably intertwined.

This original coherence of places has been systematically fractured over the last century and a half by the environment machine with its improved means of transportation and communication, by standardization and consumption, and by international styles in art, planning and architecture. The result is that the communal activities which were once a defining feature of place have become geographically fragmented, and communities are now defined as much by common interest as by common location—as in "the business community," for example. The meanings and symbols of many places have either been destroyed or commodified. Distinctive landscapes have been demolished, or, if exceptionally distinctive, copied everywhere else. Even what remains of old places often takes on new meaning because they are identified with "heritage," and labelled with historical plaques, discussed in tourist brochures, and made subject to planning controls intended to protect their distinctive features. This special recognition of old places merely serves to illustrate the lack of distinctiveness in the hard, angular, modernist straight-spaces of city centers, airports, expressways and industrial subdivisions. In such domineering or vacuous environments, it is hard to develop a sense of place, for there is nothing in them to promote affection or a sense of belonging. The quaint spaces of post-modern townscapes are less alienating, but their interesting facades and textures usually turn out to be superficial cladding. They are places that by appearance alone mimic real places. These post-modern environments are "nice lies."

Styles of Place Reclamation

From the perspective of the instant environment machine, places are not significantly important. Yet a concern with place and sense of place has become an important theme in several different professions and academic disciplines since the early 1970s. Place has also become a frequent focus in popular culture, as is apparent from articles in magazines like *Esquire* and *Harpers*. This emergent concern can be understood in at least three ways.

From one perspective, the interest in place is a desperate rearguard action first mounted as the full force of modernism became apparent in the late 1960s and early 1970s. In this case, the interest in place is a form of romanticism and nostalgia—a reaction against the decay of personal and group identity. Its effects include the designation of historically significant buildings and districts, presumably on the principle that in the face of onslaught one saves what one can. While all these efforts are valuable, they look backward and come to terms with the environment machine only in a limited way. This approach to place museumizes the best fragments of *genius loci*. The results are often pleasant, informative and exquisitely restored, but they do nothing to challenge the placeless processes of modern development methods.

In a second, more compliant sense, the recent concern with place has been an attempt to improve the products of the environment machine by making pleasant, arresting spaces, like the Barnyard, instead of the dreary angular ones that were often built in the 1950s and 1960s. The principle here appears to be that if we have to live with a monstrous machine, we might as well decorate it to look attractive. One might question whether this approach constitutes place making at all, or whether it is some form of subtle co-option by the agencies of the environment machine. Such "placey" environments can be the product of intensive technical and behavioral research used to manipulate a supposed sense of place, and in such cases the chief purpose seems to be to persuade a docile population to spend money and not to worry about environmental dilution.

A third, more radical concern with place has attempted to come to an understanding of its existential importance and has been critical of the instant environment machine. The aim has been to reclaim the specificity and originality of places by thinking carefully about their nature and the ways in which it might be possible to make new types of places without simply copying outdated approaches. Perhaps this radical concern has been based partly in the conviction that a heightened sense of place is an essential aspect of any attempt to redress the enormous injustices and dangers to survival that threaten us all. This approach attempts to break free from ideology and technical abstraction and to contact people, things and landscapes directly. This approach has led to a growing awareness that places do matter to people, and that they need to be reclaimed as integral parts of human environments.

Place Reclamation and Place Making

Place reclamation is not a simple task. The environment machine, with the full weight of development corporations and government agencies behind it, has acquired a powerful momentum so that it is not easy even to deflect, let alone stop or reverse. A direct confrontation is likely to be futile. And more sophisticated design techniques make about as much sense as prescribing better quality wines as a cure for alcoholism. Kevin Lynch

(1981), Christopher Alexander (1977, 1979) and others have recognized these difficulties in dealing with modern environments,
and they have found it necessary to make proposals for place making and environmental design that owe very little to conventional
approaches. Within most of these proposals lies a straightforward
idea that is central to all issues of place and place making—one
that offers the possibility for the emergence of *genius loci* and
that challenges the environment machine without necessarily being co-opted by it. This idea is simply that *places have to be made
largely through the involvement and commitment of the people
who live and work in them; places have to be made from the inside out.* The role of professionals and outsiders is to provide direction and advice based on their special skills and breadth of
experience that allow them to resolve specific technical matters,
overcome parochialism, and see the broader effects and implications
of local actions.

What I am suggesting is that there must be as much community involvement in place-making as possible. In the developed
world, this participation is necessary for the very practical reason
that, as population growth declines, the major design problems will
be those of redeveloping and reclaiming placeless environments and
their communities—for instance, trying to make modernist city
centers more vital and modernist housing developments more hab-
itable. Failure to attend to the needs and wishes of established pop-
ulations can only result in resentment, political confrontations,
awkward compromises, and poorly realized designs. Furthermore,
local involvement can perhaps help to redress the standardized results of hyperplanning and the worst excesses of commodification.
Both of these problems are grounded in relatively detached and abstract approaches that are insensitive to the specific attributes of
places. While locally initiated developments are unlikely to do away
with extended standards and superfluous consumer goods, they
might at least be able to adapt them to local circumstances.

There is also a conceptual reason for community involvement in
place design because the essential characteristics of place derive
precisely from such involvement. A place is a whole phenomenon,
consisting of the three intertwined elements of a specific landscape
with both built and natural elements, a pattern of social activities
that should be adapted to the advantages or virtues of a particular
location, and a set of personal and shared meanings (Relph, 1976).
The realization and the fusion of these elements are simply too difficult to achieve except by allowing the people who live and work in

places to participate in making them as they would wish them to be. Let me demonstrate this point in more detail.

A specific landscape or physical form is the aspect of place most obviously capable of being affected by architectural design. The landscape can be arranged to create spaces and settings that might breed affection and a sense of place among the residents and users (e.g., Alexander, 1977). Whether such rearrangements are successful depends very much on the ability of individual designers to appreciate the virtues and spirits of place, and their skill in using this ability to create attractive forms. Even then the oppressive constraints of hyperplanning and corporatisation are likely to reduce these forms to banal commodities, or perhaps the residents will change the designs to suit their own needs, as happened with Le Corbusier's houses at Pessac (Boudon, 1979) and Christopher Alexander's Mexacali project (Alexander, 1985; Fromm and Bosselman, 1983–1984). In other words, the possibilities for place-making solely through physical design are limited. Indeed, good forms may not always be necessary for the development of communities with a strong sense of place. Hareven and Langenbach (1981) have demonstrated that working-class communities in apparently dreary row housing surrounded by factories often seem to have developed a powerful attachment to place almost in spite of the visual and spatial character of the landscape. The relationship between built form and place is, in other words, an imprecise one.

The patterns of social relationships which are a part of all places are equally indeterminate. We are linked to our places by patterns of activities that are so varied and subtle that they cannot all be identified. These activities include shopping, getting to work, talking to neighbors, raking up leaves in the front yard, distributing community newsletters, and so on. Some of these activities are observable, but even then their significance is difficult to know clearly. Because we indulge in a particular activity does not mean that it reinforces our sense of place. For example, for Jane Jacobs in Greenwich Village putting out the garbage could be part of a morning ritual (Jacobs, 1961, p. 54), but for me in Toronto it is just a chore. So while it is through patterns of activities and personal relationships that people actually encounter places and get to know them, it is not always possible to make useful generalizations about the importance of certain patterns or relationships.

This vagueness is important, for were it absent theories of architectural and environmental determinism might indeed hold true, and merely by erecting the appropriately shaped surroundings it would be possible to create a sense of place among the inhabitants. There would then be no opposing the environment machine, and the only questions we could raise would have to do with its relative degree of efficiency in manipulating behaviors and attitudes. So long as there is indeterminacy in social activities, the only way that they can be effectively accommodated into physical designs is by allowing for community involvement in the design process and by providing scope for future modifications, additions and changes in social behavior.

A place is above all a territory of meanings. These meanings are created both by what one receives from and by what one gives to a particular environmental context, and they are not detachable and transferable, though similarities between places allow for some comparison of meanings. What is received from a place includes pleasure or displeasure, loneliness or companionship, a sense of security or danger. Contributions to a place can be constructive and visible, such as erecting a building or tending a garden, or they can take the invisible forms of personal obligations, political commitments and social involvements. The meanings a particular place has for individuals are shared, at least to some degree, because they derive from a common context and are expressed in terms of a common language and a common social background. There is unlikely to be unanimity in this sharing or intersubjectivity, but it is usually sufficient for us to be able to comprehend the reactions and attitudes of others. And it is the basis for a sense of community in place.

Qualities of Place Meaning

The qualities of place meaning can be glimpsed through the landscape in at least two ways which I call *imperfection* and *generosity*. Where there is some restrained imperfection of finish, we can be confident that this place is one which is invested with significance, for it suggests that the inhabitants have put something of themselves into it. John Ruskin wrote that "imperfection in some sort is essential to all that we know of life . . . to banish imperfection is to destroy expression, to check exertion, to paralyze vitality" (Ruskin, 1851, p. xxv). Only machines and machine-made products are perfect and precise, and where we see perfection we also see lifelessness and the suppression of self-expression and human meaning. What might be called "careful" imperfection indicates involvement and the freedom to make mistakes. Such imperfections, however, cannot be too great, for the result is the meaninglessness of chaos. Imperfection is a condition of an environment that qualifies and mollifies order without destroying it. For Ruskin, imperfection was manifest especially in the craftsmanship of gothic architecture, but it can also be seen in such things as unexpected juxtapositions of different architectural styles, unpredictable variations in street patterns, illegally parked cars and hand-made signs and all the other ways in which place identity resists perfectly rational and professional finishes. Such imperfections are the mark of life.

The second manifestation of place meaning lies in what might be termed generosity. This is the constructive gesture of individuals and groups giving us rather more than we would expect from a purely efficient or commodified landscape. Generosity is manifest in flowerbeds in front yards, in idiosyncratically decorated houses, in storekeepers sweeping their sidewalks, and perhaps even in landscaping and urban design that improve the appearance of a place but probably do little to increase profits or win votes. This spirit is an expression of spontaneity and creativity, often made in today's environments in spite of all the instant environment machine does to deny it. Generosity is doing something for its own sake, without an ulterior motive, and is an indication that someone cares for a place simply because it is his or hers.

Conclusion

The word "place" is best applied to those fragments of human environments where meanings, activities and a specific landscape are all implicated and enfolded by each other. I cannot insist that everyone use "place" in this same way, nor do I expect them to. I do believe, however, that this restricted meaning proves useful in reminding us that places are far more than interesting groups of buildings, or well-formed street spaces, or just foci of social and economic enterprises.

If I am challenged on this idealistic view of place, or told that I am being unduly shrill about instant environment machines and their consequences, I will probably confess that my real, everyday view of things is somewhat more ambivalent than I imply. On one hand, I take a certain perverse pleasure from many of the more absurd landscape products of corporations and planning departments, and a genuine pleasure from the comforts and conveniences with

which they wrap my life. On the other hand, I am keenly aware that
there is something elusive missing in the midst of this comfort and
convenience. Daniel Boorstin, the American historian, expresses
the same concern (Boorstin, 1973). He acknowledges that the technological and social changes that have so greatly improved modern
standards of living have led to a geography of few surprises, and he
asks rhetorically: "Did the very instruments of life enrichment,
once available to all, somehow make life blander and less poignant?"
(p. 389). For me, what is missing in modern landscapes is *genius
loci*, the spirit that imbues places with meaning and appropriate-
ness. The question now is how to recover this quality without deny-
ing the benefits of the social and technological changes that eroded
it. There is no handbook answer.

Genius loci cannot be designed to order. It has to evolve, to be
allowed to happen, to grow and change from the direct efforts of
those who live and work in places and care about them. Here, the
technical methods employed in corporatisation and the electronic
media are of no value. No matter how sophisticated technical knowledge may be, the understanding of others' lives and problems will
always be partial. Just as outsiders cannot feel their pain, so they
cannot experience their sense of place. I believe, therefore, that it is
impossible to make complete places in which other people can live.
And, in a world dominated by international economic processes and
global telecommunications, there can be no return to an environment of integrated and distinctive places.

Nevertheless there is an important role for architects, landscape architects, planners and social scientists to play in reclaiming
and making places. Their task is, first, to develop a sensitivity to the
attributes of places and then to find ways of initiating and directing
locally committed developments. These ways must simultaneously
acknowledge the global character of almost everything in modern
life. In short, the task is to find some means of balancing local considerations with broader social and ecological concerns. How this is
done will surely vary enormously from situation to situation, but it
always has to be based on the recognition that places are the contexts of human life and in some manner are themselves alive, for
they grow, change and decline with the individuals and groups who
maintain or ignore them. Trying to design or reclaim places is,
therefore, rather like trying to make or modify life itself. In this effort, it is wisest to adopt the gentle and patient manner of an environmental midwife, while rejecting utterly the machine-driven
arrogance of some environmental equivalent to a genetic engineer.

By such gentle means places might flourish again, but also the world might become less threatened.

Notes

1. An earlier version of this essay was given as a keynote address for the conference, "Place and Place Making," held in Melbourne, Australia, June 1985, and sponsored by PAPER (People and Physical Environment Research).

References

Alexander, C. (1977). *A Pattern Language*. New York: Oxford University Press.

———. (1979). *The Timeless Way of Building*. New York: Oxford University Press.

———. (1985). *The Production of Houses*. New York: Oxford University Press.

Boorstin, D. (1973). *The Americans: The Democratic Experience*. New York: Random House.

Boudon, P. (1979). *Lived-in Architecture: Le Corbusier's Pessac Revisited*. Cambridge, Massachusetts: MIT Press.

Cullen, G. (1961). *Townscape*. London: The Architectural Press.

Davies, R. (1978). "How to Design a Haunted House", in *One Half of Robertson Davies*. London: Penguin.

Fergusson, J. (1873). *History of the Modern Styles of Architecture*. London: John Murray [first edition 1862].

Fromm, D. and Bosselman, P. (1983–1984). Mexacali Revisited: Seven Years Later. *Places, 1:* 78–96.

Hareven, T. and Langenbauch, R. (1981). "Living Places, Work Places and Historical Identity," in D. Lowenthal and M. Binney (eds.) *Our Past Before Us*. London: Temple Smith.

Jacobs, J. (1961). *The Death and Life of Great American Cities*. New York: Random House.

Lynch, K. (1981). *A Theory of Good City Form*. Cambridge, Massachusetts: MIT Press.

Meyrowitz, J. (1985). *No Sense of Place.* New York: Oxford University Press.

Mumford, L. (1964). *The Pentagon of Power.* New York: Harcourt, Brace, Jovanovich.

Norberg-Schulz, C. (1980). *Genius Loci.* New York: Rizzoli.

Relph, E. (1976). *Place and Placelessness.* London: Pion.

———. (1981). *Rational Landscapes and Humanistic Geography.* London: Croom Helm.

———. (1987). *Modern Urban Landscapes.* New York: Johns Hopkins University Press.

Ruskin, J. (1851). "The Nature of Gothic," in *The Stones of Venice.* New York: Wiley.

Strabo (1959). *The Geography.* Cambridge, Massachusetts: Harvard University Press.

Chapter 3

Thoughts on a Non-Arbitrary Architecture[1]

□

Karsten Harries

The Austrian novelist Hermann Broch (1955, p. 43) suggested that we may read the essence of an age from its architectural facades. Applying this suggestion to what was built in Vienna in the last decades of the nineteenth century, he arrived at a very negative judgment: only a decadent society could have produced such an arbitrary, eclectic, and theatrical architecture. This had been the heyday of neo-baroque, neo-renaissance, and neo-gothic building. To Broch such a turn to the past seemed the cynical attempt of a rational age to cover up its own poverty. Reason, and this meant first of all economic considerations, determined what and how one built. But reason proved not enough; something was felt to be missing. So, an ornamental dress was thrown over fundamentally utilitarian structures, and lacking the strength and conviction to create an ornament and a style equal to what earlier ages had produced, architecture took to borrowing. The riches of the past had to compensate for the poverty of the present.

Such negative comments on the eclecticism of the nineteenth century are part of the situation that led to the rise of the modern movement. Think of Adolf Loos' much more vehement attack on the same architecture criticized by Broch, or of the hopes that led to the establishment of the Bauhaus: The modern world would finally find its own proper style. Gropius promised to heal the rift between beauty and reason, form and function; once more architecture was to be all of a piece. Today, those dreams also belong to the history of architecture. We have learned to look with different and more loving eyes at architecture that to Broch demonstrated cynicism and the decadence of the age. But was he wrong? Or have we grown only more resigned, not to say, more cynical?

Today, the age that built Vienna's Ringstrasse, the age of operetta and the *Backhendl* (the Vienna fried chicken), seems quite wonderful if irretrievably lost; slipped away into a past when the Danube was always blue. And, strangely enough, today we find architects returning to the eclectic architecture of the nineteenth century somewhat as the nineteenth century returned to the stronger styles of the preceding centuries. Eclecticism has been raised to a higher power; so has arbitrariness. Historicism has become meta-historicism. Consider what has been called "post-modern classicism" (Searing and Reed, 1981).

There is an important difference between this post-modern eclecticism and the eclecticism of the nineteenth century. The nineteenth century took seriously the historical paradigms it had adopted, just as those who insisted on the neo-gothic architecture of so many American college campuses still took its medieval precursors seriously, not only or even primarily as artistic models, but because they wanted to preserve at least a trace of the ethos that produced the original. Today such reverence for the past seems a bit naive. Not that we side with the harsh criticism directed against nineteenth century eclecticism by the Modern Movement; we lack the conviction such fervor requires. Today most would agree that Gropius and his co-fighters failed to resolve the tension between the functional and the aesthetic as they had hoped. As Drexler remarks, "We are still dealing with the conflict between art and technology that beset the nineteenth century" (Drexler, 1979, p. 17). Once more there is a willingness to accept such tension and an architecture of decorated sheds; once again there is an attempt to relieve the dreariness of functional architecture with borrowed decoration, although today there is little conviction in such borrowing. This may be put positively: Post-modernist eclecticism takes itself less seriously than did its nineteenth century predecessors. It is freer, more playful, less intimidated by the past. But, by the same token, it is also less convinced by its borrowing and less able to convince.

Aesthetics and Architecture

In *Complicity and Conviction,* William Hubbard writes that:

> if there is one characteristic that links the diverse art movements of the modernist period, it is perhaps a hyperawareness of the fact that one's personal sensibility could have been otherwise. A modernist artist is so deeply aware of this possibility of otherwise-ness that he feels a deep unease about simply accepting his own sensi-

bility. He feels a need for some reason that will convince him that
he ought to feel one way and not another (Hubbard, 1981, p. 5).

This statement invites challenge: To be sure, there is greater
awareness of the "possibility of otherwise-ness," and it is not con-
fined to artists, but is simply a corollary of our greater freedom. The
less nature and culture determine what we have to be, the greater
our freedom; the greater also the dread of aribitrariness. But does
successful art not deliver us from such dread, and not because it
gives us a reason to feel a certain way? As a self-justifying whole,
having its telos within itself, the well-made work of art promises to
banish the specter of arbitrariness, quieting our restless freedom, if
only for a time. Such a work should present itself as having to be
just as it is. Do we need reasons to convince us of this? An artist who
feels the need for such reasons would seem to be anxious about
his or her own creative power. Has the glory of aesthetic experience
not long been tied precisely to its ability to deliver us from the need
for reasons?
     One might thus insist that the answer to the problem of arbi-
trariness in architecture can only be given by architects who are
first of all artists. But such insistence misunderstands the problem.
Unlike paintings or sculptures, buildings cannot be autonomous
aesthetic objects; architecture cannot just serve the demands of
beauty. Indeed, if beauty is understood as self-justifying aesthetic
presence, then beauty in architecture is essentially something beyond, or added on to, what necessity dicatates. The autonomy that
modern sensibility has granted to the aesthetic realm, an autonomy
that calls for art for art's sake, has to lead also to a view of architecture as essentially caught between the demands of beauty and
those of life.
     Venturi's claim that "architecture is necessarily complex and
contradictory in its very inclusion of the traditional Vitruvian elements of commodity, firmness, and delight" must be taken seriously,
as must its consequences (Venturi, 1977, p. 16). The aesthetic approach—which for more than two centuries has dominated both reflection about art and artistic practice—has to lead to an architecture of decorated sheds. Given such an approach, the proper focus of
aesthetic concern is in a deep sense never more than just decoration. But if so, the link between decoration and shed cannot but
strike us as arbitrary, no matter how much the decoration may
present itself to us as a self-justifying aesthetic presence—as arbitrary as the relation of a strong painting to the wall on which it
happens to hang. The problem of arbitrariness in architecture has

one root in our aesthetic approach; the other lies in our inability to view buildings apart from any consideration of dwelling, just as sources of aesthetic delight. There can thus be no merely aesthetic answer to this problem.

Venturi does not seem to me to take his own insight into the complexity and contradiction of architecture seriously enough. He still subscribes to the traditional view that a successful work of art, while incorporating and becoming stronger because of ambiguities and tensions, must yet be an integrated whole. Venturi holds architects to the same standard: "But an architecture of complexity and contradiction has a special obligation toward the whole: Its truth must be in its totality or its implications of totality. It must embody the difficult unity of inclusion rather than the easy unity of exclusion. More is not less" (Venturi, 1977, p. 16). But how can the demands of life and beauty be reconciled? Venturi's call for inclusion strong enough to master complexity suggests a renewal, albeit in a different key, of Gropius's dream of the complete building, a dream that amounts to a subjection of the demands of life to the demands of aesthetics, and harks back to Wagner's *Gesamtkunstwerk* (Harries, 1980). Against this, I would insist on the essential difference between aesthetic objects and dwellings. The very self-sufficiency of the former, which bids us keep our distance, makes them essentially uninhabitable. An architecture of decorated sheds should give up all claim to the creation of aesthetic wholes. But to give up that claim is to give up also the claim to all merely aesthetic answers to the problem of arbitrariness in architecture.

Function and Architecture

I have linked the problem of arbitrariness to our greater freedom. To this, one may object that freedom has here been grasped inadequately because only negatively: True freedom is not freedom from constraint, but rather to be constrained only by what one really is, by one's essence.

This suggests that the problem of arbitrariness might be met by returning to what is essential. Some such reasoning supported the modern movement. Loos condemns the aestheticizing architecture of his time for heeding merely subjective aesthetic whim, leading both the individual and architecture to lose their place in that larger whole to which they should belong. He likens a villa built at an Alpine lakeside to an "unnecessary screech." "Why", he asks, "is it that every architect, whether he is good or bad, harms the lakeside? The peasant does not. Nor does the engineer who builds a railway to the lake or plows deep furrows in its bright surface" (Rykwert, 1972, p. 27). The peasant is at one with nature. Hence the look of necessity of his dwellings. With its emphasis on the subject, modernity has broken that bond. The look of arbitrariness of its architecture testifies to that breach. The engineer, however, once more has to attune himself to nature and to her laws. From the engineer, Loos expects a healing of the rift that our subjectivism has opened up. Structures like Maillart's bridges prevent us from simply dismissing such expectations.

But by now trust in engineers and their attunement to nature is harder to come by. Our deteriorating environment has forced us to be suspicious of technocracy. And we have become less convinced of the functional character of the heroic architecture of the modern movement, which is often better described as having the look of functionality than as being truly functional. From the point of view of a strict functionalism, this look of functionality is as superfluous as any ornament. It might yet carry conviction if we could share the almost evangelical hopes in technology that many had when the modern movement gathered strength. If today we are likely to be made uneasy by the look of functionality, this is not just because we see it as just another form of architectural decoration, but because the ethos that it communicates strikes us as one-dimensional and dehumanizing. Once again we are forced to acknowledge that the problem of arbitrariness in architecture is not first of all an aesthetic one.

The struggle between modernists and post-modernists is thus not adequately understood just as a struggle between aesthetic sensibilities, but between those who prefer less and those who want more. Aesthetic sensibilities carry ethical implications. The struggle becomes one between different determinations of how human beings are to exist. It is with good reason that Venturi quotes August Heckscher:

> The movement from a way of life as essentially simple and orderly to a view of life as complex and ironic is what every individual passes through in becoming mature. But certain epochs encourage this development; in them the paradoxical or dramatic outlook colors the whole intellectual scene (Venturi, 1977, p. 16).

Venturi would have us understand his theorizing and building as a contribution toward an architecture for a world come of age.

The question, however, is whether coming of age is understood here in a way that lets freedom become negative, ironic, and destructive. In *Either/Or,* Kierkegaard (1959) has given us an unsurpassed analysis of such an aesthetic lifestyle, an analysis that shows convincingly that such a lifestyle must suffer shipwreck on the reef of the arbitrary.

History and Architecture

It is this charge of arbitrariness that Hubbard levels against the work of Venturi, Graves, Eisenmann, and Meier: "Looking at post-modern buildings, we become so aware of how easily the arrangement could have been otherwise that we feel imposed upon; the arrangement feels capricious and we are dissatisfied" (Hubbard, 1981, p. 7). The same may be said of the use of traditional elements in novel, and therefore, interesting ways. Consider Graves's use of the keystone motif in the Plocek house. Kierkegaard's discussion of the interesting illuminates this version of post-modernism (Kierkegaard, 1959; Harries, 1968, pp. 49–60). Such aesthetic play with elements drawn from the past cannot lead to an architecture that carries conviction.

When thinkers despair both of freedom and of finding a natural measure, they tend to appeal to history. Heidegger, to cite just one example, writes in *Being and Time* that "the sole authority which a free existing can have" is that of "revering the repeatable possibilities of existence" (Heidegger, 1962, p. 443). Historicism in architecture may be similarly defended. The difficulty with this suggestion is that history does not speak with one, but with many and often conflicting voices. Where do we find a non-arbitrary, i.e., binding, reading of history? If every individual has to offer his own reading, picking and choosing as he sees fit, then the problem of arbitrariness is raised to a different level. If history is to offer an answer to the problem of arbitrariness, it must be experienced not as a reservoir of more or less interesting motifs which we can pick up or discard as we see fit, but as a tradition that determines our place and destiny, in which we stand and to which we belong.

This is how Hubbard would have us move beyond the arbitrariness of post-modern architecture. The history of architecture may be looked at as a history of changing conventions concerning what constitutes good building. In that history certain structures possess paradigmatic significance. Implicit in these structures is an evolving ideal image of people: "The architect has in mind an ideal about how people ought to live, and he has chosen those particular conventions because he sees a way in which he can use them to express that ideal" (Hubbard, 1981, p. 155). Relating his structure to precursor buildings, while yet attempting to make an orginal contribution, the architect adds a link to what is a continuing chain. Hubbard invites us to take Harold Bloom's interpretation of poetic achievement as a creative reading of precursor texts as a model for understanding achievement in architecture (Bloom, 1973).

The difficulty with all such views is that just as we moderns have fallen out of nature, so we have fallen out of history. We may know much more about history today than ever before, but precisely in making the past an object of scientific investigation, the sense of belonging to the past is lost. We have removed ourselves too effectively from the past to still belong to it. Time has been reduced to a coordinate on which we move back and forth with equal facility. With this the past must lose much of its authority. It tends to become no more than a reservoir of material that we may incorporate in our constructions as we see fit. But with this, the problem of arbitrarines re-enters.

There is another, more serious question raised by Hubbard's Bloomian account: If we can look at great architecture as offering a creative misreading of some past structure or structures, and that is to say also, as departing from these precursor structures, what gives direction to the departure? Hubbard appeals to an ideal of how people ought to live. If that ideal were to be rejected, the architecture that communicates it would also meet with little sympathy. But Hubbard also believes that ideals are human creations and that one function of architecture is to infuse reality with such ideals: "We in society want to be able to believe in ideals about the places we inhabit, but we know that such ideals are indefensible" (Hubbard, 1981, p. 153). The architect can count on this will to believe. Architecture helps to replace meaningless reality with a theatrically, or rather architecturally, transformed reality, which draws us in and, as we surrender to it, grants us an illusion of meaning. We become actors on a stage that lets us forget the reality it conceals. Somewhat like Sartre, Hubbard has faith in people's ability to create meanings in a meaningless world. This faith "says that of course the world, as given, doesn't make sense, but that we can make sense of it and we are the only ones who can" (Hubbard, 1981, p. 158).

This is, I am afraid, a vain faith. Meaning cannot finally be made or invented; it can only be discovered, where such discovery will also be a self-discovery. All meaning that presents itself to us as freely created must seem arbitrary, and precisely because of this it cannot convince. Without an ideal or an essence to guide our manner of departure from precursor structures, such departures must lack direction. The chain will be broken. Architectural theory cannot dispense with dreams of an ideal architecture, an architecture that would do full justice to the requirements of human dwelling.

The Primitive Hut and Architecture

Such a requirement is of course not at all novel. As Joseph Rykwert explains,

> The return to origins is a constant of human development and in this matter architecture conforms to all other human activities. The primitive hut—the home of the first man—is therefore no incidental concern of theorists, no casual ingredient of myth or ritual. The return to origins always implies a rethinking of what you do customarily, an attempt to renew the validity of your everyday actions, or simply a recall of the natural (or even divine) sanction for your repeating them for a season. In the present rethinking of why we build and what we build for, the primitive hut will, I suggest, retain its validity as a reminder of the original and therefore essential meaning of all building for people: that is, of architecture. It remains the underlying statement, the irreducible, intentional core, which I have attempted to show transformed through the tensions between various historical forces (Rykwert, 1972, p. 192).

The difference between Rykwert's claim and any conventionalism is evident. Conventionalists will seek to escape from arbitrariness by grounding practice in an on-going tradition. But we moderns have become too reflective, too critical, to simply entrust ourselves to what has been. No longer are we willing to repeat what has long been done, just because it has become part of a tradition. At the same time we are not satisfied with departures from tradition because of some merely subjective whim. We have no choice but to attempt to articulate what is essential or natural. Such articulation is the point of speculation about the appearance of the original or primitive hut. The primitive hut has played a part in architectural theory that parallels that of the social contract in political theory. Whether there ever was such a hut matters as little as whether there ever was such a contract. Both are constructs of

reason meant to legitimate a certain practice; in this they are characteristic expressions of the Enlightenment and of its confidence
that the authority of reason and nature could replace divine sanc-
tion. And although we have grown less confident about the power of
reason, our confusions leave us no reasonable alternative to reap-
propriating the lessons of the Enlightenment. We, too, have to try to
recover origins, where the return to origins is not so much a turn
back to the past as a turn to what is essential. In this sense the
speculation of the ex-Jesuit Marc Antoine Laugier may be said to
present an abiding challenge.

Not that we are likely to be convinced by Laugier's *Essai sur
l'architecture* (Laugier, 1755). We have learned to be wary of appeals
to nature. All too often such appeals have been unmasked as historical prejudice claiming a dignity for what is proposed that does
not belong to it. Consider the way in which Laugier arrives at his
version of a natural language of architecture. Laugier begins with
people in the state of nature. Among their needs is the need for shelter, a need which cave and forest meet only inadequately. The attempt to remedy that inadequacy leads to the construction of the
first house, the paradigmatic building. Architecture, in this view,
may be said to be both: the image of the cave and the image of the
forest (cf. Norberg-Schulz, 1965, p. 125).

As Laugier presents this system, the forest is allowed to triumph over the cave. Only columns, entablatures, and pediment,
representing the supporting uprights, the horizontal members they
carry, and the inclined members that make up the roof of the primitive hut, are considered essential parts of architecture. Walls, windows, doors, and the like are permitted, but are said to make no
essential contribution to beauty. The turn to the primitive hut does
not mean a functional approach to architecture. What lifts architecture beyond mere building is its power of representation. Successful
architecture represents building. As a variation on the theme
stated by the primitive hut, all great architecture recalls us to an
ideal of genuine dwelling.

Supposedly born of the need for shelter, and informed by the
natural shelter provided by caves and forests, the primitive hut
turns out to look rather like the then much revered and imitated
temples of antiquity. Not that Laugier thought the architecture of
antiquity beyond criticism. The past too has to be questioned. Only
reason can endow past structures with the legitimacy that makes
them models worthy of imitation by showing that they are representations of the archetypal building. But was the Greek temple

constructed in the image of Laugier's primitive hut, or was that hut constructed in the image of the Greek temple?

When Laugier thinks of exemplary structures, he is not only thinking of the architecture of the ancients. Gothic architecture with its forest of columns is given a similar legitimacy and takes its place beside the architecture of the ancients as a second paradigm. Laugier's *Essai* has been shown to have encouraged neo-gothic architecture (Worner, 1979). But this only reinforces suspicions that his hut owes more to cultural preferences, characteristics of the region and the period, than to the voices of reason and nature. It leads to an architecture of sheathed skeletons, appropriate to a heavily forested region, rather than to an architecture of continuous surfaces, appropriate to a region where the natural building materials are mud, brick, or stone. Laugier's "nature" speaks with a regional voice. And Laugier's interpretation of this voice is very much shaped by his historical situation.

Region and history help determine what we find natural and hence inevitable. But the less an individual is bound to a particular place in space and time, the weaker that determination, and the greater the uncertainty about what is to count as natural. This helps to explain why the problem of the arbitrariness of architecture is characteristically modern. We have greater difficulty constructing our ideal hut than Laugier did.

Nevertheless, if there is to be responsible criticism of what has come to be established and accepted, it must be possible to challenge conventional wisdom by appealing to a more primordial understanding, less subject to the prejudices of the time. Even if ideals are never given but precariously constructed, inevitably tarnished by cultural prejudice, this does not mean that they are therefore arbitrary. What gives their construction direction is the tension between conventional wisdom, and what more profoundly claims and affects us, between what one says and does and what one feels should be said and done. Even if we can never seize the dream of a building that would do full justice to the demands of dwelling in such a way that we could say with confidence that we have provided architectural practice with a firm foundation, as a source of regulative ideals such dreaming is indispensable. Laugier's speculations have thus an exemplary significance, as does the Vitruvian account of the origin of building to which it harks back. We are still not done with the Enlightenment. That goes for its architectural theory as well as for its political theory.

Dwelling and Architecture

To say that we are still not done with the Enlightenment is not to suggest that we can simply return it. To appropriate it we have to question and rethink what it thought. One aspect of Laugier's account of the primitive hut that invites questioning is his tendency to equate the need for building with the need for material shelter. But the need for building cannot be reduced to the need to achieve physical control of the environment. Equally important is the need for spiritual control. We cannot live with chaos. Chaos must be transformed into cosmos. Building has thus been thought traditionally an analogy to divine creation: God as the archteypal architect.

Such analogies may mean little today, but one task of architecture is still that of interpreting the world as a meaningful order in which the individual can find his place in the midst of nature and in the midst of a community. Time and space must be revealed in such a way that human beings are given their dwelling place, their ethos. When we reduce the human need for shelter to a material need, we lose sight of what we can call the ethical function of architecture. I agree with Hegel's claim that the highest function of all art is not to entertain or to amuse, but to articulate a binding world view; to express to human beings who they are and who they should be. When works of art come to be for art's sake, that is to say, when the point of art is reduced to that of furnishing occasions for aesthetic delight, that highest function is lost.

Architecture, by its very nature, resists such reduction. That is why, given a view of the art-object as a self-justifying whole, architecture has to appear as an impure, a compromised art. But just because architecture is not merely a source of aesthetic delight, but invites a fuller response, because it shapes the time and space of lived experience, it is unavoidable that we should judge it by how ill or well it carries out what I have called its ethical function. Hubbard is right to link the problem of arbitrariness in architecture to that of articulating ideals of dwelling. Any reappropriation of Laugier's primitive hut has to begin with a rethinking of the meaning of dwelling.

One modern philosopher who has thought deeply about dwelling is Martin Heidegger (1971). His description of a Black Forest farmhouse may be read as his attempt to give content to the ideal house that haunts our dreams of genuine dwelling. It deserves being quoted at some length:

> The nature of building is letting dwell. Building accomplishes its
> nature in the raising of locations by the joining of their spaces.
> *Only if we are capable of dwelling, only then can we build.* Let us
> think for a while of a farmhouse in the Black Forest, which was
> built some two hundred years ago by the dwelling of peasants.
> Here the self-sufficiency of the power to let earth and heaven, di-
> vinities and mortals enter in *simple oneness* into things, ordered
> the house. It placed the farm on the wind-sheltered mountain
> slope, looking south, among the meadows close to the spring. It
> gave it its wide overhanging shingle roof whose proper slope bears
> up under the burden of snow, and which, reaching deep down,
> shields the chambers against the storms of the long winter nights.
> It did not forget the altar corner behind the community table; it
> made room in its chamber for the hallowed places of childbed and
> the "tree of the dead"—for that is what they call a coffin there: the
> *Totenbaum*—and in this way it designed for the different genera-
> tions under one roof the character of their journey through time. A
> craft, which, itself sprung from dwelling, still uses its tools and
> frames as things, built the farmhouse (Heidegger, 1971, p. 160).

There is a sense in which Heidegger's farmhouse may seem to
lie more thoroughly behind us than Laugier's primitive hut. If
Laugier thinks of his hut in relation to the individual, Heidegger
seems to be thinking in terms of the extended family, extended also
through time. The farmhouse articulates "for the different generations under one roof the character of their journey through time."
Not only space, but also time, are shaped by it in such a way that
the individual gains his dwelling place as member of an ongoing
community. Heidegger thinks of his farmhouse as located in a definite region. It is born of and a response to that landscape. This
thinking of genuine dwelling is thus regional, as it is generational.
But what power do such contexts have over us moderns? Must we
not develop an understanding of dwelling more appropriate to our
changed situation? Or does the shape of modernity threaten genuine dwelling?

A Language of Natural Symbols

Heidegger understands genuine building as an interpretation
of a more original being-in-the-world that strengthens people's natural sense of place. This being-in-the-world is misunderstood when
we think of it, as Hubbard seems to do, in terms of a subject facing

a mute world of objects, which the subject then has to endow with meanings. The understanding of the world as a collection of meaningless facts rests on a distorting reduction of experience that must lose sight of the significance of things. As Schopenhauer points out, first of all and most of the time, things "do not march past us, strange and meaningless . . . but speak to us directly, are understood, and acquire an interest that engrosses our whole nature" (Schopenhauer, 1969, p. 95). First of all, things speak to us. That speech is silenced only by the reduction of things to mere objects, a reduction presupposed by science. But we have to learn to put science in its proper place; we have to reappropriate the truth expressed when we speak metaphorically of the language of nature or of natural symbols. If it is to recall us to a genuine dwelling, architecture must make use of these symbols.

By natural symbols, I understand symbols that can be derived simply from an analysis of people's being in the world. They are not tied to a particular culture or region, although, inevitably, different cultures will appropriate them differently. The term being-in-the-world, which I take from Heidegger, already implies a rejection of interpretations that would reduce experience to a relation of a subject to objects. First of all, people finds themselves not before the world, confronting it as if it were a picture, but in the midst of things, experiencing them for a particular place. Heidegger suggests that our first encounter with things is "ready-to-hand" (Heidegger, 1962, p. 95 ff.). The reference to the hand here is significant. I reach for something—it is too high. The body provides me with a natural sense of distance and proximity: What is in back of me is less available than what is in front of me. Or we can say, the body provides me with what we can call a set of coordinates, very different from the x, y, and z coordinates of geometry, and different especially in that the different coordinates carry different meanings. Up and down, left and right, front and back—all carry value implications which are brought out when we think of the metaphors these terms have furnished.

Up, for example, has a very different significance from down. We cannot simply turn a building upside down or rotate it; but we can design buildings to look as if they could be inverted or rotated rather easily. The curtain wall invites such a look of invertibility; so do certain simple geometric shapes, such as the sphere, the cube, and the cylinder. We can also design buildings that seem to discourage all such attempts. Think of the gabled roof: its presence seems to resist inversion. I am not arguing here for either a look of invertibility or a look of rootedness. All I want to say is that whatever choice we make when designing a building, such choice will communicate a particular ideal of being in the world. And if up and down carry a different meaning, so do vertical and horizontal, inside and outside, dark and light. Light serves to remind us of the way the language of space is also a language of time. Natural light is essentially moving light, changing with the times of the day and the times of the year.

I cannot do more here than provide a few hints as to how one might go about developing an understanding of the natural language of architecture. Perhaps the term "language" is misleading, for if we can speak of a language at all, this is a language addressed, first, to sense and imagination. Before attempts are made to articulate it in words, it needs to be felt. The arts, and more especially architecture, are in a much better position to teach us to listen to this language than philosophy. I can imagine courses that would explore it, but such courses would have to rely on images. There might be, for example, courses just on windows or on doors, or on roofs; or on stairs; but the list is endless. Besides architecture, poetry and painting would help to teach what to listen to. From such courses would not flow prescriptions. They would teach something like a vocabulary. Learning that vocabulary is a necessary, but not a sufficient condition for the creation of buildings that are experienced as necessary rather than arbitrary.

Natural symbols are intertwined with conventional symbols tied to a particular time and region. Consider the cross. Given our tradition, the reference to the cross on which Christ died suggests itself. There are thus architectural motifs that have acquired quite definite meanings. Any pyramid we erect harks back to its Egyptian precursors and to the function of these structures. The pyramid form is thus particularly suitable for grave monuments. But although a conventional symbol, I would suggest that there is something about the simple geometry of the form that makes it not an accident that Egyptians seized on it as they did: the conventional symbol presupposes and builds on a natural symbol. The cross also illustrates this point. But let me give one other example: in church architecture we find quite commonly that the arch separating the nave from the more sacred choir is conceived of in terms that recall a Roman triumphal arch. The analogy between the triumph of Christ and the triumph of an emperor like Titus is deliberate, although intelligible only to someone who is familiar with the conventions involved. And yet there is something about the arch form that invites such use.

Often the conventional symbolism of architecture rests on the authority of particular texts. Thus the symbolism of a traditional church cannot be understood without the Bible. Beyond that, a quite specific understanding of things as signs is being presupposed. To interpret a gothic, and still a baroque or rococo church, we have to do something very much like decode a message that yields its secrets only when we understand the language in which it is written. This language was thought to derive from figures found in God's two books, the Bible and the book of nature; both speak to us of our life and death, condition and destiny. But do they still speak to us? How seriously can we take the stories of the Bible? And can we still understand nature as a book addressed to human beings?

Between us and such a view stands the characteristically modern and, it seems to me, questionable privilege granted to univocity, to the simple and literal meaning of the text, and to an accordingly strict, or better, narrow conception of meaning. We owe such insistence on literalness both to science and to the reformation. It is part of modernity, but with this it becomes impossible to make sense of anything like the medieval interpretation of the spiritual significance of things. I would, however, suggest that even if this particular symbolic language lies behind us, even if Scripture no longer offers us the key to decoding the hidden meanings of things, these meanings still speak to us. Indeed, even that conventional vocabulary has not become completely meaningless, for in it still lives a natural symbolism. If architecture is to illuminate and shape the space of everyday life, it will have to open itself to these natural symbols.

There is yet another kind of symbolization that deserves mention. A great deal of the symbolism we find in nineteenth and twentieth century architecture takes the form of a repetition of the no longer understood, or devalued, symbols of the past. Such repetition is raised to a higher power by much post-modern architecture. Instead of trying to recover what I have called architecture's natural symbols, the architect represents and plays with the symbols of the past. Symbols now become representations of symbols and are therefore *meta-symbols*. The architecture of Las Vegas so praised by Venturi is rich in such meta-symbols. Or think of Charles Moore's *Piazza d'Italia*. Such play cannot escape arbitrariness. What we need is not meta-symbols, but something like an archeology of conventional symbols, an approach to symbols that is not so focused on what is merely conventional that it is unable to understand these conventions as particular responses to something more universally human. Such an archeological approach is also necessary when considering a metaphor like that of the book of nature. While it belongs to a culture irrevocably past, that metaphor can be understood as one attempt to articulate an aspect of human being in the world essential to genuine dwelling and to genuine building.

Home and Temple

Our being in the world is a being with others. We need to feel at home in both our natural and social environment. Architecture inevitably offers interpretations of both. An obvious weakness of Laugier's account is his neglect of the social dimension. Like the natural men of Hobbes and Locke, Laugier's primitive man is an atomic self, endowed with reason, facing natural needs. Laugier thus shares the subjectivism that is a presupposition of liberal thought. In this respect there is a noteworthy difference between Laugier's and the Vitruvian account. Vitruvius begins not with the singular but the plural, with brutish men brought together, and brought to language and building, by an accidental fire.

Like Laugier's hut, Heidegger's ideal building is also a house, although that house is now thought of as the dwelling place of a family, extending through different generations. But such emphasis on the house must be questioned. In this connection it is well to remember that architectural theory has turned not around one but two paradigms: An ellipse that has one focus in the house, tied to the family more than to the individual; the other in the church or temple. Thus while the idea of the original house has haunted architectural theory, so has that of a divine structure of sacred origin. If the former addresses itself more to the need for physical control, the latter addresses itself more to the need for spiritual control. We should not forget that a good part of what is considered in histories of architecture is sacred architecture. Thus, through many centuries, the history of Western architecture is reduced pretty much to a history of church architecture. The church building gained its legitimacy, not as a representation of the first house, but of real and imagined structures that were thought to have God as their real architect, including the Temple in Jerusalem and, even more importantly, the City in Heaven of which Revelation speaks. This reminds us of the fact that sacred architecture has traditionally had a public function as the house did not.

I spoke of an ellipse that has its foci in the house and in the temple. The distance between them is related to the distance that separates the private and the public. The ethical function of architecture is first of all a public function. Sacred and public architecture provides a community with a center or centers. Individuals gain their sense of place by relating their dwelling to those centers. We may thus think of private architecture as furnishing a ground illuminated by the figures furnished by public architecture. Think of a medieval town, dominated by its church, by the horizontal of an enormous sheltering roof and the vertical of a tower that the traditional consecration ceremony allows us to link with the ladder of Jacob's dream, a ladder that connects heaven and earth. The traditional church is another Bethel, a place of divine promise of enduring community. There is a temporal analogy: The everyday with its mundane concerns may be considered a ground illuminated by festive times. The ability or inability to celebrate festivals is closely tied to the ability or inability to establish structures or places that let a multitude understand itself as a community joined by a common destiny.

Modern architecture, however, no longer knows building tasks to rival the traditional church, although we do of course continue to build churches. But the church has become just one building type among others, and hardly one to which most architects would grant terribly much importance. There is no single building type today that could claim to possess the public importance once possessed by the church, just as there is no institution which can claim to have taken over the traditional function of the Church as guardian and interpreter of our vocation. Increasingly, value is located in the private. A corollary of this is the increasing emphasis placed on the house, which has often been discussed in terms that attribute to it almost the sacred quality of a church. Think of the Victorian conception of the house, which even knew its angels. Heidegger's celebration of the Black Forest farmhouse similarly represents a view of architecture that has replaced my ellipse with a circle, having its single focus in the house. Presupposed is the disintegration of genuine community into a multiplicity of individuals and families; a corollary is the formal approach to the law and to the state, both born of self-love and its remedy. And if the disintegration of community should extend to marriage, which threatens to be reduced to no more than a formal and increasingly temporary arrangement between individuals, the house, as Heidegger celebrates it, will also become an anachronism.

But being in the world is essentially both: Being a self and being with others. We cannot sacrifice one aspect to the other without doing violence to human nature. Not that these two aspects of human existence will ever coexist without tension. Building must recognize and respect that tension. Every building distributes in its own way the weight to be given to the private and to the public: Each is concerned not with just one, but with both foci of my ellipse, where energies once focused on the church, may today turn to public areas, such as squares, streets, and parks. Perhaps yesterday's church architects will be tomorrow's urban planners. Weren't churches thought to prefigure a city?

An Architecture of Commitment

Problems of building and dwelling cannot finally be resolved by theory; theorizing can, at most, hope to call attention to possibilities and perhaps help to recall us to what matters. But without commitment there is no escape from arbitrariness. The problem of arbitrariness in architecture is finally an ethical problem. It will be solved only to the extent that architects and those for whom they build are joined by an understanding of what human existence is to be. This is not to suggest that architecture should therefore subordinate itself to moral philosophy. The philosopher's formulations are necessarily abstract and one-sided. As Schopenhauer remarks, "Where it is a question of the worth or worthlessness of existence, of salvation or damnation, not the dead concepts of philosophy decide the matter, but the innermost nature of man himself" (Schopenhauer, 1969, p. 271). The philosopher's words are less likely to touch this inner nature than the built environment. Architecture is at least as likely to edify as philosophy.

Notes

1. This article was originally published in *Perspecta, 20* (1983): 9–20. The author and editor are grateful to Yale University for permission to reprint the article here.

References

Bloom, H. (1973). *The Anxiety of Influence*. New York: Oxford University Press.

Broch, H. (1955). Hofmannsthal und seine Zeit, *Gesammelte Werke, Essays,* vol. 1. Zurich: Rhein.

Drexler, A. (1979). *Transformations in Modern Architecture.* New York: The Museum of Modern Art.

Harries, K. (1968). *The Meaning of Modern Art.* Evanston: Northwestern University Press.

————. (1980). The Dream of the Complete Building, *Perspecta, 17,* 36–43. Cambridge, Massachusetts: MIT Press.

Heidegger, M. (1962). *Being and Time.* Trans. J. Macquarrie and E. Robinson. New York: Harper and Row.

————. (1971). Building Dwelling Thinking. In *Poetry, Language, Thought.* Trans. Albert Hofstadter. New York: Harper and Row.

Hubbard, W. (1981). *Complicity and Conviction: Steps Toward an Architecture of Convention.* Cambridge, Massachusetts: MIT Press.

Kierkegaard, S. (1959). The Rotation Method, *Either/Or,* vol. 1, trans. Walter Lowrie, D. F. Swenson, and L. M. Swenson. Garden City, New Jersey: Doubleday.

Laugier, M. A. (1755). *Essai sur l'architecture,* 2nd ed. Paris: Duchesne. [*An Essay on Architecture.* Trans. Wolfgang and Anni Herrmann. Los Angeles: Hennessey and Inglas, 1977].

Norberg-Schulz, C. (1965). *Intentions in Architecture.* Cambridge, Massachusetts: MIT Press.

Rykwert, J. (1972). *On Adam's House in Paradise.* New York: Museum of Modern Art.

Schopenhauer, A. (1969). *The World as Will and Representation,* vol. 1, trans. E. F. J. Payne. New York: Dover.

Searing, H. and Reed, H. H. (1981). *Speaking a New Classicism: American Architecture Now.* Northampton, Massachusetts: Smith College Museum of Art.

Venturi, R. (1977). *Complexity and Contradiction in Architecture,* 2nd ed. New York: Museum of Modern Art.

Worner, H. J. (1979). *Architektur des Fruhklassizismus in Suddeutschland.* Munich: Schnell und Steiner.

Chapter 4

"If the Doors of Perception Were Cleansed": Toward an Experiential Aesthetics for the Designed Landscape

◻

Catherine Howett

> *If the doors of perception were cleansed,*
> *Everything would appear as it is. . . .*
>
> ——— William Blake, "A Memorable Fancy"

These lines from Blake represent a familiar theme of visionary poetry—the poet's sense that our customary ways of looking at the world actually blind us to the reality of what is there, waiting to be known intimately and rapturously. But what is meant by "the doors of perception" that must be "cleansed" if we are to see truly? Is it our eyes only? Do we perceive the world by *seeing* it, or is our vision just one among many "doors of perception" that can be awakened to a new and more vivid experience of the world?

The act of seeing is so central to our conception of human nature that language identifies seeing with understanding—we say "Now I *see,* I *see* what you mean." Yet the degree to which any given culture attaches primacy to seeing over other kinds of sensory data is variable. The geographer Yi-Fu Tuan (1974) cites the example of an Aivilik Eskimo on Southampton Island, who depends on many more faculties than sight to deal with the environment:

> To the Eskimo, space is not pictorial or boxed in, but something always in flux, creating its own dimensions moment by moment. He learns to orient himself with all senses alert. He has to during certain times of winter when sky and earth merge and appear to be made of the same substance. . . . Under such conditions the

Eskimo cannot rely on points of reference given by permanent landmarks: he must depend on the shifting relationships of snow contours, on the types of snow, wind, salt air and ice crack. The direction and smell of the wind is a guide, together with the feel of ice and snow under his feet. . . . On horizonless days he lives in an acoustic-olfactory space (p. 11).

Culture significantly determines the choice and character of the "doors of perception" that an individual will develop as part of the process of learning to engage the environment in productive and satisfying ways. What the poets imply is that this cultural bias may needlessly narrow or suppress other innate human capacities for responding to the world around us. Moreover, that world is itself increasingly transformed in ways that reflect the same cultural predispositions. As the inheritors of late-twentieth century Western European civilization, we find ourselves inevitably cut off, at least in our everyday lives, from any possibility of encounter with the kind of primal natural landscape that challenges the Eskimo. We move about within familiar cultural landscapes, seldom asking ourselves what values are expressed by their forms and ordering, or how those values came to be embraced in preference to others. This essay takes as its premise that an examination of the historic sources for contemporary aesthetic preferences in the designed landscape may call into question the wisdom of our continuing acquiescence to a design canon that so privileges the act of seeing that other ways of experiencing the landscape are ignored or compromised.

An Inherited Aesthetic Dominated by Visual Values

Although the design of human environments is as old as civilization itself, the term "landscape architecture" was not coined until the nineteenth century. Frederick Law Olmsted and Calvert Vaux are usually credited with being the first to use this designation in an official way by referring to themselves as "landscape architects" in an 1863 letter to the Board of Commissioners of New York City's Central Park (Newton, 1971, p. 273). The rejection by the profession's founding fathers of the more familiar appellative "landscape gardening," inherited from eighteenth century practice and still in common use, was a symbolically important gesture. Its clear intention was to make the work of designing landscapes analogous with that of architecture—a virile and conceptually rigorous discipline, by contrast with gardening and horticulture, which were increasingly associated with the feminine domain.

In an essay attempting a psychohistorical analysis of Olmsted's personality, Melvin Kalfus (1981, pp. 141–147) has suggested that Olmsted had a deepseated drive to legitimize his own career, which had been marked by a series of failures in early manhood, by "surpassing his father" as a successful man of the world. Since for Olmsted, as for others of his generation, urban parks were identified with an idealized and feminine "nature in its domestic guise," it makes sense to speculate that he needed somehow to make his chosen profession seem more respectably manly in character. At the same time, he saw his task as one of providing a necessary curative to the harshly aggressive, masculine world of business by making sure that urbanites had opportunities for recovering health and serenity through contact with nature in parks and picturesque suburban enclaves.

With the founding of the American Society of Landscape Architects in 1899 and the establishment, in the opening decades of this century, of academic programs to train professionals, landscape architecture was institutionalized in a way that may be seen as reinforcing the conceptual separation between the form-giving act of design and the "raw material" that nature provided. Furthermore, the way that landscape architects design was determined to a greater degree by cultural imperatives—specifically, a limited range of acceptable *styles*—than by natural requirements having to do with advantages or constraints intrinsic to the site.

Once enough Americans had moved beyond the conditions of frontier settlement and had sufficient wealth and ambition to prompt an interest in the aesthetic aspects of town planning, architecture, and the laying out of grounds, they looked eagerly to Europe for models. Andrew Jackson Downing's *Treatise on the Theory and Practice of Landscape Gardening, Adapted to North America* (1841), as well as his other writings, enjoyed spectacular popular success precisely because Downing addressed the needs of this new audience, offering a primer of design formulas based on English practice in landscape gardening, and actual plans and views that could be copied. Olmsted's travels in England in 1850, and especially his visit to the public park at Birkenhead designed by Joseph Paxton, impressed upon his sensibility the superiority of the English "natural" style as an instrument for fostering contemplation of nature, an awareness that inspired his subsequent lifelong commitment to the principles of composition espoused by that tradition. Olmsted's vision, shared by his partner Vaux and other friends, students, and disciples, conceived of the park as absolutely different in its character from the surrounding city, a precious oasis of rural scenery intended for "pleasant contemplation" rather than for active recreation or any extension of the city's educational or cultural functions. There ought to be, in other words, as little as possible of the built world, and as much as possible of the carefully framed views of nature—great "ranges" of rolling meadow framed by trees, "sequestered and limitless" in their effect, interrupted occasionally by passages of more "rudely picturesque" woodlands or wilds (Schuyler, 1986, pp. 77–100).

Downing had introduced Americans to the notion that house and grounds together ought to form a seamless composition, a charming picture—reflecting the image either of the "Beautiful" or the "Picturesque"—that was uniquely able to express the good taste, good citizenship, and moral rectitude of the owner. He had learned from his English mentors, especially Humphry Repton and John Claudius Loudon, that the deliberate composition of pleasing views was the single most important task of the landscape designer. Olmsted was an immensely more sophisticated designer than Downing, but in his art, too, visual values have priority over all others. He used the same devices of enframement, *repoussoir,* screening, and focusing that had been the stock-in-trade of eighteenth century English practitioners creating "prospects" to enliven the walks and drives through the parks surrounding country houses—the private parks that eventually suggested a model for public ones.

Toward the close of his career—in projects such as his master plan for the 1893 World's Columbian exhibition at Chicago and his design for the grounds of Biltmore, George Vanderbilt's estate near Asheville, North Carolina, with its chateau-style mansion by Richard Morris Hunt—Olmsted embraced the emerging popular taste for landscape styles derived from Renaissance and Baroque formal traditions. Acceptance of the neoclassical revival did not, however, demand any abandonment of the underlying aesthetic of view-making that was so deeply ingrained in American practice. The so-called landscape gardening "revolution" of the English eighteenth century—in its substitution of the pastoral metaphor for the heroic, the countryside for the court, naturalism for the self-conscious display of art, the subtle motions of the soul in a gentleman of refined taste for the large gestures of Baroque tableaux or opera—had never abandoned the fundamentally *scenographic* approach that had informed the art of landscape design since the Renaissance.

The use of a term borrowed from theatrical production establishes, in fact, the link—an underlying continuity of artistic intention that is more germane to the argument here than superficial stylistic differences—between the landscapes of Renaissance and Baroque classicism and those of the English landscape gardening school. John Brinckerhoff Jackson (1980) has pointed out that the use of the word "scene" to describe a location in the real world rather than simply a theatrical "stage" came into popular use no earlier than the sixteenth century. Among the factors that might have made this usage seem appropriate, Jackson cites "the development of theatrical production as a formal art with its own rules and conventions and its own environment; a widespread belief that the relationship between people and their surroundings could be so expertly controlled and designed as to make the comparison appropriate; and, most important of all . . . people's ability to see themselves as occupying the center of the stage" (pp. 67–68). Further, the origins of modern theatrical art in Italy were tied to the earlier development there of the science of perspective, which made possible "the whole illusion of space achieved by the skillful use of light, color, and form: the space of a make-believe world which revolved around the presence of actors" (ibid.).

Thus the revolutionary aspect of the eighteenth century English landscape gardening style had to do with certain philosophical premises of the new art—especially an attitude toward the person-nature relationship that was to find expression in a new formal vocabulary—but left unchallenged the basic assumption that the design of landscape was analogous to the art of stagecraft. One might say that the dramatic "text" was new—a new storyline, a new setting, a new cast of characters—but that the authors-architects never dreamed of inventing a fundamentally new genre. Instead, the art of landscape design was still perceived to be essentially an art of forming spaces and manipulating visual effects in such a way that the landscape's meanings were communicated to its audience—the viewers—and stimulated the desired response, whether awe and admiration, delight in recognizing iconographic allusions, a pleasing melancholy, or (as was increasingly the case for nineteenth century inheritors of this tradition such as Downing and Olmsted) a sense of pride in identifying oneself with a refined and progressive cultural tradition. Few arts in modern times have been so conservative.

In the late twentieth century, for all our sense that the modern world is fundamentally different from that of our forebears, we are still so much under the sway of this post-Renaissance tradition, so culturally predetermined to look at landscape design through its lens, that it is difficult to recognize that it is an arbitrary, not an absolute, aesthetic system. How can we, accustomed to seeing things as we do, imagine a work of landscape architecture that does not give priority to how a place *looks,* that does not expect the designer to impose conventional forms upon the chaos "out there" in which the act of design originates, transforming it into a pleasing object of contemplation?

An Experiential Aesthetics

A body of scholarly work and criticism has emerged in recent years that seeks to explore the possibilities for radical revision or supplanting of this dominant aesthetic model (Berleant, 1985; Evernden, 1985; Howett, 1987; Seamon, 1987). Philosophers, geographers, environmental psychologists, design professionals, historians and critics, and other contributors to this dialogue share a common purpose in wishing to expose the limitations of the aesthetic in which a wide range of sensory, emotional and symbolic values are sacrificed to the primacy of compositional criteria determined by the act of seeing. Taking as their starting place the fundamental human experience of *being-in-the-world* described by philosopher Martin Heidegger (1962), they argue for the necessity of an *experiential* aesthetics to replace the operative one derived from Cartesian subject-object dualism, distancing us physically and spiritually from a world in which we are actually immersed. Aesthetics, according to Neil Evernden (1985), ought to be "a way of being, a stance toward the world; an aesthetic experience requires a relationship between a seeking subject and a responsive world. But scenery is a stockpile of usable commodities" (p. 54).

In a related discussion of the "commodification" of the contemporary urban landscape, Edward Relph (1987) illustrates the close connection between the idea that the world outside ourselves is a resource to be manipulated and managed in response to economic or other functional motives, and environmental design that is informed almost exclusively by theatrical and scenographic values. He cites a number of familiar examples—"McDonald's and clowns, housing developments marketed in terms of rural romanticism, package tours of the literary landscape of England"—and the fairly typical case of Monterey, California, a town whose vibrant life early in this century was made famous by John Steinbeck's novel *Cannery*

Row, and which has now been transformed into another kind of place that blurs the boundaries between "fiction and reality, location and imagination, history and invention, until they are no longer distinguishable" (pp. 188–89). It is impossible to live in today's world without being aware of how increasingly prevalent are such efforts to manufacture a once-or-twice-removed-from-reality "sense of place."

All of us are equally aware, when we begin to reflect upon it, of what it is like to have an authentic experience of place. I teach in a school of environmental design. In an introductory studio course, I have asked beginning design students to think back through their lives trying to remember the deepest, most profound, or happiest experience of place they have ever had. I then challenge them to make something that will communicate to others the nature of that experience. None of the students has ever described a *view* as the occasion of such an experience, even when what is being recalled took place in a spectacular natural setting. Instead, they summon up a much more complicated set of circumstances, rich in specific sensory and psychological details, but ambiguous or elusive in *logical* significance. Almost without exception, the places and experiences described relate to childhood. But why does one particular evening that a boy spent sitting in a tree, surveying a familiar house and yard through a maze of branches as he had done many times before, stand out with such vividness that the memory of it survives with a visceral freshness years later? A child, Yi-Fu Tuan (1974) reminds us, "places little importance on picturesqueness. . . . Nature yields delectable sensations to the child, with his openness of mind, carelessness of person, and lack of concern for the accepted canons of beauty" (p. 96). Tuan suggests that adults who allow themselves to recover a childlike, unselfconscious involvement with the physical world will discover that "an environment might break all the formal rules of euphony and aesthetics, substituting confusion for order, and yet be wholly satisfying" (pp. 96–97).

Is it reasonable to propose that the development of an experiential aesthetic might stimulate the discovery of ways to make familiar kinds of designed landscapes—in cities, towns, and suburbs, on highways and commercial strips, in parks and gardens—more "wholly satisfying" than they are at present? Olmsted was right, after all, in recognizing that landscape architecture is a work of culture, not of nature. Our form-giving is an inevitable condition of our inhabiting the planet. But if the environmental movement of the last several decades has taught us anything, it is that there is no place outside of nature. A plaza no less than a park becomes a sign of how we think about our place in the world—on the earth, under the sky, in a web of fleeting moments, rhythmic cycles, and seen and unseen energies. *All* landscape architecture may be presumed to engage the natural world—at least to be "about" nature at some level. Yet the image of nature common to most design is severely simplified, abstracted, and controlled, even when it is "naturalistic," or of informal design, as was the case with Olmsted's parks. Marc Treib (1979) has said of such purportedly "natural" landscapes that they are "actually *more* formalistic in concept; that here man not only says that we are able to channel nature into manmade order, but that man understands nature so well, that nature can be controlled or created in nature's own image" (p. 34, italics added). The active authority of the designer energetically shapes an image of nature that suits his or her own purposes, while nature plays the part of "resource," passive supplier of the material of the designer's art.

John Fowles (1979) believes that both the scientist and the artist have educated us to expect this utilitarian approach to nature. The technocratic culture of the modern world conditions us to respond to the natural environment in a way that distances us from any possibility of real experience in the passing moment. We develop a propensity for categorizing and objectifying what we experience that ultimately is able, Fowles says, "to cast a mysterious veil of deadness, of having already happened, over the actual and present event or phenomenon" (p. 61). He concludes that:

> We lack trust in the present, this moment, this actual seeing, because our culture tells us to trust only the reported back, the publicly framed, the edited, the thing set in the clearly artistic or clearly scientific angle of perspective. One of the deepest lessons we have to learn is that nature, of its nature, resists this. It waits to be seen otherwise, in its individual presentness and from our individual presentness (ibid.).

Practical Directions for an Experiential Aesthetics

Any effort to introduce a more holistic experiential aestheti in the design of outdoor environments must surely begin with tl search for design ideas that work against the distancing and dea ness that Fowles describes, creating instead opportunities for ir tensely vivid and immediate encounters with the natural world. W might begin by restoring the concept of "spirit of place"—*genius loci*—to nature. The root meaning of this term posits a living, indwelling spiritual presence or energy in a particular place that is antecedent to human awareness and responsive place-making. Contemporary design needs to invent forms that restore equity to the nature-culture equation. In this way, the unique character of each specific site might be made manifest instead of being suppressed. We have amply demonstrated our capacity to overcome whatever features of a particular site challenge our intention to impose a *kind* of landscape, filling the world with "generic" shopping centers, subdivisions, office parks, and downtowns. Now we must find a way to listen, to yield, to discover the *natural,* not just the existing or potential *cultural* meanings of a place, exactly in the way that we come to know other human beings as individuals having unique characters and personalities.

Furthermore, if we are to abjure the sterility and blandness that characterize so much contemporary landscape architecture, the forms we devise need to express the realities of the *nature* of a place that run counter to conventional notions of the pleasing, the tasteful, the beautiful—even, perhaps, the comfortable—just as our experience of nature in "wild" places confronts our expectations and keeps us vitally alert and attentive to where we are. Since modern urban society increasingly severs us from opportunities for contact with nature, designed environments must reintroduce us to a full sense of our participation in nature, in the "web of life" of which ecologists speak, even in the midst of the built world.

As designers, we might allow ourselves to think metaphorically of allowing nature to intrude itself, to "take over." Imagine an army of trees—or better, a feisty ragtag remnant of some original vegetation—"occupying" a square, blocking certain of its paths to force us around and through them. Imagine an urban place that was designed to provide habitat for creatures other than squirrels and pigeons—a tangled, thorny thicket replacing the manicured planters. Imagine transparent retaining walls—like the one proposed by artist Alan Sonfist to reveal the layers of earth strata uncovered during construction of an underground metropolitan rail station serving the High Museum in Atlanta (Sonfist, 1979, pp. 1–3). These walls remind us of an "underworld" that literally and symbolically supports human life. Imagine places that compelled us to pay attention to rainwater moving through drainage devices or, conversely, that made seasonal drought and desiccation impinge upon us forcefully—a "fountain" from which precious drops of water appeared sporadically, each one resonating somehow in the struggle of other lifeforms to endure in that place. Landscape architects are trained to "inventory" slopes and soils, hydrological patterns, existing vegetation, solar orientation, prevailing wind directions, and a wide range of other relevant natural and contextual factors intrinsic to each site, as a basis for the environmentally sensitive design decisions they hope to make. But seldom do the designs that emerge make awareness of these complex natural systems accessible to the bodies and psyches of the ordinary people who use these places in the course of their daily lives.

Thoreau (1961), communing ecstatically at the crest of Maine's Mt. Ktaadn, asked his fellow men and women to "Think of our life in nature—daily to be shown matter, to come in contact with it— rocks, trees, wind on our cheeks! the *solid* earth! the *actual* world! the *common sense*! *Contact*! *Contact*! *Who* are we? *Where* are we?" (p. 93). Thoreau, like Fowles, was convinced that all human beings share a "common sense" that they are a part of nature and desire fulfilling contact with the natural world "in its individual presentness and from our individual presentness," to use Fowles's words. Such experience is radically different from the perception of nature as scenery or of ourselves as spectators, and landscape design that deliberately engages us in a more complex immersion in the "thisness" of a place would help us, as a society, to move in the direction of more appropriate aesthetic and environmental values.

A corollary of this commitment to environmental design that reveals the true *nature* of places is a shift away from thinking of the designed landscape as a product in favor of a celebration of both landscape and design *processes*. Here Olmsted and Vaux's renaming of the profession and the subsequent institutionalization of landscape architecture as a design discipline have probably reinforced the illusion that outdoor environments ought to be designed in the way that buildings are, from plans that show precisely how all the elements are to be arranged. The influence that this conception of the profession must have had in imposing an aesthetic of visual simplicity, clarity, order, and abstraction seems obvious. An architect can potentially number every nail and screw a building will require, and the data will even remain constant over time, but no planting plan can begin to program the ecological diversity of a single six-foot-square patch of wild nature, even one studied at a single moment of a single season. Hence the pressure to simplify and the prevalence of landscape designs that exhaust visual interest before the rest of the body has a chance to become involved.

In reporting on a study showing that citizens of Sacramento, California, attached very different meanings and values to a city park than they did to a selected group of community gardens, Mark Francis (1987) describes how even non-users of the gardens preferred their appearance to the admittedly "attractive" expanses of lawn and trees in Fremont Park. Although "the value of the gardens as permanent open space was discounted by all officials who were interviewed," most other respondents clearly favored the sensory diversity and intensive social exchange the gardens offered. Twice as many garden users said they liked or loved the gardens as did park users affirm that they liked or loved the park, and many more garden users said that their "ideal open space" would be similar to the community garden. Francis concludes that the study "calls into question the need for strict unity, harmony, and formal aesthetics applied to most urban spaces and still taught in design schools" (p.111). It may suggest as well the appeal of landscapes that manifest active, open-ended process over time rather than static completion and closure.

Several of the Sacramento community gardens studied by Francis flourished in spite of having temporary or ambiguous legal status, since the sites were not owned by the gardeners. The existence of the gardens consequently seemed precarious, the investment of time and energy they demanded somehow more quixotic. This very vulnerability, and especially the degree to which the gardens were perceived as being nevertheless cared for devotedly, seems to have enhanced the favorable response of the community-at-large. The gardens had overcome the objectification that made the park seem "boring" to some users; they were not landscape "things" but landscape actions—tangible, lively, and "beautiful" physical signs of political, social, and natural processes to which any citizen might relate, if only to affirm the validity of such alternatives.

Alternative Views of the Designer's Role

The suggestion that amateur gardens of any sort might provide a useful model for "high style" landscape architecture will seem subversive to some, and yet reflects, perhaps, an openness to the"environmental humility" proposed by Relph (1981, p. 164), rooted in the Heideggerian notion of "appropriation" and asking us to value and protect—and by implication, to design—environments that we come to know "as they are in themselves, and with neither domination or subservience" (ibid.). An aesthetic based on theatrical visual effects promotes the myth of the designer as heroic genius, in the tradition of those Renaissance and Baroque masters who engineered elaborately contrived landscape features to dazzle the eyes of audiences at courtly festivals and masques. An alternative aesthetic might aim at offering people the opportunity to participate interactively in landscapes that, physically and spiritually, express the power and presence of the natural world as it is embodied in a particular place, however modest. Nature, as Thoreau intuited, still suggests answers to the ancient questions that people ask of the world, and enforces awareness of limitation, incompletion, and cycles of life and death—realities that our society often prefers to ignore or conceal. The heroic and formalist tradition in landscape architecture ignores these existential realities as well, substituting an idealized arcadian or utopian imagery that fails to engage us critically—to rouse us from our waking sleep, as any great art must.

We cannot invent a new landscape architecture every Monday morning, to paraphrase a famous remark of Mies van der Rohe about the vainglorious pursuit of new styles in architecture. But the profession of landscape architecture does need to examine and refresh the philosophical foundations that determine the goals and values informing landscape design. It is simply not enough, at this juncture in the evolution of environmental discourse, to design *with* nature. Design that seeks merely to mitigate the harmful effects of human action does not go far enough. We need to design places in which we are invited to experience nature—and ourselves in community with nature and with each other—more profoundly, more intimately, more physically, than is possible when conventional scenographic values are enforced. Most of all, we need designers willing to take risks, to improvise, and to abandon Olmsted's self-conscious ambition to associate the profession's work with architecture and engineering, in favor of a self-effacing reaffirmation of its ties to the garden and to nature.

References

Berleant, A. (1985). Towards a Phenomenological Aesthetics of Environment. In D. Ihde and H. J. Silverman (eds.) *Descriptions* (pp. 112–127). Albany: State University of New York Press.

Downing, A. (1841). *Treatise on the Theory and Practice of Landscape Gardening, Adapted to North America.* New York: Wiley and Putnam.

Evernden, N. (1985). *The Natural Alien: Humankind and Environment.* Toronto: University of Toronto Press.

Fowles, J. (1979). Seeing Nature Whole. *Harper's, 259* (November): 47–60.

Francis, M. (1987). Some Different Meanings Attached to a City Park and Community Gardens. *Landscape Journal, 6:* 101–111.

Heidegger, M. (1962). *Being and Time.* New York: Harper and Row.

Howett, C. (1987). Systems, Signs, Sensibilities: Sources for a New Landscape Aesthetic. *Landscape Journal, 6:* 1–12.

Jackson, J. B. (1980). Landscape as Theater. In *The Necessity for Ruins, and Other Topics* (pp. 67–75). Amherst: University of Massachusetts Press.

Kalfus, M. (1981). Olsted: A Psychohistorical Perspective. In B. Kelly, G. T. Guillet, and M. E. W. Herr (Eds.) *Art of the Olmsted Landscape* (pp. 141–47). New York: New York City Landmarks Preservation Commission and The Arts.

Newton, N. T. (1971). *Design on the Land: The Development of Landscape Architecture.* Cambridge, Massachusetts: Harvard University Press.

Relph, E. (1981). *Rational Landscapes and Humanistic Geography.* New York: Barnes and Noble.

————.(1987). *The Modern Urban Landscape.* Baltimore: Johns Hopkins University Press.

Schuyler, D. (1986). *The New Urban Landscape: The Redefinition of City Form in Nineteenth-Century America.* Baltimore: Johns Hopkins University Press.

Seamon, D. (1987). Phenomenology and Environment-Behavior Research. In G. T. Moore and E. Zube (Eds.) *Advances in Environment, Behavior, and Design* (pp. 3–26). New York: Plenum.

Sonfist, A. (1979). An Interview with Alan Sonfist [conducted by L. Lieberman, S. Sharshal, and D. Talley]. *Atlanta Art Workers' Coalition Newspaper, 3* (May–June), (pp. 1–3).

Thoreau, H. (1961). *The Maine Woods.* New York: Thomas Y. Crowell [originally published in 1864].

Treib, M. (1979). Traces upon the Land. *Architectural Association Quarterly, 2* (Winter): 28–39.

Tuan, Y. (1974). *Topophilia: A Study of Environmental Perception, Attitudes, and Values.* Englewood Cliffs, New Jersey: Prentice-Hall.

Part II

Interpreting Architecture and Landscape

Chapter 5

The First Roof:
Interpreting a Spatial Pattern

❐

Murray Silverstein

Much of the wonder of a great building comes from the form of its roof.[1] From the domes and vaults of monumental architecture to the timber frames of barns and peasant huts, there is something about the experience of roof forms—both inside and out—that goes to the heart of people's deepest feelings of place and shelter. Perhaps this is because the roof is the most primitive element of architecture. Many of the first buildings were nothing more than a roof on the ground, and a strong roof form inevitably strikes deep chords of meaning.

In the symbolic languages of nearly every culture, one finds instances of simple roof form with profound associative meaning. In

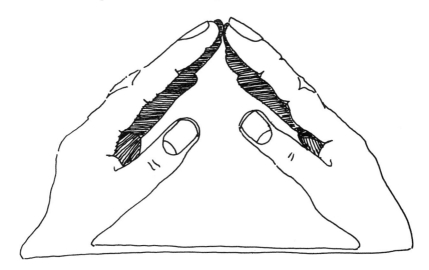

Figure 5.1. Beginning the sign for home in American Sign Language.

American Sign Language, for example, the sign for "home" begins with the sign for "roof": two hands leaning together touching at the fingertips to form a gable (figure 5.1). Similarly, the Chinese ideogram series for dwelling starts with a simple gable roof. By adding various symbols underneath, 'roof' is transformed into 'family', 'peace', 'resting-place' and 'ancestral altar'. The ideogram for 'cold' shows a roof sheltering a man on a mat with firewood (figure 5.2).

Figure 5.2. The Chinese
ideogram for 'cold'.

In the built language of architecture, the classical Western tradition begins with a celebration of the form and symbolic content of the primitive roof. Perhaps the primary pattern of the Greek temple is the pediment, the sacred gable, raised up on its columns, establishing a home for the gods, as in the Temple of Concord, Akragas (figure 5.3). Many examples of this sort can be collected. The point is that the very concept of "roof" seems to be consistently associated with values that are at the center of each culture's image of a good life. But not only is the idea of the roof commonly associated with the things people value. The form itself—the spatial pattern called 'roof'—has for centuries been stable and persistent. It seems as if there is an archetype of roof form that lies at the core of each person's sense of being at home in the world. This archetype I shall call "the First Roof." This article examines the underlying dimensions of the First Roof pattern, and describes its expression in two examples—the Jewish huppah and a house recently designed by our firm, Jacobson Silverstein Winslow Architects, in Berkeley, California. The article concludes that the First Roof pattern is one of the building blocks of architecture and can provide a valuable focus for sensitizing people to both the experiential and symbolic significance of buildings.

Figure 5.3. The sacred gable: Temple of Concord, Akragas.

The First Roof

The spatial pattern suggested by intuitions of roof form has its origins in the past, at the very dawn of architecture long before towns were built. This pattern is the form of the hut—the womb of space—for one person, a few people, or a family. In the first buildings, this hut consists of nothing more than a roof on the ground, covering a single space, shaped to make the people within feel as though they occupy, or are gathered around, the center of their world. When we speak of the First Roof, we do not speak of a thing—the roof—but of an instinct to create a relationship between things. The First Roof archetype is not an object in space, but an age-old pattern of space, a pattern which unites the roof and the earth it rests upon with the space inside and around it.

The precise shape of this patten varies through time and place. It may be circular in plan and conical in section, as the tepees of the American Plains Indians; or circular and domical, as the igloos of the Eskimos. It may be rectangular in plan and conical in section, as the ancient cruck houses of England; or rectangular and vaulted, as the *mudhifs* of the Marshmen of Southern Iraq or the

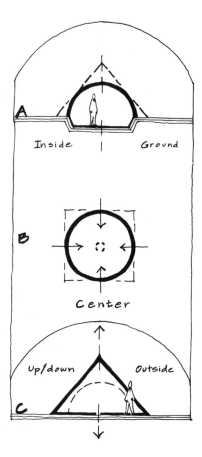

Figure 5.4. The First Roof Pattern: (A)
Section, (B) Plan, and (C) Elevation.

longhouses of the Iroquois. But whatever the particular appearance, the pattern itself is remarkably consistent: There is always
the little house formed by a roof on the ground that shelters and
"centers" the life within it. This spatial archetype has three fundamental characteristics:

> 1. It consists of some sort of frame or membrane which captures a
> bubble of space and sits directly on the ground (figure 5.4A).
>
> 2. This form has the geometrical effect of "centering" the space in-
> side; it creates an interior center on the ground (figure 5.4B).

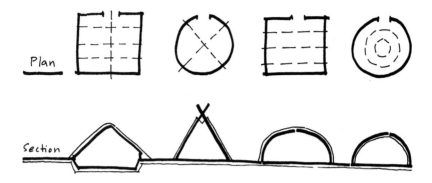

Figure 5.5. Cruck, tepee, mudhif, igloo: All possess this pattern of space.

3. On the outside, space is organized symmetrically around this form, as it rises from the earth toward the sky with diminishing scale along an invisible central axis (figure 5.4C).

Figure 5.5 shows four examples of primitive house types embodying these three characteristics. This pattern is so persistent in history that it bids strong as the starting point for any study of the way people build and use space. From this point of view, the roof is the first pattern of architecture. If we were sitting down to tell a child the story of architecture, this is where we would begin (figure 5.6). We can begin to understand the power and persistence of the First Roof pattern by remembering the times when we have experienced places that embody it. Perhaps it was the "little houses" one made as a child—the blanket strung between two chairs, and later the forts and caves; or those parts of buildings that have always been special places of shelter and refuge—the attic room, the loft, dormers and alcoves; or those places that make symbolic and ceremonial use of the primitive roof—the wedding tent and the canopied marriage bed, aediculas, gazebos and booths; or those structures complete in themselves that embody this pattern—vacation huts and cabins, garages and barns, temples, pavilions and tents.

What is it that makes our feelings for such places so haunting? It is always difficult to try to understand why something is intuitively appealing. Part of the nature of the appeal is that the thing, finally, is not reducible to analytic categories. This is particularly true of architectural form, where attraction is partly grounded in ineffable perceptions and feelings of overall rightness. But just this difficulty also suggests a line of approach: If the appeal of the First

Figure 5.6. Once upon a time . . . the first building (after Viollet-le-Duc).

Roof archetype lies in one's perceptions of its wholeness, then understanding should begin with this fact and proceed by examining the ways that the fragments of our experience are brought together and "made whole" by this form. This is the approach taken in the next three sections of this paper (also see Jacobson, Silverstein and Winslow, 1990). I argue here that the First Roof archetype is intuitively attractive because it works to unify experience by embracing and holding in balance three basic distinctions:

1. the formal distinction between inside and outside;

2. the symbolic distinction between self and the world;

3. the functional distinction between the practical and the ideal.

1. Inside and Outside

Let us make an elementary analysis of the form of the first roof pattern. First, notice that the pattern has the rough shape of a simple bowl turned upside down. One thinks of a family of shapes that includes dishes, baskets, kettles, boats—in short, all the primitive vessels (figure 5.7). As a type of vessel, the roof's function is to *contain something and thereby split the world in two: to establish simultaneously an inside which contains and an outside which excludes.* Just as the bowl or the tightly woven basket is shaped to contain water and set it aside from the rest of the world for a human end, so also is the roof shaped to contain people and claim and protect a piece of the earth for human use.

Figure 5.7. A primitive effigy vessel: A form that contains and excludes.

We immediately recognize an obvious fact: With a single stroke, the primitive roof creates both inside and outside. While it is easy to grasp this fact intellectually, we can never quite experience it, for we can never be inside and outside at the same time. The power of the roof lies in this duality. At any moment, we are either inside and contained by the roof or outside and excluded from what is inside. These two experiences are distinctly different. From the *inside* we are the contained thing. We are surrounded, and experience our container as a hollow, concave space, like a cave in an infinite solid. We feel the closeness and intensity of the place, the feeling of being within a compressed, diminutive bubble of space. Looking up, we see the structure of this fragile bubble that narrowly but decisively excludes the rest of the world. Looking down, we see the ground, the piece of earth we claim and upon which we sit. At any point within, the shape of the space gently orients us to a center that we have claimed. Out of the disorder of the world the roof helps us fashion a safe place, set apart and sheltered from everything outside (figure 5.8).

From the *outside,* in contrast, the roof is not a hollow concave space, but a solid mass in silhouette rising up along a vertical axis. The roof is a strong figure against its background. There is a sense of steady, urgent energy pushing up from the ground, aimed at the sky. At any point upon this form, we are oriented not to a still center but to the sky and the landscape beyond. While the interior shape creates its own world, the exterior shape takes its place like a sentry in the world, looking out, organizing the space around it, and claiming the space within (figure 5.9).

In the ways that it expresses both the inside and the outside, the primitive roof brings into play a fundamental contrast of human experience. It is at once an intense place of refuge *from* the world and an expansive place of confrontation *with* the world. That so simple a form can bring to life these polarities is perhaps the central mystery of roof form. The contrast between the inside and outside experiences of roof form can be seen in the following two examples provided by students asked to describe a memorable built place from their past.[2] One woman described the lake cottage her family shared for a few weeks each summer (figure 5.10):

> At the cottage we kids had to sleep in lofts. This was a wonderful state of affairs for us. The loft was reached by a ladder and, but for a low wall, was open to the room below. We had the excitement of watching over mysterious adult games like pinochle played by

Figure 5.8. Inside.

Figure 5.9. Outside.

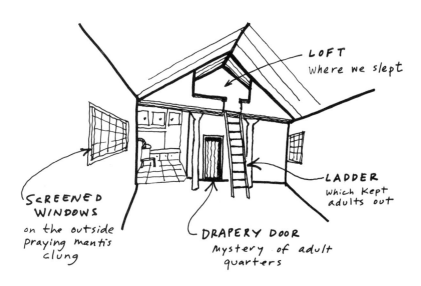

LOFT
where we slept

LADDER
which kept
adults out

SCREENED
WINDOWS
on the outside
praying mantis
clung

DRAPERY DOOR
Mystery of adult
quarters

Figure 5.10. Remembering the inside.

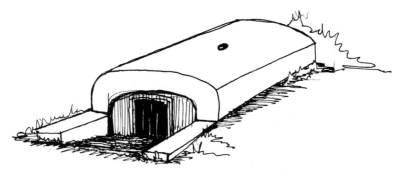

Figure 5.11. Remembering the outside.

various aunts and uncles who in town only watched TV and went early to bed. And when all were asleep on such nights, in the loft you felt part of one huge family.

Another student remembered a storm cellar in a field behind his childhood home (figure 5.11). From across the field, this structure appeared simply as a low arched roof on the ground. It had long been abandoned, and he was not allowed inside. He imagined it flooded with water and full of "poisonous cotton-mouth water moccasins." He and his brother were drawn to this roof form and spent many hours on top of it:

> . . . peering through a hole—three to four inches in diameter—waiting for our eyes to adjust to the dim interior. And if you waited long enough you were sure you could detect the silent fluid move ment of thousands of serpents. We disposed of uncounted bugs, frogs, pebbles and a few plastic cowboys by consigning them to that hole. Or we lay on our backs on our gently arched haven from the ground and told cloud stories to each other of the things we saw moving across the sky. We often fell asleep and took our nap there.

Though these memories are unique, they contain themes and associations that run through other students' accounts of remembered places. The memory of the cabin, for example, becomes a memory of family and the shared experiences that constitute the web of family life. The recollection moves from the loft and the excitement of "watching over mysterious adult games" to that moment on the edge of sleep when "you felt part of one huge family." There is a widening circle that goes from roof to family to the fusion of self and family. In contrast, the memory of an exterior space like the storm cellar begins with the feeling of being excluded and on the outside looking in. The "dim interior," with its snakes and lost cowboys, is first studied from outside through the hole in the roof. Then there is a shift and new orientation: The boys roll over and the roof becomes the "gently arched haven" lifting them up from the ground and from which they watch clouds go by and tell stories. Here, the association jumps from the outside experience of the roof as sheltering a mysterious inside, from which one has been excluded, to the roof as platform upon which a new frame of reference is established. Each culture and each individual plays upon the basic duality of outside/inside in different ways, as various points of balance between self and world, center and horizon, are explored and affirmed. This explication points toward the psychological overtones of roof form. We begin to see the frame, as it were, upon which specific meanings may be fastened.

2. Symbolic Foundations

For human beings, all forms are not equal. Some are more compelling and alive than others. These favored forms, however they arise, attract us. They feel mysteriously right, and we identify with them. This experience of attraction and identification is based on the intuition that, somehow, this form is like us. In it, however dimly, *we see ourselves.*

The charismatic quality of the primitive roof form may be explained by considering its relationship to other vessel forms. As we have already seen, the First Roof is a member of the morphological family of primitive vessels. As such, it is connected by threads of meaning and association which tie these forms together in language and imagination. The primary symbolic equation of this family of forms is *vessel = body = woman.* This equation is explored at length by Erich Neumann in *The Great Mother* (Neumann, 1972). Neumann presents the vessel shape in all its manifestations, from cradle to hut to coffin, as the central motif in the symbolic constellation he calls the "Great Round." He argues that the experience of the body as vessel is universally human:

> All the basic vital functions occur in this vessel-body, whose "inside" is an unknown. Its entrance and exit zones are of special significance. Food and drink are put into this unknown vessel, while in all creative functions, from the elimination of waste and the emission of seed to the giving forth of breath and the word, some-

thing is "born" out of it. *All* body openings . . . as well as the skin, have, as places of exchange between inside and outside, a numinous accent for early man. They are therefore distinguished as "ornamental" and protected zones, and in man's artistic self-representation they play a special role as idols (p. 39).

Neumann goes on to claim that this experience of body as vessel, while common to men and women, is primarily an experience *of the feminine:*

Woman as body-vessel is the natural expression of the human experience of woman bearing the child "within" her and of man entering "into" her in the sexual act. Because the identity of the female personality with the encompassing body-vessel in which the child is sheltered belongs to the foundation of feminine existence, woman is not only the vessel that like every body contains something within itself, but, both for herself and the male, is the "life-vessel as such," in which life forms, and which bears all living things and discharges them out of itself and into the world (p. 42).

This equation of forms may be summarized in the diagram of figure 5.12, which I have adopted from Neumann's more intricate presentation of the symbolic foundations of the feminine. This diagram provides one way to understand the intuitive power and the charismatic quality of First Roof forms. We are attracted to these simple shapes, we find meaning "in" them, because they are like mirrors reflecting the very ground of our self—an inside and an outside, a body born of the mother.

Following this line of thought, we may say that in the language of symbolic form, a building that embodies the First Roof pattern "stands" for the human being, inside and out. The symmetrically shaped roof on the ground with its interior womb and exterior thrust—the essence of the First Roof—is a symbol of that duality of self which we experience as inside and outside, feminine and masculine, our "inner" self and our "outer" self. Further, as a form which unites the contrasting realities of inside and outside, the First Roof is a symbol of that elusive ideal, the whole self that somehow unites its inner and outer natures.

3. The Fusion of the Practical and the Ideal

Beginning as an instinctive response to the conditions of the environment, the First Roof becomes a symbolic form, reflecting

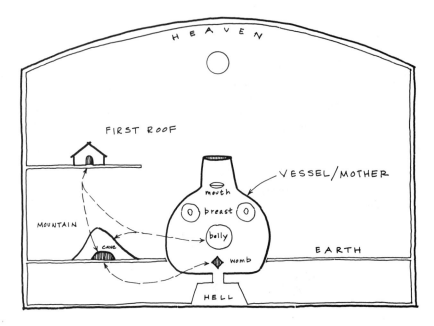

Figure 5.12. The symbolic foundations of the First Roof form.

people as they are in relation to the world. In effect, we begin by burrowing into the ground, piling sticks and skins together, seeking shelter in the mother, and in no time the form becomes sacred. Frank Lloyd Wright referred to this relationship between the utilitarian and the symbolic when he made the insightful comment that architecture is a gift of the practical self to the ideal self. One can think of this idea as a fable: The practical self, wet and cold, defenseless at night, craving a safe place, invents shelter, builds the First Roof, gets inside and lives there. Out of such inevitabilities, the practical self, now dry and warm, perhaps more at home, discovers the pleasures of material comfort. But something else is waiting to be found. For this roof that has been built, this practical extension of the practical self, is like its builder, in some sense, *is* its builder. In this identification, I suspect, lies the origins of the sacred. In the practical, the sacred is found. But who finds it? The ideal self, in Wright's terminology—that part of a person that craves for more than the practical, more than material comfort; that part of us that longs for meaning. Architecture, Wright seems to be saying, arises from the tension in the human soul between the practical and the ideal. At its best, architecture can be a gift that resolves this very tension.

This conjunction of the practical and the ideal in a single object is another facet of the wholeness that lurks in First Roof forms. This relationship becomes clearer when we shift our focus from the finished object—the hut or the house or the temple—to the process of building it. We must never forget that our precursors *built* these structures by hand, generation after generation, over many thousands of years. This fact is often noted by architectural theorists as part of the argument for user-participation in the design and building process. Here, I wish to emphasize the *experience* of this activity and its inevitable effect on the human psyche. Try to imagine what it feels like to need shelter, to gather materials and build a hut, and then to live in it, waking up in it, going out and returning day after day. Perhaps the most dramatic moment in the building process comes when the materials have been stacked, woven or tied. Suddenly the overall skeleton of the building becomes apparent. A new form comes into being.

At once, this new thing seems greater than the sum of its parts. We are familiar with the pieces—the sticks and stones, and thatch—but when they come together in place, there is a moment of surprise. Experiencing this jump from parts to whole must have been common to prehistoric builders. Though it is less familiar to us, anyone who makes things from scratch, from idea to realization, can recognize the feeling. Throughout the gathering and assembling, we are guided by practical concerns—the nature and cost of the materials and the ease of gathering and transporting. When the frame rises, however, the whole appears, and the practical gives way to the symbolic. In this sudden perception of wholeness, *a feeling for the ideal is born*. Later, living with the form, it is all of a piece—a single process from parts to whole, fusing the practical and the ideal.

The Huppah

One concrete example of the First Roof pattern is the Jewish huppah, which is an intriguing case because it is a form whose essence is not actual shelter but a compressed experience with the meaning of shelter. The huppah is the symbolic roof under which Jewish wedding ceremonies are held (figure 5.13). It is a kind of canopy, framed in wood, roughly square in plan, with posts at the four corners held up by family and friends. The roof of the huppah may be arched, gabled or flat and is covered with fine cloth or leafy branches and flowers. This form echoes the original huppah, a

Figure 5.13. *Huppah* form on Jewish marriage coins and marriage contract.

special tent in which the bride and groom consummate their marriage. The word huppa means literally a "covering" and is associated in the Talmud with the tabernacle—the sacred tent that the Jews carried during their wanderings from Egypt to Palestine.

The huppah is used in the wedding ceremony to create an elementary spatial distinction: The canopy symbolically marks and centers a *place*—the new household created by the marriage—and sets it off from the world around it. The four relatives or friends are the community; they hold up the structure but must stand outside. The marriage blessing that is prescribed by the Talmud makes it clear that this ceremony consecrates not only the couple under the canopy but renews the community, the life outside the canopy, as well.

This relationship between home and community illustrates the twofold nature of the huppah—it simultaneously centers a life within and re-establishes the sense of place in the wider community around it. As inside, it is the safe place where life may be created and nurtured; as outside, it takes its place in a community of other such forms and thus creates the public world. At the same time, it is a charismatic form that transcends the practical concern of shelter and becomes a symbol of the ideal of human wholeness. The huppah ceremony also incorporates the existential reality of First Roof form. The Talmud asks that the little roof be built for the ceremony, from scratch, by the father of the bride. Further, instructions are given that the frame of the huppah be made from trees planted for this purpose at the birth of the child—cedars for boys and pines for girls. In this way, the archaic meaning of the wedding is made tangible. Through building the huppah, the patriarch sees the new whole emerging from the parts he has planted, the union of cedar and pine.

A pre-Talmudic legend describes the wedding of Adam and Eve in Paradise: "The Holy One . . . made ten wedding canopies for Adam and Eve in the Garden of Eden." Joseph Rykwert (1972) interprets these canopies as the primordial House, alluded to but never described in Scripture. Viewing the huppah as the original image of human, as opposed to God-like, wholeness, Rykwert writes:

> Whatever [the huppah] was made of, clearly it was not meant to keep the weather out, or to perform any of the functions attributed to building, besides providing physical enclosure. The shelter provided by the huppah was notional. Although it was notional, it was

nonetheless necessary. Its floor was the earth, its supports were living beings, its trellised roof was like a tiny sky of leaves and flowers: to the couple sheltering within it, it was both an image of their joined bodies and a pledge of the world's consent to their union. It was more; it provided them—at a critical moment—with a meditation between the intimate sensations of their own bodies and the sense of the great unexplored world around. It was therefore both an image of the occupants' bodies and a map, a model of the world's meaning. That, if at all, is why I must postulate a house for Adam in Paradise. Not as a shelter against the weather, but as a volume which he could interpret in terms of his own body and which yet was an exposition of the paradisal plan, and therefore established him at the center of it (p. 190).

The meanings associated with the huppah extend our interpretation of the First Roof pattern. As we have seen, the pattern was born of the mother and matriarchal institutions, providing a sheltered center, a point of orientation, around which life flowed. With the creation of the huppah, the First Roof becomes the sacred place where man and woman are united. The original huppah was a ceremonial tent that contained the marriage bed, the place where the sexual bond was established. In effect, in the case of the huppah, the mother form becomes the sacred place where a man and woman meet *inside* to recreate the mother; in turn the life of the community *outside* is regenerated.

A Design Example

The First Roof is not only a pattern to be found and analyzed in architectural history. It is also a generative principle that can provide insight into current design problems. Let me illustrate with a project from our architectural practice. The project involves the renovation of, and additions to, a family residence in Woodside, California. The existing residence, housing a family of four—husband, wife and two children—is a two-story, 1200 square-foot building originally built by the husband before he was married. With its precise 26' by 26' footprint, its four-sided hipped roof and central skylight, the building is a strong example of First Roof form (figure 5.14).

The family had outgrown the small two-bedroom structure but was quite attached to the building and the wooded hillside on which it sits. The functional program required more than 3000 additional square feet, as well as substantial remodeling, but our first efforts to extend the building met with resistance on the part of our clients.

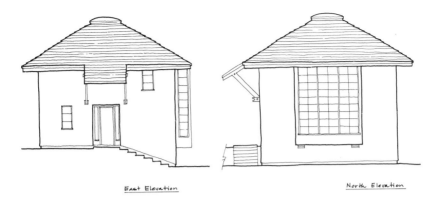

East Elevation   North Elevation

Figure 5.14. Existing residence: A strong First Roof form.

They simply did not want to see the original building "swallowed" by the new project. They loved its form, which they associated with their beginnings as a couple and the birth of their children. Though they clearly wanted more space, they hoped the new work could somehow be subordinated to the existing building.

The solution we developed lay in conceiving the project as a trio of First Roof forms—the remodeled original and two new forms, one larger and one smaller than the original. These three pavilion forms were then threaded together with circulation space like beads on a necklace set into the curve of the hillside (figure 5.15).

Our clients found this approach quite appealing. It preserved the form of the existing house and allowed the large addition to be developed as a pair of variations on the original theme. It was a case, however, of form outpacing program: Upon accepting the "First Roof necklace" as architectural parti, we spent considerable time deciding which function to place in which pavillion. After much fiddling, we finally arrived at an allocation and an organization of spaces which fit the form and seemed right. A diagram depicting this work is shown in figure 5.16.

In the diagram, the original structure (1) becomes the children's house with private studio space for the woman above. The middle pavilion (2) is the family commons—entry, kitchen, dining, library—with the couple's bedroom above. The third pavillion (3) is the garage/workshop with private space for the man above. A glazed, unheated hall connects pavilions 1 and 2, forming a courtyard; a breezeway and mud room connect pavillions 2 and 3.

In reality, of course, this allocation of spaces will change over time. While the children are young, the couple's bedroom will

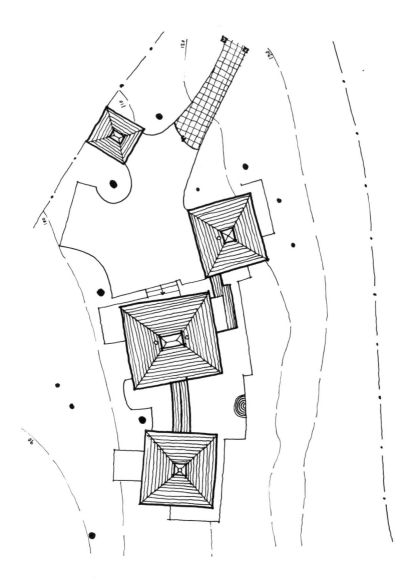

Figure 5.15. Proposed site plan: A necklace of First Roof forms.

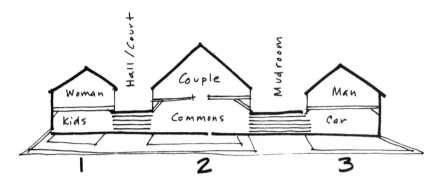

Figure 5.16. Family dwelling as a trio of First Roof Forms.

remain in pavillion 1, near them, with the woman's private space above the commons; as the children enter adolescence and more separation is in order (for the teens *and* the parents), the couple's bedroom moves to the central pavillion; and when the children leave home, pavillion 1 can be shut down or converted to a rental unit, and the couple can regroup in pavillions 2 and 3.

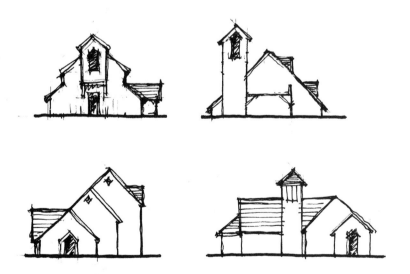

Figure 5.17. Composing with First Roof forms.

The architectural idea that remains constant in this flux of family life is this:

(a) the mother form from which the house design grows is the primitive First Roof pattern;

(b) a family dwelling may be conceived as a collection of First Roof forms, each unique yet each a member of the ancient family; and

(c) by nesting, stacking, stretching and compressing, these forms can be joined together to create large, complex versions of First Roof form (figure 5.17).

This is an idea from which many kinds of residential architecture can spring. Our design for the family in Woodside is one version, inspired by the existing conditions from which it grew. As the Woodside project developed in drawings and models, the clients expanded the program to include two more pavillions—a small storage shed forming a kind of gatehouse near the entrance to the property, and an in-law unit similar in scale to the original building and about 100' away from our "necklace". From the one-room shed to the more complex pavillion at the center of the necklace, the project became the occasion to once again explore the old form and try to make it new (figures 5.18 and 5.19).[3]

WEST ELEVATION

SOUTH ELEVATION

Figure 5.18. The new residence.

The Great Grandmother

The pattern of space that I have called the First Roof and illustrated with the huppah and the project from our office is an archetype with its origins in prehistory. It is a pattern found in architecture all over the world, in both sacred and secular forms. From ancient huts, through the ceremonial aediculas of classical architecture to postmodern "references" of our own times, the pattern persists. John Summerson (1963) finds the pattern in certain ornamental elements of Romanesque architecture and argues that these forms led directly to the development of the pointed arch in the twelfth century. Summerson believes that the Gothic Cathedrals are hierarchical compositions whose spatial "atom" is the First Roof pattern, enlarged, underlined, stacked, repeated and stretched (figure 5.20), culminating in the miraculous structures at Chartres and Amiens.

Figure 5.19. The new residence: Garage and studio.

Just as the First Roof is embedded in the language of Architecture, so also is it found in the symbolic language of our minds. As I have indicated, the pattern has been the focus of many centuries of symbolic thinking, the central axiom of which lies in the equation of the primitive roofed space with vessel, body, first body, and mother's body. In effect, if architecture is the mother of the arts, the First Roof is the great grandmother of architecture itself. Seen in this light, I would suggest that further analysis of this pattern could provide a path for practitioners into the psychology of architecture. If the structures we create—from windows to large buildings— are endowed by our unconscious minds with symbolic content, we ought to know more about the dynamics between outer and inner form. It would certainly help us to know ourselves, and might also help open doors to an ageless architecture of the heart.

Figure 5.20. Gothic compositions of First Roof forms.

Notes

1. I am grateful to Max Jacobson and Barbara Winslow, my partners in architectural practice, who provided criticism and direction in the development of this essay.

2. The examples are drawn from a class, "Introduction to Architecture," taught by the author in the adult extension program of the University of California, Berkeley. The first assignment in the class is "remembering a place." Students are asked to recall a memorable built place from their

childhood and describe it. Each time this assignment is given, a good many students respond with a "roof story" of one sort or another.

    3. Figures 5.18 and 5.19 are from drawings by Ken Martin.

References

Jacobson, M., Silverstein, M., and Winslow, B. (1982). Choosing the Right roof: How the Shape of the Roof Influences the Spaces Below. *Fine Home Building, 10* (August–September), 26–29.

—————. (1990). *The Good House: Contrast as a Design Tool.* Newtown, Connecticut: Taunton Press.

Neumann, E. (1972). *The Great Mother, an Analysis of the Archetype.* Princeton, New Jersey: Princeton University Press.

Rykwert, J. (1972). *On Adam's House in Paradise: The Idea of the Primitive Hut in Architectural History.* New York: The Museum of Modern Art.

Summerson, J. (1963). *Heavenly Mansions.* New York: Norton.

Chapter 6

Toward an Architectural Vocabulary: The Porch as a Between

◻

Robert Mugerauer

Martin Heidegger's interpretation of building and dwelling provides a means to understand the nature of architecture and the possibilities of design vocabulary. Heidegger argues that the primal sense of "arche-tecture" is restored when it is understood as an opening that subsequently makes buildings and building possible (Heidegger, 1971a, b, c). The "arche" in "arche-tecture" originally meant "first principle" or "first element."[1] "Tecton," today echoed in "techne" and "technology," means "making or setting into work."[2] "Arche-tecton," then, refers to the first skill, primary craft or chief work.

But what does "arche-tecton" say? Heidegger's language presents a rejuvenating directive: architecture, in actually setting its joining capacity into concrete work, accomplishes the opening of a site where the fundamental dimensions of reality can be gathered together. Architecture is a careful attention and response to what nature, people, and their sense of the sacred need to come forward into a vital and proper relationship—that is, into a *world*. These three dimensions must be mediated in appropriate historical and regional traditions (Heidegger, 1971c, pp. 220–221).

According to Heidegger, architecture originally was the measuring which enabled the opening for a cosmos and the fundamental placement of human life. This measure was a "meting out" and a "measuring of the between," which encompassed heavens and earth, divinities and humans (ibid.). Such an architectonic was the province of the gods, who humans emulated in their building by following sacred models. From this original sense, measure as design came to be identified with architecture. As the gods have given way to humans, and we have assumed almost entirely the power to

103

measure, partaking in the measuring has emerged as a fundamental human task. We have inherited the responsibility to design appropriately, with care that all the relevant dimensions are included and balanced. We need to think of architecture as the originary opening and measuring according to appropriate standards so that we can live commensurately with the world. Since poetry was also a techne for the Greeks, we can adapt Heidegger's description of genuine poetry to architecture: "[architecture] as the authentic gauging of the dimension of dwelling is [a] primal form of building" (Heidegger, 1971c, p. 227). Recovering this prototypical understanding would help architecture's primal power to continue as an original admission to dwelling.

Suppose, following Heidegger, we accept this language used to understand and practice architecture, so that architecture appears as the opening of sites. In this phrasing, design and building attune themselves to the use and needs of things and help gather the dimensions of world. The question in regard to design vocabulary is, how to attend and respond appropriately to our traditional architecture and design elements as part of people's responsibility to provide an opening for future building and living? This question simultaneously asks about our concrete, historical manner of living and the character of specific architectural elements, particularly how they are joined into a building, and the mode in which they help a world unfold.

Developing a design vocabulary from the implications of Heidegger's approach agrees with the work already begun by Karsten Harries (1983, 1988), Christian Norberg-Schulz (1985), and Christopher Alexander (1977), all of whom focus on specific, traditional elements in their discussions of an architectural language. Both Harries and Norberg-Schulz explicitly utilize Heidegger and, in many ways, Alexander is implicitly Heideggerian (Seamon, 1985, p. 2). Harries's view is that we need an architecture based on a natural symbolism. He argues that designers might move toward a non-arbitrary architecture by patiently rethinking the fundamental dimensions of their buildings—for example, the essential nature of windows, doors, and roofs. Such basic elements, usually taken for granted, need to be explored according to their particular logic and mode of enabling human being-in-the-world to occur (Harries, 1983, 1988).

Norberg-Schulz develops the concept of dwelling by interpreting the manner in which built form and the setting into work are accomplished by concrete things such as floor, wall, ceiling, and fireplace (Norberg-Schulz, 1985). Alexander's "Pattern Language" emphasizes a "field of physical and social relationships" that is realized through interconnections of elements, many of which are archetypal (Alexander, 1977, p. xi). For example, he identifies "patterns" for a porch at the front of a house: private terrace on the street, sunny place, outdoor room, six-foot balcony, paths and goals, ceiling height variety, columns at the corner, front door bench, raised flowers, different chairs (Alexander, 1977, pp. xxxv–xxxvii). The suggestion is that an architectural form like "front porch" can be identified in terms of essential parts that make that form what it is.

Here, in a way somewhat like Alexander's, I explore *between* in terms of one architectural element—the *porch*. Whereas yard lies between house and neighborhood or nature, porch appears nestled between house and yard. The Midwestern and Texas porches with which I am familiar provide the empirical basis for this project. Other versions of the porch are considered insofar as they methodologically contribute to the phenomenological reduction, which aims to analyze and describe the essential characteristics of the Midwestern and Texan porches.[3] To look at the porch as part of a common environment does not imply that it is uniquely American. Still, according to current research, "porches in the American sense—that is, roofed but incompletely walled living areas—are rare in Europe" (McAlester and McAlester, 1986, p. 52).

What would a phenomenological approach say about the porch as a distinctive element of an American architectural vocabulary and about architecture as opening for world?

The Porch and Nature

The physical and cultural meanings of the porch are partly grounded in the manner by which it relates the house to the natural environment, especially to the weather. The porch provides refuge from frequent showers and relief from overheated interior rooms in summer's oppressive heat. Early on, American architects were aware that the porch offered one easy way to ameliorate contrasts between inside and outside the dwelling. As the influential nineteenth century architect Calvert Vaux explained, the porch provided "the simplest and most economical way to obtain . . . temporary shelter from heat, cold, or storm" (Vaux, 1864, p. 83).

Figure 6.1. A nineteenth century stone house in Austin, Texas. Note how the hood of the porch demarks a sheltering space beneath. Photographs by Robert Mugerauer.

The porch, as a mediating place between house and exterior, seems simple, yet reverberates with levels of meaning and implications. Since it shelters by *holding out* undesirable forms of weather or by *opening up to* moderating breezes, the architect seeks a porch design that will decidedly "express its purpose." As Vaux continues,

> We need something that shall indicate the protection from the weather that the porch offers, and give life, and light, and shade to the design. The result may, in a manner, be obtained by putting a boldly projecting hood over the opening . . . (ibid., p. 83).

As Vaux advocates and figure 6.1 indicates, the porch can be dramatic, even in modest form. The hood unifies the porch's physical and symbolic dimensions and demarcates a physical space beneath. The porch establishes a distinctive built place in the landscape. In time, the porch may become more elaborate, both materially and culturally. As an example, the hood may develop into a variety of more complex porch designs (figure 6.2). In his porches for country residences, Vaux (ibid., pp. 82–87) moves immediately from the introduction of the hood to designs for a timber-framed and

Figure 6.2. Victorian house in Riverside, Illinois. American architects soon designed more elaborate porches.

braced porch and then on to an enclosed wooden porch that is almost an external vestibule. Next, he elaborates an enclosed projection with a balcony over the entry arch and concludes by considering appropriate seating as well as wood, stone, marble, and tile flooring.

A constant throughout the range of design complexity is that the porch allows *lingering* between inner and outer spheres. The porch encourages and is articulated by the interplay of natural and domestic features (figure 6.3). We put plants on our porches: flowerpots on the ledge, flowing vines on trellises, houseplants set out to benefit from summer's rejuvenation. From the porch, one hears birds, shoos off squirrels, and watches hummingbirds at the bird feeder.

It is acceptable for the children to be out on the porch at night, since they are close enough to keep an eye on, and proximity is connected with safety. The porch makes a good home base from which to chase fireflies in the twilight. Adults stay outside after dark, listening to a sports event on the radio, only half bothering to think about turning off the porch light that attracts moths and mosquitoes. Or, smoking a last cigarette, one can simply enjoy the evening, with the crickets and tree frogs chirping. Because it is not as uncomfortable as the summer lawn's grass, the porch provides a pleasant way to be outside in the night. On the porch, we can allow

Figure 6.3. A bungalow in Austin, Texas. The porch mediates between house and natural environment.

ourselves to be relaxed and "vulnerable," but without risk. There are even sleeping porches.

On the porch we can linger late, letting night remain as a distinctive environment. When we are out on the town, in contrast, our experience of the night is subordinated to the activity that brought us out. Rather than encountering the night itself to any significant degree, we are likely to move through it unaware on the way to somewhere else. The porch today may be one of the few remaining places where town and city dwellers have significant access to night sky, atmosphere, and bird and animal activity. The porch enables people to be together with nature by providing an intermediate site.

With the advent of air conditioning, the porch began to disappear from the American house. The change would seem to be technological mastery of weather, a development that rendered the porch obsolete environmentally. The impact of technology alone, however, does not account for the rise or fall of the porch, since the impact of air conditioning varies across regions or has nothing at all to do with some of the porch's functions. In the upper Midwest, the summers are pleasant without air conditioning and, in southern climates, the spring and fall offer adequate time for the use of porches.

In short, porches are not intelligible solely in terms of weather. It rains no less now than it did when the first porches were built as convenient shelters. Rather, our responses to the weather, through both architecture and technology, are a facet of cultural understanding and experience. Porches were not an inevitable American solution, as is witnessed by alternatives in the rest of the world where it also is hot, cold, and rainy. For example, in some Japanese architecture, an increase in eaves' size provides the same function. Moreover, we do not add porches to every building, though the weather in a given place is the same for them all.

Architectural convention and fashion clearly play a part, as does social behavior. The phenomena of the car port and attached garage may indicate changes in perception and behavior, such as acceptance of the automobile as belonging to the home. No doubt the increased time spent before television sets interiorized American living patterns and spatial forms. The influence of modernism is also part of the story. In the early phase of the Arts and Crafts movement, porches were retained but wide eave overhangs also developed; in the later Machine Age Movement, porches were incompatible with the aesthetic of flat, smooth surfaces (McAlester and McAlester, 1986, pp. 10–11, 439–485).

Though porches tended to disappear with shifts in technology and architectural styles, they are still built. Even the much beloved suburban ranch house, for all its modern characteristics, sometimes included a minimal porch area or has had one added to it by the occupants (figure 6.4). The construction of porches has recently benefited from the desire to get in touch with the outdoors again and with attempts to discard the television and re-establish family and neighborly communication. On new houses, porches seem to be desired as part of a rejuvenation of tradition and the recovery of something lost (figure 6.5).

The Porch and Society

The porch not only provides a place to belong to the natural world but also opens a place for family and friends *to gather*. A resident gets the mail from the postman, who chats for five minutes until the unexpected shower slackens; children play monopoly during the afternoon, while their friends come and go; in the evening, the teenagers posture, whisper, and laugh. One may call from the porch, bidding a passing neighbor to come up for a glass of

Figure 6.4. Porch added to a 1950s ranch-style house in Austin, Texas.

Figure 6.5. A new house, completed in 1987, Jollyville, Texas. Porches continue to symbolize traditional values.

lemonade; a passing couple can wave to friends on the porch across the street and walk over to gossip for ten minutes.

As a place to be alone or with others, the porch is a semi-private space parallel to the semi-public space of the street. The porch does not force one to make the unattractive choice between admitting people to the full intimacy of the home or of keeping them in the distanced relation of the formal public realm. Being on a porch carries no further obligations. The result is interactions that are easy and only minimally committal, thus promoting acquaintance with neighbors and neighborhood. The porch is, therefore, multiple in its meanings. By staying open as the balance between the spheres of private inside and public outside, the porch stays open to possibility either way. It lets casual encounters remain casual and the private stay private.

As a between and joining, the porch's ability to promote lingering is often illustrated by its furnishings. Typical porch chairs are usually casual, certainly as compared to dining or living room furniture, where people maintain a much more erect and "proper" posture. On the porch, one may lean on the railing, since casual lounging is allowed in the "semi-private" intimacy that is not formal. There is also the porch swing, which has its own mode of existence, more free and less upright than even the rocking chair (figure 6.6). While the hammock seems similar, it is in fact private and usually placed in the back yard. Or in contrast to the yard's swing set for children, the porch swing is significantly adult and social, as is seen in its importance for courting and for entertaining family friends.

The range of social relationships and varieties of porch often correspond. The size and placement of the porch may correlate with the occupants' social relation to other community members. More specifically, the height of the porch above the ground generally articulates and maintains the proper range and mediation between those inside and outside. In an American culture that promotes egalitarian and democratic ideals, it is not surprising that many porches are not elevated more than a half dozen steps. The porch's floor is not above the face of someone standing outside. It reflects and supports a fundamentally *equal* social status (figure 6.7).[4]

The porch as it mediates a specific relation between inside and outside and above and below helps to establish *limits and measures* architecturally. The limits and measures, according to Heidegger, would be provided by what is joined, by what is involved in the joining. In regard to the American home, the mode of belonging for house, family and visitors would give the measure. The measuring

Figure 6.6. Greek-Revival house, Austin, Texas. The porch swing enhances the porch's casual sociability.

Figure 6.7. Frame houses in Wauwatosa, Wisconsin. Note the democratic measure: porches are not raised above the eye level of those outside.

is partially accomplished architecturally by the porch, which metes out the proper opening and thus enables a specific manner of lingering between inside and outside.

While the democratic measure for building is commonly maintained in the traditional American houses of working people, there are grander styles of houses, occupied by persons of greater than average wealth, status, or power. These houses not only tend to have a larger porch, but one more elevated above the ground (figure 6.8). Built form and social differential coincide. If the inner sphere of the occupants is high enough above the outer realm of visitor and passers-by, the egalitarian porch may give way to a secondary elevated form. Rather than a porch that promotes the lingering of equals, architecture lays out a balcony where those inside can emerge in a elevated manner (figure 6.9). Similarly, institutional buildings, where a citizen appears in "official role and dignity," usually have a balcony physically and symbolically differentiated from "ground" level. The phenomena is common in governmental architecture, such as the Student Union at the University of Texas at Austin (figure 6.10).[5]

Intermediate between egalitarian porch and hierarchical balcony, the porches of the fairly well-to-do may be ambiguous or complex. As fellow citizens, the occupants are politically equal to others;

Figure 6.8. Mansion, Austin, Texas. Grand houses tend to have a large, elevated porch and balcony.

Figure 6.9. Caswell House, Austin, Texas. An elevated
balcony helps residents to display an elevated status.

simultaneously, as bosses, managers, or professionals, the residents
are of a higher status, at least economically. Such middle ground is
seen, for example, in the Littlefield home, built by the prosperous
Austin businessman George W. Littlefield, who played a significant
role in the commercial development of the city (figure 6.11). As a
rancher and an active member of the developing Texas community,
Littlefield was not significantly distanced from other townspeople
or from students and faculty at the nearby university. Yet, as a civic
leader and banker, he was distinguished. As a reflection of his place
in the community, the lower porch of his house is elaborate but not
too grand or not too high above the ground; there is an upper balcony, or gallery, of middle height.

    Even though there is some correlation between the height and
placement of a porch and the occupants' status and power, the two

Figure 6.10. Student Union, The University of Texas at Austin. Institutional balconies differentiate hierarchies of power.

do not always correspond directly. The point is not to think about porches as a dimension of cultural practices. Fundamentally, porch and balcony provide a measure of the *mode* of residents' relation to nature and society. The architectural elements help establish the specific modulations of differentiation and participation. One's way of being in the social realm is brought forth through specific porch and balcony forms.

For example, in egalitarian multiple-family housing, only so many apartments can be at ground level. If the inside living spaces are basically homogeneous, with those higher or lower seen as no better or worse, no more or less powerful than their counterparts, the upper floors also need access to the outside, so as not to appear disadvantaged (figure 6.12). One example is the development of the New Deal's Greenbelt Towns, intended to provide low-rent

Figure 6.11. Littlefield House, Austin, Texas. An intermediate form of lower porch and upper balcony.

Figure 6.12. Student apartment building, Austin, Texas. Egalitarian balconies extend limited living space outside.

Figure 6.13. Garden Terraces, Baldwin Hills Village, Los Angeles, California. Both second-floor and first-floor residents wanted gardens to tend.

housing for low-income families. The Greendale project in Milwaukee, Wisconsin, showed that tenants wanted and would care for gardens. Consequently, in the subsequent project of Baldwin Hills Village in Los Angeles, the relation of housing units to outdoor environment was given a more sophisticated form (figure 6.13). When garden terraces were provided for first-floor residents of this housing development, second-floor residents demanded them too. Here, the height of residence does not correlate to status differential; the entire mode of access to outside is more significant.

An equal relation of dwelling place to street and natural environment is increasingly difficult to maintain as one moves from the scale of low-rise to high-rise buildings and from traditional to international styles. In large, "functional" housing forms, with their minimal balconies, distancing inevitably occurs (figure 6.14). Not only are apartments substantially removed from the ground, but the force of winds and the angle of sunlight often force residents to keep openable windows and balcony doors closed. At the upper levels of high buildings, balconies tend to be symbolic and part of the continuity of building design rather than usable. When they are used, the increased size of the building tends to diminish the balcony and remove it from life below. The greater the height, the more

Figure 6.14. Functionalist apartment building, Austin,
Texas. The higher the building, the greater the tendency
to diminish the balcony's form and power.

participation in street life is replaced by the detached aesthetic attitude of "a view." The result is a weakened or indirect relationship
between inside and outside.

The central point is that balconies need to be socially non-
distancing in egalitarian housing. In one sense, these balconies
function like porches. For occupants with no ground level entry, the
balcony, like the porch, can extend one's living space outside. A
multi-story residence may have the same sort of balcony or gallery
at each level. To be truly intermediate places, however, such balconies would need simultaneously to belong to inside and outside
realms. Whereas a porch belongs to the inside by virtue of being directly connected to doorway and threshold on the ground level, a

balcony requires a compensating manner of continuity. It needs to be an integral part and extension of the inner realm, which is possible only when the balcony is set into the building and not merely tacked to the outside. If the balcony is recessed into the building, it appears as part of the overall structure. It becomes a secure and semi-private area, providing physical and social comforts similar to those of the porch.

Further, the balcony is a place to be used on an upper floor only when it is able to support everyday human experience—i.e., providing an area where people can face each other and sit, read, eat, and play cards. It seems, then, that the balcony has its own requirements of width and depth. Ideally, the space is large enough to accommodate a table and surrounding chairs. According to Alexander, balconies "manage to gather life to them or to get used" when they are at least six feet deep (Alexander, 1977, p. 783). In the usable balcony, the form remains close to an upper-level porch, though still derivative from the porch and limited in its direct mediation between inner and outer realms.

The Porch as a Place in Itself

Between house and surroundings, the porch opens a place for the occupant to belong to both nature and community. Because it is a *site emphasizing the between and enabling gathering and lingering to occur,* the porch becomes a place of events and experiences. Vaux emphasized the importance of the porch as a place when he held that, in the design of country homes, "the porch . . . suggests itself as having the priority of claim to our notice. . . . This part of the design is the first that appeals to the attention of a visitor, and admits of much character and expression" (Vaux, 1864, p. 82). As Vaux suggests, particularly important here is the fact that the porch provides the transition between house and outside. *The porch marks a threshold.* The rise to the porch is the rise to the level of the household, a transition in spatial form and meaning. The shift is from the "rest of the world" to another place or manner of being. *The porch joins different worlds.*

The porch steps embody the difference between the realms of outside-below and inside-above. Steps commemorate the transition, concretely holding the memory of movement. In accomplishing the passage, one's embodied experience corresponds to the architectural forms. One lifts feet and legs, climbing with the body's weight up the steps. The effort of the body in ascending acknowledges the differentiation. Steps permit and memorialize this difference and transition. Architectural form, bodily action, and memory are homologous. Each enables the recognition of the privileged private world inside and the complementary public and nature worlds outside. In addition, the passage between outer and inner is also marked often by shifts in materials—for instance, a concrete walk may give way to wooden steps. The changes in built elements reflect and signal transitions in placement.

The porch brings about and extends a between, reconciling outside and inside. The porch is at rest, balanced between the spheres it mediates. The formal character of the whole shows the unity. American houses often have an arriving-leaving place already defined on the inside—a vestibule, for instance. If the world were essentially private, the inside area for greeting and leave taking would be sufficient. The realm outside the threshold could be detached and purely exterior. In an egalitarian world, however, one's own life is not only private and inside, but also public and outside. Others meet us and are welcome not only in common public ground, but also at our thresholds.

For many American houses, the private lingering place inside the threshold has been matched by a corresponding place outside. The pattern is: pure inside (covered), inside lingering place (covered), threshold, outside lingering place (partially covered, partially open), and pure outside (uncovered). Given both the place outside and place inside, the threshold remains architecturally and socially balanced. The between is kept as the middle of the balance point.

Variations From the Porch's Essential Character

As the porch becomes an articulated site, it passes through phases of enclosure. The simple hood over the entry becomes a platform that is roofed over. The open space between roof and platform may be delimited by columns. Railings or sitting walls bounding the platform may further articulate the lower portion of the space between columns, and lattice work and trellises may be added to the upper portion. The process may go "too far," and the porch loses the balance of remaining a between. With too much elaboration and substantialization, the porch becomes enclosed. An initial, but still somewhat open, screening is replaced by a stable framework with

Figure 6.15. Wooden-frame houses, Oshkosh, Wisconsin. Porches are protected and enclosed by screens and storm windows.

its own door and closed screening. In turn, the screens are replaced by storm windows, first in winter, then all year long, until finally the area is sided over, becoming another room (figures 6.15 and 6.16).

In the Southern variation of enclosing the porch to generate extra interior space, the porch may be glassed to make a sun or breakfast room (figure 6.17). That the porch belongs to and elaborates the essential character of the house in relation to the outside world is witnessed by the fact that even an enclosed porch tends to contribute to the house's style and gestalt, rather than appearing as a mere addition. The phenomenon is so strong that the house often appears completed even when the porch is obviously added as an afterthought (figure 6.18).

Perhaps the porch's betweenness is strong enough to account, albeit at an unconscious level, for the retention of a front porch, even when additional room and storage space are needed. This importance of the front porch can be seen when contrasted with the back porch which in the American Midwest tends to become a mere utility area. The back porch does not have the special functions of the front porch, but instead serves mainly as an enclosed area for transition in bad weather. It keeps the cold at a further remove from the

Figure 6.16. Remodeled house, Oshkosh, Wisconsin. The fully enclosed porch becomes another room.

Figure 6.17. House remodeled in the 1980s, Dallas, Texas. A glassed-in porch provides sunlight and an additional room.

Figure 6.18. Workers' housing, originally part of a socialist project, Milwaukee, Wisconsin. Even when added later, porches can complete a house's gestalt.

interior and facilitates donning and removing snowgear; it may become a storage space for frequently used domestic items not to be left outside or brought inside, such as coats, boots, and gardening utensils. A back porch is an intermediate space, but it does not have the front porch's full range and power to reconcile the private and public realms.

In another variation, the porch is related to portico. Though differences of power and authority remain embodied in American legislative and judicial buildings, hierarchical relationships have been replaced with a more equal social and spatial system. Vertical spatial and social differences have given way to horizontal similarities. In the Greek beginnings of our democratic tradition, public life was conducted in covered walkways or porticos. In the portico of Athens' agora, Socrates and other citizens conducted public philosophy; hence, the portico was the great public realm of passage, where one learned to live and reason. Later, the portico was used as the hall of justice. Beyond the privileged palace of king, justice in the West came out into the public sphere. Justice according to common law among peers was no longer "handed down from on high."

Lawyers and clients operated here, and democracy's business was conducted in the accessible, shared horizontal space of porticos. In this tradition, the porches on American courthouses have sometimes been places of public life and citizens' regular use.

From another angle, however, the porch has generated an essentially private, or intimate, form which perhaps results from the privitization of American life or from the ideal of "getting away from it all" and returning to family and nature. Away from the public front and the semi-private edge of adjacent property, decks and patios have unfolded from houses and backdoors (figure 6.19). The deck and patio are not just a yard, but are raised and built like the house. They are more open and informal than the front porch because they occur in the realm of the private backyard (Mugerauer, 1986). The deck echoes the porch in the way it mediates the house with the backyard. Since the deck is not covered, however, it marks a form halfway between porch and yard. If there is no backyard, the deck appears as *the* outside area—as a kind of roofless gallery or balcony removed from the street. The users are still connected to the natural, open dimension of the environment, for example, as

Figure 6.19. Deck, built on a house in 1986, Jollyville, Texas. A deck echoes the porch, mediating between house and yard.

they cook out. Porch forms continue to unfold, opening new variations on the manner in which we gather together on the outside of our homes.

Conclusion

This essay marks a beginning in describing and interpreting the porch. I explored major variations to discern the porch's essential characteristics and modulations in the way it helps to establish human worlds. A thorough phenomenology requires consideration of all spaces of betweenness—the character of door, window, vestibule, balcony, gallery, and so forth. One would also need to consider the changes in porches in relation to the entire house, and especially interior rooms such as living room and parlor. Such a phenomenology would also examine porches on buildings other than residences, especially in the civic and public spheres. The examples used here are largely Midwestern and Texas porches; these forms would need to be compared with the full range of American porches as well as with the British verandah or *piazza*, the French *galerie*, the Spanish *portale*, and the Italian *loggia*.

Though it is only a beginning, this initial inquiry provides one ground for further work. A key conclusion is that the porch is an architectural opening of a site. The porch, as a between, establishes the site for the emergence of a world. The essential features of the porch disclose the physical, environmental, social, and ontological dimensions of the betweenness in our ways of living and building. The porch simultaneously establishes its own identity and our orientation by differentiating and reconciling inside and outside, above and below, front and back in regard to natural and social worlds. The fundamentally horizontal and egalitarian mode of gathering helps establish the character of democratic private and public spaces. By gathering these dimensions together, in a built place, architecture as a between helps open and sustain a democratic mode of dwelling.

Porches disclose themselves as the scene of the gift of admittance and meeting. It is because of this admittance and meeting that people linger and enjoy themselves on the porch. "Gift," "admittance," and "history" are deeply related in Heidegger's thinking.[6] "Mittance" means to give permission to enter into a place or one's fellowship. "Admittance" refers to acceptance and reception. The household grants entry to others by way of the porch and, in turn, is granted the company of people and environment. Further, the porch's specific modes of gift and admittance help us to understand how architecture is a historical opening of sites for human dwelling.

According to Heidegger, the giving of admittance never happens once and for all, nor through architectural elements that would somehow be unchanging. Rather, the giving occurs as a continual unfolding of diverse modes of being, brought about in part by epochal changes in buildings and interpretations of specific architectural elements. Since architecture helps mediate our existence in natural and cultural contexts, it gives the gift of the between. This gift is primal, not only because it was necessary to make our dwelling possible in the first place, but because to dwell now and in the future, we always need the gift anew. In a continuous but changing manner, architecture gives what sustains us: sites for the establishment and cultivation of human worlds.

Notes

1. *Archae* has two primary meanings. In addition to the sense developed here, it denotes a beginning or origin, as in "archeology." The language of architecture involves a kind of archeology of regional responses to the dimensions of reality, of architecture's own heritage, and of the basic language of the discipline and vocabulary of design elements.

2. On "tikto" meaning "to bring forth or produce," and "techne" meaning "making something appear" or "letting appear and dwell," see Heidegger 1971a, p. 159. "Techne," as "poiesis" is a mode of "bringing-forth-into-unconcealment," or *"her-ver-bringen"* (Heidegger, 1977b, pp. 12 ff.).

3. On the phenomenological reduction, see Spiegelberg, 1965, pp. 134–137.

4. For example, Vaux and Downing's model houses and the more than 500 houses from the Sears and Roebuck catalogues all confirm the "democratic" porch height (Vaux, 1864; Downing, 1850, 1873; Stevenson and Jandl, 1986). Of the 664 houses having porches recorded in *A Field Guide to American Houses,* (McAlester and McAlester, 1986), only eleven appear to be exceptions to this range. In fact, after discounting site and water complications, one notes that only three houses out of 664 have porches with more than six steps.

5. The balconies in more hierarchial societies that ours would complete this height range. Here, the very privileged and powerful review, address, or even bless the population below.

6. I interpret "admittance" in light of "mittance"—the usual translation of the German *"Geschick"* of Being. For Heidegger, the mittence of Being is Being's fateful sending and giving of itself. The plurality of the events of givings—mittences—is what constitutes history (Heidegger, 1977a; Mugerauer, 1988).

References

Alexander, C. (1977). *A Pattern Language*. Oxford: Oxford University Press.

Downing, A. J. (1969). *The Architecture of Country Houses*. New York: Dover [originally 1850].

Harries, K. (1983). Thoughts on a Non-Arbitrary Architecture. *Perspecta, 20*, 9–20.

———. (1988). The Voices of Space. In M. Benedikt (Ed.), *Buildings and Reality*, vol. 4 of *Center: A Journal for Architecture in America*, pp. 34–49. New York: Rizzoli.

Heidegger, M. (1968). *What is Called Thinking*, J. G. Grey (trans.). New York: Harper and Row.

———. (1971a). Building Dwelling Thinking. In *Poetry, Language, Thought*, A. Hofstader (trans.), pp. 143–161. New York: Harper and Row.

———. (1971b). Language. In *Poetry, Language, Thought*, A. Hofstadter (trans.), pp. 187–210. New York: Harper and Row.

———. (1971c). ... Poetically Man Dwells.... In *Poetry, Language, Thought*, A. Hofstadter (trans.), pp. 213–229. New York: Harper and Row.

———. (1975). *Early Greek Thinking*, D. F. Krell and F. A. Capuzzi (trans.). New York: Harper and Row.

———. (1977a). Letter on Humanism. In *Martin Heidegger: Basic Writings*, F. A. Capuzzi (trans), pp. 189–242. New York: Harper and Row.

———. (1977b). *The Question Concerning Technology and Other Essays*. W. Lovitt (trans). New York: Harper and Row.

McAlester, V. and McAlester, L. (1986). *A Field Guide to American Houses*. New York: Knopf.

Mugerauer, R. (1986). Midwestern Yards. *Places, 2*, pp. 2, 31–38.

———. (1988). *Heidegger's Language and Thinking*. Atlantic Highlands, New Jersey: Humanities Press.

Norberg-Schulz, C. (1985). *The Concept of Dwelling*. New York: Rizzoli.

Seamon, D. (1985). Foundational Ecology and Christopher Alexander's *Pattern Language*. A paper presented at the national meetings of the Environmental Design Research Association (EDRA), City University of New York, New York City, June.

Spiegelberg, H. (1965). *The Phenomenological Movement,* volume II. The Hague: Martinus Nijhoff.

Stevenson, K. C. and H. W. Jandl. (1986). *Houses by Mail: A Guide to Houses from Sears Roebuck and Company*. Washington, D.C.: The Preservation Press.

Vaux, C. (1970). *Villas and Cottages*. New York: Dover [originally 1864].

Chapter 7

A Lesson in Continuity: The Legacy of the Builders' Guild in Northern Greece

◻

Ronald Walkey

Beautiful places inspire us. Even if they are distant from our everyday lives, they have the power of immediate relevance. Sometimes the inspiration is a personal one: the way a certain stair enters a room, or a grove of trees shelters a glade, or a window makes place. This inspiration is personal in that it connects to something that allows us to inhabit and to see ourselves there. At other times a beautiful place gains a wider recognition because it suggests answers in our own culture and to our own places; it may point to a quality we may have lost or have yet to recognize. Often such places become a kind of unconscious model that influences our daily work in oblique ways.

Once novelty wears off and if the inspiration is strong enough, we may be led to analyze and to make comparisons and new connections. It is almost as if we must infiltrate the emotion of inspiration with reason so that we can translate it into action. I believe that the architecture of the Aegean Islands has affected us in just such a way. The inspiration was initiated by the sketchbooks of LeCorbusier and followed by the return of many post-war travellers bringing back their slides to Doris Day's North America. The weighted curve of a Santorini vault; the Mykonos staircase; the shuttered and stone-paved streets of Hydra—all were exotic and intimate. But what led us to use the inspiration was, I think, much more than just the picturesque. What we saw, and—if we were fortunate—what we visited, spoke of invention, cohesion, and tradition. In our time of alienation and abstraction, the Aegean physical form and social reality seemed mutually supportive. In our time of endless strip development, the public room of the Aegean street and its importance to every village person was obvious. In our time of monotony and machine-like repetition, the diversity of Aegean form and the adaptation of simple shapes used in an ingenious and appropriate way stood in stark contrast. The use of the materials at hand to make walls, roofs and courtyards that responded to a harsh climatic reality was a rediscovery. And, finally, there was the inspiration of a process of design and building that could involve everyone. These inspirations from Aegean environments spring from the outcome of addressing immediacy and limited resources in a coherent local culture (Moutsopoulos, 1985; Philippides, 1985).

The traditional building of northern Greece, western Turkey and the adjoining Balkan states may offer us something even more. It is from here that a coherent culture of building spread throughout the northeastern Mediterranean. There is ample evidence that the relative security and the economic resources led to a building form based on reflection, refinement, and intellectual challenge. In this essay, I argue that these buildings and their situation in both time and culture offer a more relevant inspiration to our modern search for continuity in a pluralistic world.

What of this land that had been under Ottoman control since the fifteenth century? On the mountainous and rugged landscape, only infrequently gifted with a fertile valley, the settlement pattern and the building forms have little in common with their island neighbors (figure 7.1). Rather than a single culture, the villages and small cities of northern Greece, Albania, Southern Yugoslavia, Bulgaria and western Turkey were composed of compact yet distinct subcultures living and working in a symbiotic way (Moutsopoulos, 1967; Leonidopoulou-Stylianou, 1982). While Greek, Vlach, Turk, Bulgar and Jew maintained their separate languages and beliefs within well-defined neighborhoods, the homes built for this diversity were of a singular order. The differences are seen in slight variations in plan and in certain detail elements discussed below. The key design element was *a single housing form for a pluralistic and diverse culture.*

Travellers and scholars who have been drawn to this landscape and to these settlements can sense immediately that the history and the mix of cultures have led to something entirely different from the island architecture (Curzon, 1837; Dodwell, 1819; Furmor, 1966; Leake, 1835). The mountainous terrain that allows for measured separation, the cultural diversity and richness within the settlement, and the features of the Ottoman administration that managed this plurality all gave birth to a building process and a building form which is exceptional (Jelavich, 1983).

Figure 7.1. Vitsa, a village in the Pindus Mountains.

What the housing in this mountainous land shares with its island neighbors is a similar respect for material and climatic realities. Although the forms are different, both dwelling styles show a common sense generally associated with vernacular work. But their differences are much more pronounced:

• There is a different urban spatial organization. In northern Greece, the public street is seldom the living room of the community. The houses look inward at street level, with small and protected doorways in often large and fortified walls. Public life centers around the square, which is usually adjacent to a church or mosque.

• The large villages and the towns of northern Greece are divided into distinct residential neighborhoods, each serving a different linguistic and cultural background. Main shopping streets become the cultural meeting ground, with the neighborhood streets remaining more separate and private.

• There are grand houses and humble houses. Although they vary in size, scale and in detail, these houses have similar formal qualities and construction.

- The houses become important seats of family identity, carefully organized to maintain social functions and status. Storerooms and production facilities are within the house.

Also, there is overwhelming evidence of great building skill:

- True and precise stone walls with dressed corners and lintels.

- Continuous vertical holes in dressed corners filled with lead to cushion earthquake shock.

- Magnificently shaped timber roof trusses making wide cantilevers.

- An evocative connection between inside and outside, where both thickness and screens create spaces which are half inside and half outside the wall (figure 7.2).

- Deliberate sizing and detailing of stairs to enhance the sense of passage from one floor to the other.

- Carved stone lintels, corners and decorations (figure 7.3).

- Fine wood detailing throughout the interior.

- Ceilings inlaid with wood pieces to create geometrical patterns that enhance the centering quality of certain rooms.

- Colored glass imbedded in plaster as clerestories above window openings in important rooms.

- Paintings on walls and cabinets depicting animals, plants, distant cities, and sometimes mythical stories.

- Ornate fireplaces of formed plaster, with applied color and decoration.

- The use of color, both inside and out, to enhance the quality of the flat surface.

There is much more to these houses than the urgent solution of a resident builder with quick and humble means during a time of hardship. The work is complex and evocative—filled with the transformation of inspiration from earlier cultures. The house form is robust enough to have survived through five centuries and fluid enough to suit radically different terrains, to support local custom, and to accept foreign cultural influences (figure 7.4). Quite simply we have here the record of continuity of place in a very diverse world.

Figure 7.2. Kontou *archontiko*, Vizitsa period. Built in 1793.

Figure 7.3. House gate in Monodendrio.

Figure 7.4. Tositsa *archontiko*, Metsovo.

What might be described as most intriguing and most mature about these houses is the way in which they were built, particularly in regard to the network of designer-builders who created this continuity. These men seem to have been able to take inspiration from a detail, a foreign influence—even from the work of competing colleagues. Here is an example where rationalization and analysis of the inspiration has lead to skillful and often profound interpretations that did not erase tradition. What I would like to address is the nature of this interpretive process. Who built these places? How did they build them? And what mental and intuitive constructs shaped this lesson in continuity?

I suggest that there are three essential conditions that led to the evolution of this exceptional architecture:

> 1. The quality and coherence of this housing was spread and sustained throughout the region by a complex network of design building teams. This network was a descendant of the builders guild of medieval Byzantium.
>
> 2. Members of this guild understood a number of central qualities that a house must have and that when seen in the mind's eye gave form to an iconic house. I suspect that it was a non-verbal, fluid sort of collective intention that could be adapted to the different means and situations.
>
> 3. The central qualities and the process were the same for a small and humble house as they were for the grand mansion.

The Builders

My research on these houses indicates that the economic system of the late Byzantine Empire had fostered, as in other centers, a guild system of labor differentiation. Each trade was highly organized from within and was sanctioned by the central authority. During the unstable centuries before the Ottoman conquest, much of the commerce of port cities had been reduced by high taxes, local tyranny and banditry. After the fall of Salonika in 1387, a new and efficient form of land tenure and taxation was put in place. There are different opinions on how this system affected the guilds. One source suggests that they continued uninterrupted under Ottoman rule (Jelavich, 1983, p. 62), while another concludes that all guilds were either discontinued or disrupted, save for one: the builders' guild (Moutsopoulis, 1967, p. 102). Recognizing the need for mosques, bridges and monuments to give physical claim to the new empire, the builders' guild, or *isnaf* as it is called in Greek, was allowed to continue.

Whatever the political upheaval did bring, the builders' guild soon extended throughout the entire region as an organization to nurture the craft, to protect it from outsiders, to extend discipline and to train apprentices. There was a strict system of unwritten laws and a fixed hierarchy that was regulated by supervised examinations. Leaders were elected from within the membership, the highest of whom was responsible to the Porte to whom the guild tax was paid.

I suspect that such a system originated in the urban centers, but it was soon to spread over the whole southern Balkans to include the small and most distant villages. The relative peace of the early years of Ottoman administration brought prosperity and expansion into the mountainous areas that before the fifteenth century had been the preserve of the herders and bandits. There were at least four reasons for this new settlement. First, the nomadic people—including the Karagounis, Koutsovlachs and others, with a lineage stretching back to Roman times—began to settle in their places of winter pasture and to follow the flock only in the summer months. Second, malaria was taking its toll in the low lying areas, and many families moved to higher ground for a chance of survival. Third, banditry and oppression was not long in returning to the land; favoritism, domination of agricultural land by Turks, and neglect by central government often led to local tyrants once again having their own way. Finally, perhaps, there may have been a desire for freedom, a longing for a distance from central authority. Ottoman control was almost non-existent in these high and remote areas. Some villages were given special dispensation from taxes, were able to police and to defend themselves, and were given the right to trade directly with the world beyond the Ottoman sphere of influence (Makris, 1982, pp. 181–192; Moutsopoulos, 1975).

Economically, these villages could not sustain themselves from the local environment. Although in Byzantine times a tax write-off could be given to a wealthy merchant who sustained a mountainside monastery and its servant community, this subsidy came to an end with the empire (Makris, 1982, pp. 181–182). What did sustain these villages was the extension of urban trade and specialization. Although remote, the entire region was connected by paths and roads where goods and services could pass between settlements and beyond to distant centers. As a consequence, each village developed a specialty of its own. Rather than supporting a trade of every type, the village would specialize and become widely known for a certain skill. In Greece, Verria was known throughout the Ottoman Empire for its fine towels, Siatista for its furs, Kalarites for its fine silver filigree jewelry, and Ambelakia for the red dye that colored the fez throughout the entire Middle East (figure 7.5).

Similarly, there were builders villages that were known throughout the region for their unique skill. In Greece, the most well known of the builders' villages were in the Zagorohoria, deep in the Pindus mountains—villages such as Pirosogianni, Monodendrio, and Zoupani (now Pendalofos) (figure 7.6). The equivalent in Yugoslavian Macedonia were the villages of Galicnic, Debar and Kriva Palanka. In such places nearly all the able men were involved in this single trade.

How did these guilds operate? After beginning the new season with spring carnival, teams of from ten to twenty men would descend from the remote village leaving it in the care of the women and elderly until a return late in the fall. Led by one master, these teams, *bouloukia* in Greek, might travel hundreds of miles to a distant village to begin work under a contract concluded the previous year. In each team were journeymen and apprentices, and sometimes other special artisans such as a highly skilled joiner whose specialty was doors, or a master fireplace maker.

There were no drawings for these buildings. The only written evidence of these craftsmens' work is a number of one-page documents each describing the number of rooms to be built, how many special doors, how many fireplaces and a schedule of payment and bonuses (Moutsopoulos, 1967; Charlambos, 1983). Working throughout the season, a boulouki could usually complete one large house or a small church. The record of three churches in one season seems to be held by the team of Demos Zipaniotis in 1795 (Makris, 1982, p. 204). Very large and elaborate houses like that of Schwartz in Ambelakia took five years to complete, and another three years to paint and decorate.

Certain celebrations related to the building stages were spelled out such as the *themliatiki*, a celebration when the foundation was complete, and the paying of the "worn-out-clothes" replacement, or *mandilomata*, at the completion of the job. I have seen old and faded photographs from the last decades of the guild where women from the owner's household have draped the ridge of the completed house with new shirts and handkerchiefs for the workmen. One contract

Figure 7.5. View of Kalarites, a village in the Pindus Mountains, once famous for its silver filligree.

Figure 7.6. View of Zoupani (now Pendalofos), a builders' guild village in the Pindus.

proclaims, "We won't take anything for our food or for our clothes: only a jug of ouzo and two parties" (ibid., p. 204). Usually, it was the responsibility of the owner to provide food and clothing for the bou- louki during the summer construction time. The team members were thereby indentured to the client both as guests and workers.

The inner cohesion of the bouloukia and the isnaf was rein- forced by the fact that they had developed an argot. This secret lan- guage of the builders, *mastorika* or *koudarika* in Greek, served several purposes. It immediately set the group apart and claimed its members' allegiance, almost like a uniform. It also enabled each boulouki to protect its craft secrets. As other non-building villages gained wealth and had the means to initiate their own local build- ing industry, it was important that the house-building skills be held within the guild to protect their livelihood. Finally, this secrecy was important for self-defence. Sometimes builders were targets of local extortion, or they would be working so far from home that some an- imosity might arise with the local villagers. It therefore was very useful to be able to converse in a protected way.

Together with coherence, the isnaf fostered excellence and com- petition among building teams. The wealthy clients sought out the most skillful and best known builders. It was essential, therefore, that each team know what was happening throughout the region in the cities of Thessalonika, Plovdiv, Istanbul and beyond. Yet each boulouki managed to keep its own intentions disguised, at least un- til its next contract was complete. The master of the team would of- ten leave his signature carved on the house: "Kosmas from Zoupani" in one; "Theodoros Zoupaniotis, the great star from Zoupani" in an- other. The carving of faces into the stone work of some houses may be the portraits of the builders, clients or of no one in particular. Perhaps these likenesses help to instill symbols of life grounded in old Greek custom.

By the beginning of the nineteenth century, the reputation of the isnaf had grown beyond the Balkan states. In 1808 the team led by Kominos Kalfas was invited to Jerusalem to restore the Church of the Holy Sepulchure after it had been destroyed by fire. By the latter half of the century, however, the growing popularity of west- ern idioms were rejecting anything 'oriental', and client's instruc- tions frequently demanded an exact copy of what had been seen in a foreign capital. Neo-classicism with its frontal symmetry in Aus- trian dress became the rule of the day first for the large houses, then increasingly for the rest. At the same time, the turn of this century saw the fixing of many national boundaries in the area. The war and resettlements that led to the final decisions decimated the links of these itinerant builders. The end of the long and glorious tradition was finally sealed by the availability of reinforced concrete, which simplified the building process and required less skill. Any villager could build his own home, but craft and the old legacy were no longer needed.

The House

To understand the special qualities of the guild-built houses, it is useful to examine in detail one house that illustrates a number of building qualities common throughout the region. This dwelling, the Karagiannopoulos house, is in the village of Vizitsa, on the western slope of Mount Pelion, a ridge about half way between Thessalonika and Athens, high against the Aegean Sea. The village is some nine kilometers up a winding road from the Pagasitokos Gulf. Not far from the village's central square a number of *archontika,* or mansions, stand in the lush green hillside, their backs against the slope. They are immediately recognizable among the new one-story concrete frame houses—taller than the rest, seeming to lurch from the slope. Many of the archontika are nearly overgrown and green with vines. The cover is especially thick on those where earthquakes or years of neglect have led to the collapse of a roof or wall. The Karagiannopoulos archontika sits self-contained on a piece of land with little definition by fence or wall. The house was built by a boulouki from Zoupani in the last decade of the eighteenth century for the Papanastasiou family. Originally the small area of land in front of the house was contained behind defensible wall and gate. In the courtyard so formed, a paved open space separated the main house from a covered oven and from a small building called *paraspiti,* which held storerooms and a summer kitchen.

The house is imposing. Rising up three floors, the structure has few openings in the stone walls of its first two stories. The foundations of these eighty-centimeter-thick walls are twenty centimeters below grade except at the rear where the house is dug into the slope leaving only narrow ventilation slots into the rear storage rooms. A stone-bearing wall runs through the middle of the house parallel with the front, effectively defining a front and back for the interior spaces. Embedded in the stone at every meter of vertical rise are tie members of wild chestnut or oak that serve to distribute the load and to lessen the damage from earthquakes that are frequent in

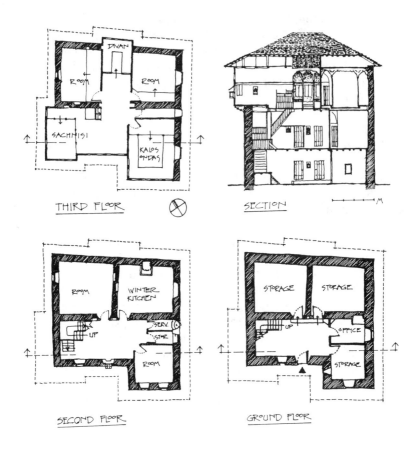

THIRD FLOOR   SECTION

SECOND FLOOR   GROUND FLOOR

Figure 7.7. Plans and section of Karagiannopoulos *archontiko*.

this area. The walls of the uppermost floor of the house to the front
are of light, plastered, woodframe construction, with many openings and the whole floor bracketed out over the walls below. Window
openings, originally without glass, are fitted with wooden shutters
hinged in a number of ways. Above the windows are clerestories of
colored glass set in plaster frames. Wide eaves supported on exposed pole rafters and trusses hold decking on which large slates
are overlapped to make a forty-ton weather protection (figure 7.7).

The single door to the house is on the front face, opening out
onto the small paved area. It is overlooked by the small window of
the plan projection and is further protected by a window directly

above that is fitted with a projecting iron grillwork. The door jambs are of dressed granite, and the magnificent one-piece stone lintel is shaped and carved in a manner known to the area. The twenty-centimeter-thick timber door is secured from the inside with an oak beam that can be heaved across it from a recessed pocket in the wall.

Darkness pervades the ground floor. The flagstoned central area is surrounded by a low stone step from which lead doors to three store rooms and an office. Trading goods and household supplies were kept here. Off to one side, the open wooden staircase turns up and passes narrowly through the exposed beam and board floor to arrive near the center of the second floor. To the front of this space, two windows overlook the view, and the wall is splayed back in both to accommodate a windowseat and to coax the meager light deeper within. This space served as the family workspace, but as in most houses all rooms served multiple purposes. Facing onto this central space are the doors to the three winter rooms. Some of these have raised floor areas, called *divans*. Another has a fireplace that serves as winter kitchen. A small door leads to a washing up area and another to a lavatory.

Once again the stair of open and delicate detail doubles back, this time to lead up to the center of the third floor. With extra space provided by the cantilevered walls and with the lightness of the walls penetrated by so many openings, the stained glass clerestories, and the delicate wood detailing, the impression is one of openness. When coupled with the breathtaking view over the hills, the space generates a sense of weightlessness. There is no ceiling over this open area and the lattice of roof timbers disappears into the dark.

To one end, and subtly defined from the central space by a row of delicate and carved columns that support a screen of carved wooden arches, is the *sachnissi,* the special heart of the house. Delimited from the central space, raised one step from it, surrounded with carpeted divans and with its own ceiling—the whole space edges out over the stone wall below (figure 7.8). At the opposite end of the central space a doorway, set at forty-five degrees, leads to the *kalos ondas,* or the "good room" for visitors and guests. Its exterior walls are of similar fenestration in light framing, but the ceiling here is closed by a painted sofit which curves to meet the intricately panelled ceiling. Wall surfaces are also painted with floral and geometric designs, in a manner that is lighter and more whimsical than the Turkish Baroque style of the period (figure 7.9).

Figure 7.8. Old photograph of a *sachnissi*.

Figure 7.9. Detail of ceiling in the *kalos ondas* of Karagiannopoulos *archontiko*.

A short hall opening to the rear of the central space through an olive arch leads to another divan also defined by thin carved columns and a raised floor. From here the windows offer a view up into the mountains. From this hall there are doors that lead to two other rooms. Around all rooms on this floor runs a continuous wooden shelf above the door head, like an inner horizon. This detail is found over the entire Balkan region. The doors themselves are made of interlocking wooden pieces assembled without nails. Above the shelf and over each window is a *fengiti,* a plaster lattice that holds small pieces of colored glass in a Turkish Baroque pattern. Throughout the house a number of small niches are let into the stone with carved wooden frames similar to the doorways. These spaces were used for the display of special objects.

In these houses there was never any furniture as we know it. The floor, built-in benches and shelves served to support life's activities. Low stools, folding tables, and heavy wooden chests for family possessions were the only moveable elements. Blankets and clothes were kept in closets that were built into the non-structural walls. In the central space the stairs are marked by a curious extension of the balustrade. Made of delicately fashioned wood, it supports a number of small drawers and a shelf. Throughout the house there is an interplay between containment and openness, strength and delicacy, and order and randomness.

The Central Qualities

One can next ask how the design coherence of a dwelling was achieved within the framework of the guild. How did each boulouki in competition without codes or a fixed curriculum of form manage to do consistently beautiful work? I would suggest that the mature members of the building team held in their "mind's eye" what I would call an *iconic house.* This iconic house was shaped by the coming together of several central qualities in a loose but generative way—a collection of intentions with regard to the built-form reality. These qualities, I suspect, were not prescriptors in the normal sense, and they seem more definitive than patterns based in behavior, for they define reoccurring geometries and the composition of the entire dwelling. What the building of these houses has required, if I am right in this speculation, is qualities that are specific and very visible. These qualities could be called up in the builder's imagination, and there was no loss of essential features despite the myriad of interpretations. The iconic house must also have been clear enough to serve for verification. Once the central quality had informed a particular building part, it would be "visible" to builders and clients alike that a particular quality had been achieved. The building would have succeeded in restating the old truth, yet in a new way. The building could be judged as a real and a valid house.

Here, I outline eight central qualities that I believe formed this iconic house. There are other qualities which may also have been part of this image, but it seems these eight are more detailed and serve to elaborate the core of each house. In attempting to define these eight qualities, I have found it interesting to speculate on their origins. Several seem to have a deep connection to metaphors of person-earth-sky. Others suggest a metaphor of the human struggle for a balance between order and chaos in both the inner and outer world. Many of the building elements of these houses, and perhaps even some of the qualities themselves, were in evidence long before the period in question. Some are more attributable than others. All seem to invite speculation.

1. The Seasonal House

The house has a room or rooms which are located and especially tuned for seasonal use. Winter rooms are within the heat-sustaining walls, with smaller window openings, fireplace, raised divans, enclosed ceilings and less decoration due to the necessity of cleaning a winter's smoke from the walls. The areas for summer use are on the upper floors, with thin and open walls, perched both for the view and the breezes. The sleeping quarters for the family changed according to the season. The winter kitchen was used for other purposes when the weather permitted the use of the summer kitchen in the adjacent paraspiti.

In a climate of extremes, with rain, snow, deluge and sub-zero temperatures that alternate with hot, arid summers, one would expect that the houses would have been designed to function efficiently. Materials are responsive, with the mass of stone and the open passage to air under the trusses of the roof. What is unique is that the basic conception of the house included a migration within it to lead a different life according to the season.

From what roots might this pattern descend? Could it be that many families had ancestors that led semi-nomadic lives, moving with spring to different pastures? This seasonal quality suggests a metaphor for an inner and an outer world that is in harmony with the growing seasons and the joys of nature.

2. Strong Back—Open Front

All the houses have a clearly defined front and back. The openings of the upper floor focus in one direction (figure 7.10). In the hillside villages, the closed back of the house sits against the slope. With flat-land houses, the front is indicated by a large and articulated opening in the garden wall (often with a roof of its own) and a pathway leading to the front door. It is obvious that any house built in an area where conflict and security is a major issue will limit openings to one side. Perhaps the origin of this particular quality, therefore, is practicality. But it is not difficult to make anthropomorphic connection. With the 'face' of the house raised high holding windows under the brow of the roof, the house feels almost like a family totem (figure 7.11).

3. Mass and Fine Detail

The buildings display the extremes of both mass/ weightlessness and protection/openness. The thickness of the walls, mass of doorway and lintels, and the expanse and weight of the roof are in contrast with the open floor construction, the stair detailing and the carving of other elements that in some places can become as fine as a fingernail. The leading tip of the last roof slate is usually no more than two centimeters thick. On the upper floors, the delicacy of columns and ceilings that define spaces within the central volume are the antithesis of the mass of the lower walls. An open lattice of wooden members support the stone of the roof. One aspect of the competition between building teams was their ability to stretch their achievement in wood construction (Moutsopoulos, 1967). Inventive detail and daring structure was the rule of the day, and this had little to do with economics.

In the best of the houses there is a specific ordering property to the combination of mass and fine detail. Certain elements are made more massive than need be, while others are made more light. Perhaps the ordering principle here is analogous to the patterning seen in the handicrafts of the area, particularly in the fabrics and kilims. Areas of solid color (mass) are brought to life with patterns of geometrical design (detail). The latter is never allowed to dominate the former; rather, it always acts as counterpoint leaving the integrity of the solid color enhanced.

Figure 7.10. Kontou *archontiko* with *paraspiti* in front and mountain behind.

Figure 7.11. House as a family totem: Vaitsis *archontiko*, Makrinitsa. Built 1761.

4. Ascending Lightness

From the massive walls rooted in the damp level, surrounded by darkness and relieved only by a single open door, up through the stairs past the arched windows on the second floor and farther up to the sunlight of the top floors—the house displays a distinct vertical gradient of visual lightness. One would expect the mass to recede with height, but the quality of light is transformed as well. At the top, light from open shutters passes delicate edges, colored light bounces around the room from the clerestories above the shelf line, and flowers and figures are painted on a light background. In addition, the memory that the sachnissi is cantilevered over the wall at some height adds a hint of insecurity to the lightness.

5. The Floating Roof

The roof of the house is invariably expressed separately from the walls as a cover floating above the house and reaching out horizontally with its long overhangs. This pattern is in stark contrast to the houses of the Aegean Islands, Crete and the southern Mainland of Greece where by setting the roof below the parapet of the wall it is transformed into a terrace. In the north the lightness of construction on the upper floors, the cantilevered sachnissi, the expression and often overemphasis on the open truss members gives the roof a feeling of lift above the mass below. Perhaps this pattern comes from the memory of a tent (Kucukerman, 1985). More likely it is a continuation of feeling of the oldest of the houses where open porches predate the closed sachnissi. The result is a strong roof plane, with life right up inside it, above the walls.

6. The Balanced Center

Until the onslaught of Austrian Neo-Classicism in the mid-1900s, nothing in these houses was built symmetrically. Yet the memory of a central space is carried up through the house by where the stairs begin and where they enter on each floor. Rooms and other elements are arranged around this central space in a loose balance (figure 7.12). Doors are often at an angle giving way to the central space and allowing cross-views through the house (figure 7.13). Larger spaces are kept from bleeding off the energy of the center by a line of columns, or a suspended ceiling, or by raising the area and surrounding it with divans. The continuous head-height shelf links disparate elements placed either in or on the wall surfaces.

Figure 7.12. Dynamic balance of Xeradakis *archontiko*
Pinakates. Built 1840.

Such play with asymmetry is no accident. Many sites offered
flat and undifferentiated opportunity for regularity, and the builders certainly had the skill to accomplish it. It may be that the reason for the odd geometries relates to the need for special room
orientation. I suspect, however, that it is the play between balance
and imbalance itself that was central to the feeling of the house: a
play between security and doubt, between dynamics and rest. The
quality of a balanced center extends into most of the finished rooms.
Shelf, fireplace, divan, ceiling with its concentric geometries, the
door on the corner—all seem to strive for a centered balance within
the room as part of the whole.

Figure 7.13. Interior showing placement of door giving way to the center.

7. The Struggle to Square

Through all the houses there is little evidence of a true right angle. In plan, elevation and detail, almost everything is seen to be slightly askew. I suggest that this is not a result of the building shifting over time, or is it for lack of skill or by reason of poor instrumentation. Rather I suspect it is a conscious decision to leave evident the dialogue with geometry. The tension is felt throughout the house: a wall slopes away ever so slightly, or it meets its neighbor at an angle of something like eighty-seven degrees, or a door does not face directly into the room.

Yet tightness and awkwardness are never tolerated. The way of dealing with irregular sites is an interesting example of this fact. The lower walls of stone would follow the property line, but not the rooms above. Because of the formal nature of these rooms and the careful balance necessary between them, severe irregularity could not be accommodated. The space had to approach more of a square or rectangular shape for the quality of the center to be achieved. Hence, the walls of these upper rooms are cantilevered out over the angled wall below to approach the right angle in the room (figure 7.14). It seems that just a certain distance from the absolute was attempted.

Figure 7.14. Macedonian house reaching to make square rooms.

No doubt part of the genesis of this central quality stems from the "balanced center" discussed above, but the predominance of the square has, I suspect, older roots. Part of the lineage may lie in the *Chahar Taq* of Persia, the place of worship. Four squares surrounded an open space symbolic of fire, form a larger square. It is a form that has long been used in the Islamic world both for mosque and for residence (Ardalan and Bakhtiar, 1979, p. 79).

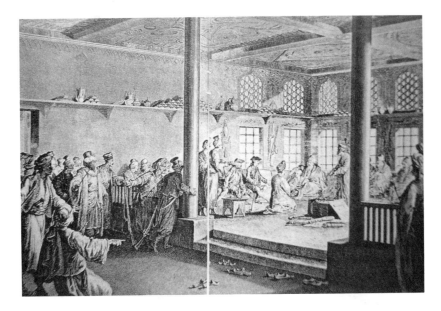

Figure 7.15. Receiving guests in the special room. From an early 19th century print.

8. The Special Room

Within every house there is a special room, or a covered balcony, which acts as the formal and the symbolic center of family life. Functionally, this room was used to receive guests and for business transactions (figure 7.15). At other times, the family used it for sleeping or dining. From the entry door, one is led up and through the house to this special room on the top floor. The plan is organized so that this room will have the best uninterrupted view. Its protrusion on brackets high over the wall, its raised floor, colored clerestories, and definition by columns speak of a conscious attempt to create a very special place around which the other rooms play a supporting role. It is as if the whole house had been orchestrated to allow this room to "float" above the rest of the house (figure 7.16). From the exterior, the projecting windows and walls suggesting a detached room are a common identifying feature of all these houses. But this pattern is far more than an element on the facade.

It may be that this space developed from the need in Christian houses to lead a social life in the evenings after local curfews were imposed. Others suggest a Muslim legacy that requires more privacy for women within the home. Kucukerman (1985, p. 22) suggests

Figure 7.16. The special center of a house.

that the notion of room is descended from the nomadic Asian tent, which was a singular and a defined space. But this possibility does little to explain why this special room is high off the ground. Although each of the many languages in the area has its own name for this room, that used in Greece—*sachnissi*—may shed some light on the question. The fact that this word means "the room of the Shah" may be more than coincidental. It may be that the origin of this special room is Persian, a transformation of the Sufic concept of *socle* which is a "revered and elevated temporal place, together with the *ivan,* the porch, both of which have very ancient roots" (Ardalan and Bakhtiar, 1979, pp. 68–70).

The calm, yet poised nature of these rooms in the houses of northern Greece—half way out over the wall and raised up to float above the world—impart just such an impression. A room "metaphysically viewed as the locus of the soul moving between the garden, taken as spirit, and the room seen as body" (ibid.). These spaces are rooms for being in. They are rooms for being.

Conclusion

Building forms and building processes from the past will always inspire us. Their quality and sense of fit with the cultural and social world offer us images and questions that help us to find ways to make beautiful work in our own time. They become the seeds of what we do when we act in an inspired way. They lead to the inspiration that we might pass on.

The vernacular building of the Greek Islands has exerted a strong influence on twentieth century architecture. This article suggests that further inspiration and insight may be found if we look to the mainland of northern Greece and to the adjacent Balkan states, for the production of housing in this region over the last four centuries has left a powerful and coherent legacy. At the beginning of the eighteenth century, the villages and small cities of what is now northern Greece, Albania, southern Yugoslavia, Bulgaria and western Turkey were composed of compact, yet distinct sub-cultures working and living in a symbiotic way. The strong physical continuity of the dwellings throughout the area speaks of a unique process that was able to embrace many sub-cultures in intimate relationship. While Turk, Greek, Bulgar, Vlach and Jew maintained distinct languages and beliefs, the houses built for such a diversity vary only slightly in their plan and detail.

The grand houses, major works of architecture though they are, were not the product of trained architects nor were they built by residents as part of a layman's vernacular. Rather, these dwellings were the product of an extensive network of "design-build" teams, direct descendants of the Byzantine builders guild, the only guild to be allowed to continue under Ottoman rule. Contact and competition among the teams produced powerful and unique buildings which are only recently being documented. Many teams worked abroad, bringing influence from major cultural centers into the form, detail, and decoration of their building. Descending from only a few mountain villages, and speaking a secret builders' dialect, these teams developed a design by calling on a number of rules, or central qualities that would suggest an iconic house. Such an image was flexible enough, and at such a deep level that it could not only adapt to site and client, but to sub-culture as well. The strength of interconnectedness within the guild and the power of the central qualities allowed influences from distant places to be integrated and transformed with great imagination.

The houses that survive from that sensitive and responsive system are a testament to an integrated process of building and culture, one based on a shared vision in which designing and building were united in craft. The eight central qualities that shaped each house have a lineage that stretches back in time across many cultures. There may be lessons from these distant places that can speak to our contemporary search for continuity with a human face—a continuity that can emerge from our own culturally diverse and pluralistic world.

References

Ardalan and Bakhtiar. (1979). *The Sense of Unity: The Sufi Tradition in Persian Architecture*. Chicago: University of Chicago Press.

Charlambos B. (1983). *Introduction to Greek Traditional Architecture*. Ed. D. Philippedes, Athens: Mellisa.

Curzon, R. (1837). *Visits to Monasteries in the Levant*. London: John Murray.

Dodwell, E. (1819). *A Classical and Topographical Tour Through Greece, 1801, 1805 and 1806*, vol 2. London.

Furmor, P. L. (1966). *Roumeli, Travels in Northern Greece*. Penguin.

Grabrijan, D. (1976). *The Macedonean House*. Ljubjana.

Jelavich, B. (1983). *History of the Balkans, Eighteenth and Nineteenth Century*, vol. 1. New York: Cambridge University Press.

Kizis, Y. (1984). *The Pillon House*. Unpublished Dissertation. Athens: Athens Polytechneon.

Kucukerman, O. (1985). *Turkish House, In Search of Spatial Identity*. Turkish Touring and Automobile Association. Istanbul.

Leake, W. M. (1835). *Travels in Northern Greece, 1805*, vol. 1. London.

Leonidopoulou-Stylianou. M. (1982). *Makrinitsa, The Development of a Community in Time and Space*. Athens: Dissertation, Athens Polytechneon.

Makris, K. A. (1982). *Magnesia, The Story of a Civilization*. Athens.

Michaelides, C. E. (1967). *Hydra, A Greek Island Town: Its Growth and Form*. Chicago: University of Chicago Press.

Moutsopoulos, N. C. (1967). *The Popular Architecture of Verria*. Athens: Technical Society Publications.

——— . (1975). *The Thessalean Ambelakia.* Tessaloniki: Tessaloniki Polytechneon.

——— . *The "Oda" in Macedonean Architecture.* vol. 10. Zygos, Athens.

Papadopoulos, S. A. (1972). *The Greek Merchant Marine (1450–1850).* Athens: The National Bank of Greece.

Philippides, D. (1985). *The Classical Revival in Greece.* Athens: Mellisa.

——— . (1985). *Greek Traditional Architecture.* Athens: Mellisa.

Chapter 8

Toward a Phenomenology of Landscape and Landscape Experience: An Example from Catalonia

◻

Joan Nogué i Font

A phenomenological geography deals with the nature of environmental experience and behavior. Geographers have traditionally worked with such concepts as region, space, place, and environment, and each of these themes can have a phenomenological interpretation (Relph, 1985). Another important geographical focus that can be considered phenomenologically is landscape, which has varied connotations and interpretations (Cosgrove, 1984; Meinig, 1979; Relph, 1981). This article asks whether there can be a phenomenology of landscape in its own right, or whether there exists only a phenomenology of landscape as particular individuals and groups experience that landscape.

I argue here that both phenomenologies exist and do not exclude each other. *They are simply there,* a fact which I attempt to demonstrate in relation to Garrotxa, a region in Spanish Catalonia of some 325 square miles located in the foothills of the Pyrennes about ninety miles north of Barcelona (Figures 8.1, 8.2 and 8.3). My empirical focus is a set of twenty open-ended interviews conducted with two groups of people familiar with Garrotxa in different ways: farmers and landscape painters. I examine what Garrotxa is as a landscape and environment for both groups and consider to what degree the descriptions indicate a Garrotxa landscape that is a "thing-in-itself." I conclude that the Garrotxa landscape has important meaning for both farmers and landscape painters and that their descriptions point to certain shared characteristics that mark out the essential nature of Garrotxa as an environment and place.[1]

The Garrotxa landscape's climatic and botanic qualities are related to an Atlantic and Mediterranean ecological type. With high rainfall and fertile soil of volcanic origin, the Olot Valley—the

Figure 8.1. The location of Garrotxa in Catalonia.

geographic core of Garrotxa—is the site of small villages and farm-
houses. Despite recent social and economic changes in Catalonia as
a whole, the Garrotxa landscape is still largely agricultural, and
farmers are an important group. Olot, a small industrial city of
30,000 inhabitants, is the capital of Garrotxa and is known for its
century-old school of landscape painting, which is still active today
(Grabolosa, 1974; Miralles, 1983). There are a large number of
professional and amateur landscape painters and art galleries in
Garrotxa. These galleries are all located in Olot and generally sell
only landscape paintings. This tradition of landscape painting in
Garrotxa began in the mid-nineteenth century with a group of
nationally and internationally outstanding artists including Enric
Galwey, Ivo Pascual, Melcior Domenge, Josep Berga i Boix, and Josep

Figure 8.2. A typical landscape of Garrotxa.

Figure 8.3. The Valley of Brac, one of many small valleys around Olot.

Figure 8.4. Joaquim Vayreda, *Fall Landscape,* no date [late 19th century], oil on canvas, 0.430 x 0.555m. Reproduced with the permission of the Garrotxa Art Museum, Olot, Catalonia, Spain.

Berga i Boada (Fontbona, 1979). Probably the most significant of these artists was Joaquim Vayreda (1843–1894), who was influenced by Barcelonan Marti í Alsina and particularly by the "Barbizon Group" of French landscape painters, including Corot, Daubigny, and Teodor Rouseau. Vayreda interpreted the Garrotxa landscape as a mirror of the artist's emotions and emphasized direct contact with Garrotxa as a place (Benet, 1922). Vayreda had a great capacity for synthetic vision and portrayed Garrotxa as a humanized rural landscape expressing color and life (Figures 8.4, 8.5 and 8.6).

A Phenomenology of Landscape

A phenomenology of landscape explores "the way in which the natural geography of a site and region contributes to an atmo-

Figure 8.5. Joaquim Vayreda, Untitled, no date [late 19th century], oil on canvas, 0.485 x 0.355m. Reproduced with the permission of the Garrotxa Art Museum.

sphere, character, and sense of place" (Seamon, 1986, p. 20). The argument is that landscape is synergistic and its parts and inter-connections make an environment into a whole "which is greater, but less visible than its material parts and their sum" (Coates and Seamon, 1984, p. 7). Drawing on the insights of Heidegger (1971), the architect Christian Norberg-Schulz (1980) is one scholar who

Figure 8.6. Joaquim Vayreda, *Bracken,* 1891, oil on canvas, 0.655 x 0.495m. Reproduced with the permission of the Garrotxa Art Museum.

attempts a concrete phenomenology of landscape. For Norberg-Schulz, the landscape in which people live is not just a flux of changing phenomena but contains a constant structure and meaning that phenomenological explication can reveal and interpret.

Norberg-Schulz presents five essential qualities that he argues characterize a landscape: thing, order, character, light and time. Further, he suggests that various combinations and juxtapositions of these qualities lead to four general types of landscape: romantic, cosmic, classical, and complex. The *romantic* landscape, perhaps best illustrated by the Nordic forest, is an environment in which the forces of nature work vigorously, particularly because of seasonal change. The romantic landscape is characterized by "an indefinite multitude of different places. Behind every hillock and rock there is a new place, and only exceptionally the landscape is unified to form a simple, univocal space" (ibid., p. 42). In contrast is the *cosmic* landscape, best illustrated by the desert, where there is a dissipated and eternal order hardly disturbed by time. The cosmic landscape contains no "individual places, but forms continuous neutral places . . . [people do] not encounter the multifarious 'forces' of nature, but experience its most absolute cosmic properties" (ibid., p. 45). Third, Norberg-Schulz speaks of a *classical* landscape, which is situated between environmental homogeneity and variety. Represented, for example, by the regions of Greece, the classical landscape is characterized by the intelligible composition of related elements: "In general the classical landscape may be described as a meaningful order of distinct, individual places" (p. 45). Last in Norberg-Schulz's typology is the *complex* landscape, in which the characteristics of the other three landscape types integrate themselves in different proportions. Examples that Norberg-Schulz gives are Naples, Venice, and the Champagne region of France.

Norberg-Schulz's discussion is significant because it indicates one general way in which a phenomenology of landscape might proceed. There has been little research, however, that identifies and describes phenomenologies of particular landscapes, such as Garrotxa. Seamon (1986) offers one general discussion of how a concrete phenomenology of landscape might proceed and emphasizes the importance of complementary efforts that involve: (1) secondhand cerebral knowledge gained through interpretation of such landscape "texts" as literature, photography, landscape painting, and vernacular architecture; (2) firsthand understanding of the landscape that would involve "experiential discovery and awareness of landscape character" (ibid., p. 20). Seamon divides this second effort into two distinct phases. The first phase involves learning to look phenomenologically at the elements of the physical surroundings which constitute landscapes—for instance, water, light, color, winds, rocks, and so forth. The second phase involves understanding experientially how these diverse phenomena interrelate in a specific landscape to endow it with a specific sense of place.

Phenomenology accepts the intersubjectivity of experience, awareness and knowledge. This intersubjectivity allows the researcher to examine the environmental experience of others, as long as the researcher classifies these experiences through methods that promote clarity and intersubjective validity. Spiegelberg (1975) suggests two methods through which phenomenological research can be conducted practically. First, *imaginative self-transposition* involves phenomenological research where the researcher imagines himself or herself in another person's place and studies his or her experience. Second, *joint encounter and exploration* involves research where the researcher and the subject of the study participate in mutual exploration of experience. It is this latter method of joint encounter that is used in this study. I interviewed ten farmers and ten landscape painters in depth in their own environment, surrounded by the landscape they normally use or contemplate. At all times I tried to reach the maximum degree of empathy possible towards the landscape and the person before me. I talked with the farmers in the middle of the forest or during a break from their labors. With the landscape painters, I made excursions into the landscape and visited art galleries. I also spent much time alone in the Garrotxa landscape, seeking to experience and understand it as deeply as I could. I travelled on foot, whenever possible, to saturate myself better in Garrotxa and to integrate myself sensorily.

The Farmers' Experience of Landscape

I chose the ten farmers in this study in such a way that they would provide a representative picture of the farming experience in Garrotxa. These farmers are from different geographic parts of Garrotxa and come from different socio-economic backgrounds. They include both men and women whose ages range from thirty-five to eighty years. The profound understanding that these farmers have for their landscape is perhaps the single most striking characteristic that arises from their descriptions of Garrotxa. Their work allows them to maintain a daily relationship with landscape that is both direct and intense. They know in depth its way of functioning, its rhythm and changes. These farmers have received through "family transmission" an enormous amount of knowledge and an exceptional wealth of vocabulary related to their landscape: the smallest depression, the most insignificant ridge, the most unexpected precipice, the most hidden pasture—all have names. This detailed awareness of the environment is something obvious for them. As one farmer explained, "Of course, everything has a name. Cliffs, woods, rivers, fields, paths—I know everything. If not, what could you tell about them? Things must have a name."

The experiential landscape of the farmers includes a range of elements that can be summarized in terms of contrasting environmental scale. Mountains and valleys mark the largest environmental elements. This level of landscape description incorporates topographic features that structure the farmers' landscape and constrain their experience of place and environment. The second level of environmental scale refers to those smaller environmental qualities that fill out and embellish Garrotxa's mountain and valley base. These elements range from more to less tangible and include soil, water, forests, sky, light, colors, sounds, smells, and sense of space and time.

The Garrotxa farmers are totally conscious of the fact that they live halfway between the plains and the high mountains. As one farmer explained, "We are 'in the middle' because we have big mountains on one side and the plain on the other." The mountains that encircle and define the farmers' valleys are not the high snow-covered peaks of the Pyrenees seen on the distant horizon. The Garrotxa mountains are smaller but with a distinct character and personality: accessible, of manageable proportions, and—most importantly for the farmers—covered by forests (Figure 8.7). Valleys are also an essential component of the farmers' experiential landscape. The valley bottoms are covered by cultivated fields, planted today in corn, wheat, soybeans and potatoes. The farmers' descriptions point out that the experience of living in each valley is different in spite of the fact that to the outsider all of the valleys may seem very much the same: "There are a lot of valleys in Garrotxa. They all have something similar, but they are all different. For example, the simple fact that some have more sunlight than others is enough to make them different."

Beyond the emphasis on general qualities of mountain and valley, the farmers' descriptions mention more detailed environmental features. A section of Garrotxa, especially around Olot, is of volcanic

Figure 8.7. The farmers' landscape of mountains, woods and fields with a typical Garrotxan farm in the right foreground.

origin and is marked by volcanic cones, depressions, and basalt pillars. For the farmers, this volcanic soil is an important landscape trait, giving the earth a peculiar color and texture: "Volcanoes are like mountains here. They are completely covered by forest and it is sometimes difficult to distinguish them. It is the volcanic soil which makes you realize where you are and what kind of land you are working." Volcanic soil is for farmers around Olot what karst landscape is for farmers in other parts of Garrotxa. Cliffs, sinkholes, and caves are important in these farmers' descriptions of landscape because, like volcanic soil, these geologic elements affect the colors, texture and light of the landscape. A farmer who lives in the northeastern part of Garrotxa explains that the karst stone of his area "is peculiar. It is broken and it 'breaks' the landscape. It gives light to the place."

Water is another environmental element that the farmers mention frequently, mostly as it relates to rainfall, streams, and springs. One farmer explained that "this is a bountiful land because of the water. There are springs everywhere and the water is good."

The annual amount of rain, especially in the Olot area, is high. This considerable rainfall, together with fertile soil, has a direct impact on vegetation: "We are lucky in this area because rainfall is high and the soil is good. As the old saying goes, 'Olot is the Heaven's chamberpot'." Farmers' accounts also mention the importance of springs in Garrotxa, some of which have become places of informal social interactions and collective experiences. In these cases, the spring is not only a pool of water but also a space—called a *prat* in Catalan—for talking, picnicking, and dancing. As one farmer explained, "I like going to the spring. In the old days, we celebrated more events there. But I still like to go because I always meet someone to chat with."

The forest is another important element in the farmers' landscape descriptions. "This is a land of forests and cliffs", says one farmer, while another explains that "there is a great variety of trees, like persons." Intimately tied to the mountains both physically and symbolically, the forest is an environment that incites the imagination and brings to mind legends and memories. The farmers speak of the woods as the perfect integration of four types of interrelated elements: geology, vegetation, animals, and human-made artifacts. As one farmer explained, "forests are not only trees. The woods have caves, cliffs, animals, and many things made by people." Other geologic elements mentioned include gorges, sinkholes, and small streams. Pine, oak, and beech together with an underbrush rich in grasses and all types of prickly plants are mentioned as vegetation types associated with the forest, while animals include birds, squirrels, and wild boars. Human-made elements that the farmers speak of include paths, pastures, fences, forest trails, wooden bridges, springs for watering livestock, shelters for shepherds, property border markings, abandoned churches, houses in ruins, overgrown roads, and unused fields overrun with scrub. For the farmers, the forest is a part of their life and, therefore, a humanized landscape: "Our forest is different from the high-mountain forest that is away from people and their activities. Like our forefathers, we go into the forest and use it and enjoy it."

One of the most essential Garrotxa traits as indicated by the farmers' descriptions is a person-nature equilibrium that seems to have existed since the earliest human settlements (Figures 8.8, 8.9 and 8.10). Farmers are conscious that they live in a human-made landscape shaped through generations of work, and they see vernacular buildings as an integral part of the landscape, little different from woods or mountains. Today, as Garrotxa loses population,

Figure 8.8. The traditional agricultural landscape of Garrotxa: farmers harvesting wheat by hand.

Figure 8.9. The vernacular architecture of Garrotxa: a traditional Garrotxan farm building with animals housed on the ground floor, family residence on the second floor, and grain and hay storage in the loft.

Figure 8.10. A traditional stone-and-wood barn of Garrotxa.

the farmers seem to hold this feeling for buildings even more strongly. As one farmer explained, "those stones and walls you see over there in the forest were farms, cottages and barns just a few years ago. It is like people when they die: things return to the land."

In the farmers' comments on Garrotxa, colors, sounds and smells are also frequently mentioned and integrated into a whole through direct everyday contact with the landscape: "You see the seasonal changes in the landscape. And you do not only see them, but you 'feel' them. It is not only the color. It is everything." The green of woods and fresh crops, the yellow of wheat, the brown-yellow of corn fields in the summer, the brown of cultivated lands, the blue of sky—all are significant colors. Sometimes, descriptions from the farmers suggest that a sense of color is what unifies the diverse elements of landscape to give it a particular character, for example: "The cliffs, woods and fields all go together. Cliffs are highlighted by the greenness of woods, and the shade of the woods changes according to the color of the fields down in the valley."

At the same time, the farmers' descriptions also referred to a strong sense of light that varies from location to location and supports a sense of at-homeness and heightens a sense of place. As one farmer explained, "the light we have is different from our neighbor's light. It is different from the ones they have on the coast and in the Pyrenees." Tactile and olfactory experiences are also mentioned in the farmers' landscape descriptions. Paths, for example, are spoken of according to their surface—stony, muddy, with or without grass, and so forth. If there is doubt about the name or the qualities of a plant, the first thing a farmer will do is smell it. Smell, even more than appearance, is the most important vegetative trait for farmers in the case of medicinal plants: "You do not only use the eyes. Smells help you to know different plants."

Overall, the farmers' descriptions of Garrotxa point to a particular sense of space and time. Places for the farmers are intimately and profoundly connected to each other at both a physical and experiential level. Each path leads to a different "place": to the spring, to the river, to the wheat fields, to the neighbor's house, to the forest, and so forth. The name of these paths varies and is dependent on the "place" that the path leads to and on the type of geographic features over which it passes. Through their work and daily observations of a changing nature, farmers live with a cyclical and spatial conception of time. Distances are measured in term of time required to travel on foot between two places, thus one hears a farmer say that "between the village of Castellfollit and Olot there is 'an hour on the path'." Very seldom do farmers utilize the corresponding physical distance of four miles. At the same time, the pace of seasons, days and hours mark spatial-temporal rhythms that are lived in depth. Time is cyclical, multidirectional, spatial and adapted to the rhythms of nature.

The Landscape Painters' Experience of Landscape

Ten landscape painters, both professional and amateur, were included in the group interviewed; all were members of the Olot School. Eight painters live in Olot and two in small surrounding villages. Unlike the farmers, all of these artists were men, ranging in age from thirty to seventy years old. There are only a few women landscape painters in Garrotxa—none of them professional—and I was unable to interview them because they were not in the area while I was doing my fieldwork.

The landscape painters are also in direct contact with the Garrotxa landscape, but their relationship is not as corporeal, practical or constant as the farmers', nor is the artists' specific environmental knowledge as profound, detailed, or pragmatic. What is clear, however, is that these landscape painters, following the philosophy of the Olot School, need direct contact with the landscape: "To paint out of doors", said one artist, "is the basic condition necessary to captivate Garrotxa's spirit." These painters perceive the landscape as a balanced set of forms, masses and colors, the interrelationship of which gives a concrete pictorial composition. My interviews indicate that it is difficult for the painters to specify the elements that make up their landscape because the experience is holistic. As one artist said, "landscape is something global and its elements can not be individualized without difficulty. I am used to looking at the environment as a combination of colors, volumes and forms."

In spite of the artists' explicit reference to the unity of landscape, certain elements reappeared in several of the interviews. A first element frequently mentioned was mountains and valleys, also important in the farmers' descriptions of Garrotxa. The immediate horizon of Garrotxa is always limited by low mountains of 5,000 feet or less. These mountains are high enough to mark out a landscape of small, encircled valleys. Mountains therefore, generally occupy the background of the Garrotxa artists' pictures and serve as a reference point: "In Garrotxa, the immediate horizon is always limited by mountains. They occupy the background of the canvas. These mountains define small and beautiful valleys, which have something in common but at the same time are all different. They are small worlds in an already small world." The valley bottoms are generally cultivated, and these fields are a significant part of painters' experiential landscape: "Size, color and texture of crops change from season to season, and these changes are extremely important in the landscape as a whole."

In addition to mountains, valleys, and fields, the landscape painters also mention, like the farmers, the importance of the soil, but for the artists, it is its color that gathers their attention: "the soil gives a special tone to the landscape that not everyone perceives at first." Not all the artists know the specific material characteristics of the Garrotxa soil, but they are all aware that the vegetation they paint depends on that soil, as well as other factors. For instance, the artists mention how qualities of water contribute to the ambience of the Garrotxa landscape: "Water is important in this landscape, especially in the Olot area. You do not have to be near a spring or river to realize that fact. You 'feel' the quality of water everywhere." Following Olot School tradition, these landscape painters usually include water in their work—for example, a river, spring, pond, or rainstorm.

Another geologic element that the painters mention is Garrotxa's frequent cliffs, which break the smooth valley landscapes and sometimes pose a problem of presentation: "These cliffs present challenging difficulties to the painter. Their color, light and texture are greatly different from the qualities of the soil." These cliffs command attention and inspire respect. Their vertical arrangement forms significant landmarks and barriers of which the artists take special note: "The cliffs are an important structure in the landscape. They are present. You see them. They are powerful."

Like the farmers of Garrotxa, the landscape painters note that mountains are generally covered by forests, some of which change color and tonality depending on the season and type of tree: "Like crops, the trees offer a great variety of colors throughout the year, even if they do not change their leaves." Importantly, there is a difference in the forest experiences of the farmers and landscape painters. The farmers see the forest as an integration of geology, vegetation, animals and human-made artifacts. This is not the case among landscape painters, who experience forests from another scale and viewpoint, generally related to the trees' aesthetic qualities: "The oak, the pine the holm-oak—all of them are trees with different aesthetic qualities. These trees have very little in common in terms of color and character." The landscape painters hold in particularly high esteem the riverside woods—forests along streams. Today, these woods are rare because of clearing and ecological damage. At the beginning of the century, however, they were venerated for their great beauty and inspiration for poets, writers and artists. Today, the painters sometimes include riverside woods in their paintings even though these forests may not be present in the actual landscape. As one painter explained, "They cut them down in the name of economic efficiency. They were a cultural and ecological heritage that is now lost."

When painters work in the landscape, their primary aim is to absorb the whole atmosphere of the place: "When you stand in front of the canvas, surrounded by the landscape, you look at everything, and everything has an influence on you: the color, the smell of crops, the sounds coming from the farms." When the painters represent fields and vernacular buildings on canvas, however, they often transform them and present them as they might have been a century ago. For example, buckwheat is no longer a major crop in Garrotxa, yet the painters frequently include it in their work because it has become the symbol of traditional Garrotxa and a way of life that have practically disappeared. Buckwheat flowered in September and appeared frequently in Garrotxa paintings, photographs, and literature at the turn of the century (Nogué i Font, 1985). As on painter explains, "Of course I realize that landscape changes and the old crops are no longer there. But still I like painting buckwheat instead of these new and foreign varieties of corn. Buckwheat has been here for centuries. Because of its beauty, Vayreda, Berga i Boix and many others painted it."

In the same way, the Garrotxa painters may creatively manipulate the human-made landscape, leaving out modern agricultural machinery, television antennas, and plastic and metal structures that have invaded the farms during the last twenty years. Instead, these artists present the human-made environment as it was at the turn of the century, when stone, wood and iron were dominant building materials. Certainly such traditional constructions still exist and give character to Garrotxa, but there are new elements which seem not to be "seen" by landscape painters. As one painter explains, "There are more and more ugly agricultural buildings in the surroundings, and the only option I have is not to paint them. It's a matter of getting rid of things that do not fit in the landscape. On my canvas, landscape recovers its virginity." Or, as another painter said:

> I was born in the village I paint. I have pictured it from many different points of view, but you will never see that horrible factory painted on my canvas. I do not paint the factory because I do not like it. This is not its place.

Sounds, smells and the sense of touch also form a significant part of the landscape painters' experience. As one painter explained, "While painting outside in the fresh air, I notice sounds and smells that influence my painting. A certain aroma, for example, can have the effect that the landscape you are painting takes on a particular mood." The landscape painters have a special ability to capture the sense of light of the landscape of Garrotxa. The interviews suggest that three interrelated elements underlie this sense of light: sky, clouds and changing seasonal colors of Garrotxa's vegetation. Almost a third of the typical canvas is normally reserved for the combination of form and color established by sky and clouds: "The sky is difficult to paint because it is not a smooth or uniform layer. The sky is living, filled with shades, colors, and vibrations." The gamut of colors and tonalities that the landscape painters recognize is enormous: blues and grey-whites in the sky and all kinds of greens, yellows and browns in the vegetation. The sense of color and, by extension, the sense of light, are strongly tied to a sense of time. Garrotxa's color, light, and atmosphere change continually, especially in the spring and fall. As one artist described the landscape's totality:

> The Olot landscape is like a garden. It has a serenity of lines and colors that live and always change. In time you learn how to capture the almost invisible shades of light and air. It is very difficult to describe these things. You have to see them.

Garrotxa as a Place

The preceding sections identified elements that are part of the farmers and landscape painters' experiential Garrotxa landscape. Are there commonalties in these two sets of descriptions that point to the essence of Garrotxa as a place and region? As has been shown, mountains, valleys, cliffs, soils, water, woods, fields and buildings are present in the landscape experience of both groups. What varies is the different perspective and intensity through which the two groups "live" these elements. In spite of differences of emphasis, however, there appear to be certain commonalties that arise from the interaction of these elements, and these similarities are useful in articulating the "character" of Garrotxa.

Particularly, both sets of interviews highlight the following clusters of themes: rainfall-vegetation, rainfall-volcanic soil, cliffs-woods-fields, and mountains-forests-vernacular buildings. The first descriptive cluster suggested in both farmers and painters' interviews is rainfall and vegetation. "Garrotxa is water and trees," one farmer says, and a landscape painter adds that the high rainfall and vegetation give "a special tone" to the Garrotxa landscape. The cliffs-woods-fields cluster refers to the fact that the Garrotxa landscape is wild and abrupt (cliffs), but at the same time is human-made (fields). Woods, cliffs and fields represent a transition from wilderness to cultivation, with more presence in some parts of Garrotxa than in others, but always a softening feature that binds the three elements into one. As one farmer said: "Cliffs, woods and fields all go together."

A third cluster of themes common to both groups involves mountains, forests and vernacular buildings. These elements indicate a particular sense of place that is observable neither in the nearby high mountains—for example, the Pyrenees; nor in the nearby plain regions—for example, the western Emporda region visible from most elevations in Garrotxa. The height of the mountains is not important here but, rather, their relationship to the forests and vernacular buildings. These last two elements transform the character of mountains, softening them and endowing them with living qualities.

A particular sense of light mentioned by both farmers and painters indicates another important aspect of Garrotxa's character. This quality is perhaps one of the most precise ways to express the special "togetherness" of Garrotxa's landscape elements. The Garrotxa light is not brilliant, although both farmers and painters mention how its brightness varies throughout the year. Garrotxa is essentially dark green and closed between mountains; its light is muted accordingly. Sometimes, this light quality was mentioned in reference to travels to other places with greatly different light qualities. As one farmer explained in regard to travel to Figueres, a city outside of Garrotxa: "When I go to the Figueres market, I notice exactly when I leave my home because each time, at the same point, I must put on my sunglasses. I am not used to the brightness." Or, as a painter explained, "There is no light in Garrotxa. It is dark. After a long time painting here, I feel that my paintings become more and more dark. This landscape absorbs you, sometimes too much."

There is another shared theme in the two groups' descriptions that points to the central character of Garrotxa, and this theme has to do with Garrotxa as a home. The label that people give their home region is often an important indication of the key elements characterizing that place. Landscape painters and, especially, farmers use the noun *"garrotxa"* or *"garrotxes"* (plural) to summarize the landscape's character. In Catalan, "garrotxa" means "tangled, wild, difficult terrain" (Fabra, 1980), and certainly a large part of Garrotxa's landscape is such, especially its northern and northeastern parts. As one older farmer said, "This land is 'garrotxa'. Indeed, it is so. It is rugged and difficult. It is hard to find other 'garrotxes' like this in Catalonia." In many parts almost inaccessible, the Garrotxa landscape is full of forests, precipices and gorges. In most of the farmers' and artists' descriptions, one finds mention of a harsh, imposing landscape that inspires a certain respect, especially today when emigration has left the region largely uninhabited and isolated.

Conclusion

As the above interpretation illustrates, the experience of the Garrotxa landscape is in some ways different for farmers and painters. There are, however, certain environmental qualities and experiences of Garrotxa that are shared, and these similarities indicate that a phenomenology of landscape in its own right exists. These similarities are environmental qualities and interactions that are normally hidden and taken-for-granted, but that can be identified and described through a phenomenological approach.

In terms of Norberg-Schulz's fourfold typology (Norberg-Schulz, 1980), one can conclude that Garrotxa is a special kind of romantic landscape. In its geographical variety, one finds the "indefinite multitude of different places" (Norberg-Schulz, 1980, p. 40). This environmental diversity marks the key distinguishing characteristics of a romantic landscape and, in the case of Garrotxa, is identified by the complex topography, seasonal changes, fluctuating rainfall, and other natural forces.

If regional character can be identified through the phenomenological approach, does one have the basis for a new regional geography? Could a phenomenology of landscape provide another way for geographers and other environmental researchers to identify the sense of place for a particular region? In this respect, Norberg-Schulz's landscape types are useful, though perhaps too general in that a landscape like Garrotxa becomes a specific kind of romantic landscape different from Norberg-Schulz's Nordic examples because of latitude, different geology, and so forth. Future studies need to develop ways to identify landscape character more thoroughly and precisely, and this article provides one potential approach that can be applied to other regions and human groups.

In most general terms, the present research offers one innovative method to explore the ways that people experience places and give them meaning, especially in regard to the landscape qualities of these places. Any external intervention in a place should consider the essential characteristics that define that place from the *inside,* and a phenomenology of landscape provides on important vehicle for this understanding. In modern society, it is crucially important to know the integral character of a place because technology can so readily change, remake, or destroy environments. With a knowledge of place and landscape, people—particularly the insiders of a place—have a foundation from which to provide environmental description to others, including outside experts. In this way, specific environments can be worked with and maintained in a way that respects and supports their essential character, which at least partially is grounded in the natural landscape.

Notes

1. This study of farmers and landscape painters is part of a larger research project that also explored the Garrotxa landscape as experienced by tourists, hikers, and recently arrived residents who were formerly urbanites. See Nogué i Font, 1985.

References

Benet, R. (1922). *Joaquim Vayreda*. Barcelona: Publicacions de la Junta Municipal d'Exposicons d'Art.

Coates, G. and Seamon, D. (1984). Toward a Phenomenology of Place and Place-Making. Interpreting Landscape, Lifeworld and Aesthetics. *Oz, 6,* 6–9.

Cosgrove, D. (1984). *Social Formation and Symbolic Landscapes.* London: Croom Helm.

Fabra, P. (1980). *Diccionari General de la Llengua Catalana.* Barcelona: Edhasa.

Fontbona, F. (1979). *El paisatgisme a Catalunya.* Barcelona: Destino.

Grabolosa, R. (1974). *Olot en les Arts i en les Lletres.* Barcelona: Dirosa.

Heidegger, M. (1971). *Poetry, Language, Thought.* New York: Harper and Row.

Meinig, D. W. 1979). *The Interpretation of Ordinary Landscapes.* New York: Oxford University Press.

Miralles, F. (1983). *Història de l'Art Català. L'època de les Avantguardes 1917–1970.* Barcelona: Edicions 62.

Nogué i Font, J. (1985). *Una lectura geográfico-humanista del paisatge de la Garrotxa.* Girona: Diputacio de Girona i Collegi Universitari de Girona.

Norberg-Schulz, C. (1980). *Genius Loci: Towards a Phenomenology of Architecture.* New York: Rizzoli.

Relph, E. C. (1985). Phenomenology. In M. E. Harvey and B. P. Holly (eds.), *Themes in Geographic Thought* (pp. 99–114). London: Croom Helm.

———. (1985). Geographical Experiences and Being-in-the-World: The Phenomenological Origins of Geography. In D. Seamon and R. Mugerauer (eds.), *Dwelling, Place and Environment. Towards a Phenomenology of Person and World* (pp. 15–32). Dordrecht: Martinus Nijhoff.

Seamon, D. (1986). Phenomenology and Vernacular Lifeworlds. In D. G. Saile (ed.), *Architecture and Cultural Change* (pp. 17–24). Lawrence, Kansas: School of Architecture, University of Kansas; reprinted in *Trumpeter, 8* (1991), 201–206.

Spiegelberg, H. (1975). *Doing Phenomenology.* Dordrecht: Martinus Nijhoff.

Chapter 9

Toward a Holistic Understanding of Place: Reading a Landscape Through its Flora and Fauna

◻

Mark Riegner

To "read" a landscape, the student must prepare inwardly to be receptive to the whole, to be moved by it, and to approach the details with the attitude that each is a gateway to something more than itself. Striving toward an understanding of wholeness through a study of the natural landscape is a prerequisite for asking how one can design dwellings, workplaces, communities, and agricultural landscapes in harmony with a particular place. How, in other words, can each detail of the human-built environment approach a significance through which the individuality of a place can become present?

Relph (1979, p. 28) explains that to "come to know the individuality of a landscape through careful seeing and reflection is a considerable achievement; but to identify the broader principles implied in that landscape requires . . . an effort of imagination that makes it possible to grasp the whole nature of something of which we know only a fragment." In this article, I propose that a fragment, or part, when approached phenomenologically, becomes a revelation of the whole that informs it. Specifically, the living elements of a landscape—its plants and animals—provide focal points through which the character of a place becomes present. The organism and its world are intimately united, and each can be used to read the other.

This essay applies a style of phenomenology grounded in Goethe's way of science (Arber, 1950; Bortoft, 1986; Brady, 1977, 1987; Goethe, 1988; Lehrs, 1958; Seamon, 1978; Steiner, 1968, 1985, 1988), expressed particularly in his dictum: "Seek nothing beyond the phenomena; they are themselves the theory." As an innovator in the study of morphology—a term he coined that refers to the principles of form in the organic and inorganic worlds—Goethe devoted much of his life to developing a qualitative, descriptive natural science. He believed that an active yet receptive observing and seeing are the key to apprehending inherent patterns and principles in the natural world. By participating empathetically within the sphere of phenomena, the student can discover the in-dwelling significance of the whole as it declares itself through the interrelating of parts. Through such a way of looking, the forms themselves become their own interpretation; they become language (Bortoft, 1986).

Besides providing a way to read plant and animal forms, this approach also enables one to read landscapes—the contexts in which plants and animals are situated. Although landscapes are complex entities with many facets such as geology, climate, hydrology, and so forth, each environmental detail is nevertheless a partial disclosure of the whole and bears a simultaneous relationship to the whole and to all the other parts. Accordingly, it is through the parts that the whole is encountered (Bortoft, 1985).

In the first sections of this essay, I examine plants as parts through which the character of a landscape comes to presence. If one considers a plant's morphology as a kind of language, one can follow how that language varies from place to place. A landscape's plant forms become expressions of the qualities that characterize a place—for example, light intensity and moisture. In later sections of the essay, I explore how, in a parallel manner, an animal's morphology can be interpreted as a form language that reflects the qualities of its environment. I maintain that elements of an animal's form can indicate, for example, whether an animal lives in a moist or dry landscape. In the final section, I consider both plants and animals together as the living components through which the wholeness of a landscape comes forth.

The Language of Plant Morphology

An ecological perspective requires that the student consider characteristics of an organism within the context of the environment in which that organism lives. Organism and landscape form an inseparable unity. Ecologists apply this knowledge practically by identifying "indicator" species from whose presence can be deduced a spectrum of physical conditions that infer the ecological context. Many terrestrial plants serve as precise indicators of soil chemistry, moisture content, and thermal regime of a particular environment.

For example, the presence of milk-vetches, a large group of plants in the legume family, is typically diagnostic of relatively high concentrations of selenium in the soil, while members of the mustard family generally prefer soils rich in sulfur (Odum, 1971). The suitability of land for agriculture can often be determined by surveying the native plants. Peasant farmers in Peru, for example, know exactly where to plant certain crops by the presence of telling "weeds."

On a global scale, different plant associations occur in different geographic regions and indicate the climatic and geologic conditions of those areas. Because these vegetational associations may appear superficially alike in geographically distant regions with a similar climate and geology, they constitute identifiable types, or *biomes,* such as desert, tundra, tropical rain forest, and temperate deciduous forest (see Holdridge, 1947). A biome, however, is not a homogeneous entity, but a mosaic of local areas each typified by a particular combination of environmental factors, like humidity and temperature. As the environmental factors vary from locality to locality, so does the vegetation (Walter, 1985). Striking examples of intraregional variation in vegetation are often seen in comparisons of north- and south-facing mountain slopes. On the north coast of Tenerife of the Canary Islands, for example, the vegetational variations are related to differences in solar radiation, wind exposure, and precipitation. Prevailing oceanic breezes from the north transport misty, moisture-laden air inland, which is intercepted by north-facing slopes. The south-facing slopes, in contrast, not only receive less moisture, but they have a more direct exposure to the sun and thereby experience an evaporation rate greater than that of the northern slopes. Consequently, there is less moisture on the slopes with a southern exposure, where sparse vegetation stands in stark contrast to the luxuriant growth on the adjacent north slopes.

In a similar vein, the vegetation of the oak-pine belt of the Upper Sonoran Zone in central Arizona varies with changing topography and water availability. Ponderosa pine and evergreen oaks, with small, stiff, leathery leaves, predominate on most arid canyon slopes. On cooler, shady, north-facing slopes, however, broad-leaved Gambel oaks take root. And, if a sandy wash is present, a ribbon of cottonwoods will grow, their broad, delicate, light green leaves quivering with the slightest breeze. Thus, plant communities within a biome can be seen to reflect a region's varying environmental factors differentially.

The ability of plants to reflect an image of their ambient conditions is also evident at smaller scales. A given species growing in different locales characteristically exhibits varied growth habits if

the environmental circumstances differ. This relationship is documented by ecologists who observe that plants show variations in
growth habit with changing altitudes (Clausen et al., 1948). A plant
on a mountaintop, for example, tends to have a shorter stem, more
compressed form, and more finely differentiated leaves compared
with a specimen of the same species found at sea level. This relationship was also observed by Goethe (1974, p. 26), who noted that
"the same species of plant develops smoother and less intricately
formed leaves when growing in low damp places, while, if trans-
planted to a higher region, it will produce leaves which are rough,
hairy and more delicately finished."

One also discovers that plants growing in the same locale exhibit differences in morphology that reflect the precise conditions of
the place where the individual plant is rooted (Bockemuhl, 1986).
For instance, a dandelion growing in a shady, moist spot near a forest edge has a tall, erect, pale green stem and upright-pointing
leaves that describe a cone. In contrast, a dandelion growing nearby
on a well-drained, sandy soil in full sunlight has a relatively shorter
stem with a reddish tinge, and smaller, more incised dark green
leaves that are prostrate. Other plants in these same "micro-
environments" express similar contrasting growth habits. This pattern indicates that a given plant species has different growth habits
in different micro-environments, while different plant species grow
similarly in the same place. Every plant bears the signature of the
place where it is found. Conversely, the individuality of a place
comes to expression in every plant present.

In describing plants this way, no claim is made regarding cau-
sality—that is, how the ambient qualities actually come to be expressed in the plant. Rather, a *way of seeing* is indicated through
which a part illustrates an aspect of the whole. Every detail of a
plant—leaf shape, orientation of foliage, form and color of flowers
and fruits—is in harmony with the character of the species and
with the particular context in which the specimen lives. If one
strives to read plant forms as words of a text, meaning can come to
presence. The challenge is to view plant form within an appropriate
context so that meaning emerges simultaneously with the recognition of interrelationships.

To extend this way of looking, one can compare the above
contextual observations with observations of an individual plant's
form (Amrine, 1987; Bockemuhl, 1981, 1985, 1986; Goethe, 1974,
1988). What is disclosed through a plant's morphology? To begin
with, one can examine the leaf sequence from the base of a typ-

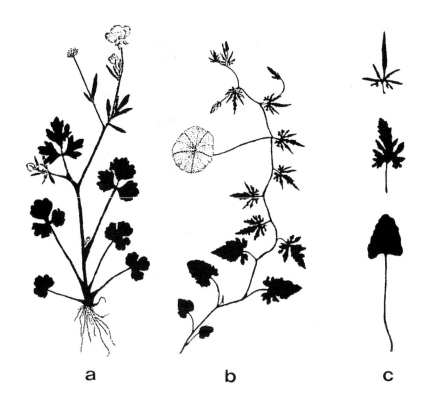

a   b   c

Figure 9.1. Leaf sequences of three herbaceous plants: (a) a buttercup, *Ranunculus marginatus;* (b) a bindweed, *Convolvulus tenuissimus;* (c) detail of three leaves from a bindweed, *C. althaeoides,* arranged according to relative placement on the plant's stem. In each of the drawings, note the increasing differentiation of leaf shape from the basal leaves upward (from Suchantke, 1982a, p. 59, and used with permission).

ical non-woody, seed-producing (i.e., herbaceous) plant up the stem to its apex (figure 9.1). One notes that the shape changes successively from one leaf to the next. In other words, each leaf can be seen to represent one step—a frozen moment—within an orderly continuous transformation.[1] As figure 9.1 illustrates, a particular quality of this transformation is the increasing *differentiation* from the basal leaves upwards; the leaf shape becomes more elaborately formed before ultimately contracting. This phenomenon is well known among plant morphologists (Sinnott, 1960). Hammond (1941), for example, studied the increasing degree of complexity in leaf shape from node to node up the stem in various varieties of

Figure 9.2. Leaves of five varieties of cotton (a-e) from the first node above the ground (bottom row in figure) to the fifth node (top row) (after Hammond, 1941, and used with permission).

cotton (figure 9.2); from the ground upwards, the leaf shape becomes more deeply cleft in each of the five varieties illustrated.

One interpretation of this pattern is that those leaves nearest the solid and moist earth—the oldest leaves—are more round and less dissected, while those farther up the stem nearer the light source, and more exposed to desiccating air, exhibit a greater articulation, incision, and differentiation. Whereas the lower leaves are more substantial, the upper ones are, in Goethe's words, "more delicately finished." It is as if the leaf blades are progressively "cut away" and formed from the periphery. In the terminal leaves, located just below the flower (see figure 9.1), the "cutting away" gesture is often so exaggerated that the blade appears insubstantial—a mere vestige of a leaf, compared with the earlier shapes of the sequence.

Before considering the relationship between plant and landscape in more detail, it is essential to clarify the emphasis on this particular leaf sequence, since not all herbaceous plants undergo a foliar transformation, and for others that do, the direction of differentiation may be reversed. An adequate understanding would require an examination of each example within the context of its spatial and temporal environment. For instance, the foliage of the goldilocks buttercup, *Ranunculus auricomus,* a common plant distributed throughout Europe, undergoes what appears to be a typical transformation except that the last leaf on the stem reverts to a simple, rounded shape. As it produces this simple leaf, however, the plant also prepares next year's shoot within the soil. Although the last leaf formed, the rounded leaf is actually the first leaf of next year's growth and is therefore the initial leaf in the transformative series.

The question remains, however, as to why I choose the increasingly differentiated leaf sequence as representative, even though it is not a pattern common to the majority of herbaceous plants, which display a wealth of morphological diversity in their foliage. This question draws attention to an important aspect of Goethe's scientific method. Whether he studied botanical, meteorological, or chromatic phenomena, Goethe sought examples in which nature was especially revealing. He described such an example as a gateway to the experience of "an instance worth a thousand, bearing all within itself" (Bortoft, 1986, p. 15). The configuration of such a critical phenomenon need not be the most frequent motif observed; commonality is not a criterion for its important status. Rather, its value lies in its being a particularly clear window through which to behold the pattern of a natural principle. In this sense, I maintain that the increasingly differentiated leaf pattern described above has important revelatory power in understanding the plant's relationship to its landscape and in disclosing the individuality of place.

Air, Soil, and the Plant

To place the above observations into a broader context, one can examine how a plant is situated in relation to the environmental factors necessary for its survival, especially illumination and humidity. To a naive observer, illumination and humidity each presents itself ideally as a continuum existing between *polarities*— illumination, between qualities of light and darkness; and humidity, between extremes of dryness and moisture. A plant meets, as it were, the quality of light as it grows toward the sun,

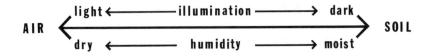

Figure 9.3. The polarity between air and soil.

expanding into the surrounding light- and air-filled space. In contrast, the quality of darkness is met most fully within the subterranean sphere of the roots and, to a lesser degree, in the lowest leaves of the stem, which are nearest the soil and often shaded by upper foliage. In a parallel way, a plant encounters dryness in its upper parts, where moving air facilitates evaporation. Moisture, on the other hand, is concentrated in the soil, where the roots are located. By identifying these qualitative relationships, the "realms" of air and soil can themselves be seen to constitute a polarity between, respectively, light/dry and dark/moist conditions (figure 9.3). These two realms, however, are not mutually exclusive, since moisture permeates air, and air permeates soil. Despite this interpenetration, each realm can be associated with dominant qualities: air accommodates light and dryness; soil, darkness and moisture.

A detailed consideration of the leaf transformations in figure 9.1 provides a morphological illustration of the polarity between air and soil. The lowest stem leaves are nearer the moist, dark soil, while the upper ones unfold farther into the dry, sunlit air. Accordingly, the less differentiated, rounded gesture of the basal leaves is associated with the qualities of moisture and darkness (which characterize the soil), while the highly differentiated, incised, and ultimately contracted gesture of the upper foliage bears a relationship to the qualities of light and dryness (which prevail in the air). One can also see this formal relationship in trees. Walter (1985, p. 197), in describing the crown of a solitary deciduous tree, distinguishes between sun leaves, which are peripheral and thereby exposed to full sunlight, and shade leaves, which are innermost and sheltered from direct light. By comparing the leaves morphologically, Walter concludes that the sun leaves are "smaller and . . . have a denser nervature." In the sense described above, one could say that they are more expressive of light/dry qualities. Talbert and Holch (1957) found a similar relationship in trees from the foothills of the Rocky Mountains (figure 9.4).

Just as a plant's upper leaves, which expand into the sunlight, are generally the most differentiated, so is the entire foliage of many plants found in environments of intense light, such as mountain and desert landscapes. Consider, for example, montane plants,

Figure 9.4. Sun and shade leaves from seven representative species of deciduous trees from the foothills of the Rocky Mountains. The leaf on the left of each pair is a sun leaf; on the right, a shade leaf (based on Talbert and Holch, 1957, p. 656).

which grow at elevations where reduced atmospheric filtering exposes them to strong solar radiation. These plants often show a marked degree of differentiation and incision in their leaves. Under conditions of extreme light intensity and aridity, the foliage of desert flora is typically either highly incised or contracted, as seen in, respectively, the white bur sage and creosote bush, two dominant plants of the Sonoran Desert of the American Southwest (figure 9.5). In the cactus family, the gesture of "cutting away" and hence leaf blade reduction is so pronounced that nothing of a leaf blade remains; instead, there are only spines.

The lower leaves of a plant's stem, on the other hand, are nearer the moist earth and farther from the sphere of light and desiccating air. Just as these leaves are generally less differentiated and more simply contoured, so is the entire foliage of many plants in shady, moist environments, such as the tropical rain forest. Growing in plentiful moisture and constant shade, the leaves of many rain forest species converge in their shape and have elliptical, smooth-edged blades (figure 9.6). "It is remarkable," observes Richards

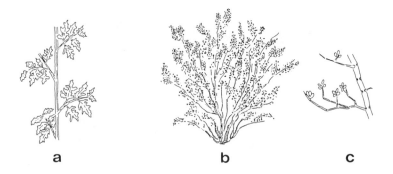

Figure 9.5. Leaves of: (a) white bur sage, *Franseria dumosa;* and (b) creosote bush, *Larrea tridentata;* (c) detail of creosote bush (from Larson, 1977, pp. 47 and 97, and used with permission).

(1981, p. 83), "how the rain-forest environment seems . . . to mould the foliage of all species coming under its influence to one particular form." Some eighty percent of rain-forest trees have leaves with entire margins, according to several comprehensive studies (ibid.). Oaks and maples, for example, which in the temperate zone have intricate leaves that vary considerably in shape, have representatives in tropical rain forests with simple, oblong leaves that taper gradually to a point.

This rounded, smooth-edged quality seen in the foliage of plants of moist habitats comes to fullest expression in aquatic and semiaquatic vegetation. Just as water in the archetypal image of a droplet adopts a smooth, rounded form (Riegner, 1989; Riegner and Wilkes, 1988, 1989; Schwenk, 1965; Schwenk and Schwenk, 1989), so do many plants of tranquil, aquatic landscapes exhibit a watery motif in their smooth, rounded leaves. In water lilies, for example, the leaves assume a flattened disc shape, while the marsh-marigold, mud-plantain, and skunk cabbage—plants common to northeastern North American freshwater habitats—also have broad, rounded, smooth-margined leaves (figure 9.7). A plant's foliar morphology, therefore, can be seen to reflect characteristics of its surroundings.

The Plant in the Landscape

Although plants in a landscape will converge in their qualities to express the individuality of that place, there is typically a diver-

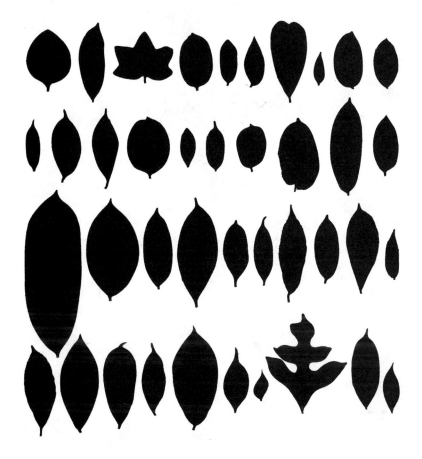

Figure 9.6. Leaves of representative plants from an African rain forest (from Richards, 1981, p. 82, and used with permission).

sity of plant species, and hence morphologies. Moreover, within any environment, there usually occur a wide range of ambient conditions such as illumination and humidity. One can ask which environmental qualities are embodied most conspicuously in a particular species. Some plants, for example, express in their morphology the qualities of soil, while others reflect the qualities of air. Consider typical deciduous trees of a mid-Atlantic North American forest (figure 9.8). The leaves of the seventeen species illustrated here vary in their degree of incision. Studying the overall leaf shape and relative length of the leaf stalk, or petiole, one notes that the

Figure 9.7. Marsh-marigold, *Caltha palustris*, a plant of freshwater habitats (photograph by author).

Figure 9.8. Leaves from representative trees of a mid-Atlantic North American forest; top row (from left to right): swamp white oak, northern red oak, scarlet oak, white ash; second row: American beech, sweetgum, yellow-poplar, slippery elm; third row: sassafras, American holly, sycamore, eastern hophornbeam, flowering dogwood; bottom row: sugar maple, red maple, silver maple, American chestnut (based on author's observations and leaf presses).

simpler, less dissected leaves have a
shorter petiole compared with the
more formed, deeply cut leaves. If
one compares these leaf shapes with
those of an individual herbaceous
plant of figure 9.1, one sees that the
short-stalked, less formed leaves,
like the shapes of the basal leaves of
a single plant, reflect the soil qualities described above, while the long-
petioled, highly differentiated
forms, like those typically located
higher on a plant's stem, suggest the
qualities of air (figure 9.9). The
lengthy petiole can be interpreted in
its gesture as an extension in which
the leaf blade is lifted out into the
light-permeated air and thereby
away from the branch, which has an
earthy, substantive quality.

This relationship is also supported by an examination of the leaf
morphology of the white mulberry
(figure 9.10). In each leaf, the edge
closest to the branch is less indented
and elaborate than the edge facing
the sun. As an example of a plant
where the two tendencies of air and
soil are equally represented morphologically, one can examine the
compound leaf of the white ash (fig-

Figure 9.9. From top to bottom:
scarlet oak, swamp white oak,
American beech; compare with
figure 9.1c (author's drawing).

ure 9.8, uppermost right): the leaf shape itself suggests an attunement to the air, whereas each of the seven leaflets, with their simple
form and short "petiole," expresses soil qualities.[2]

From this perspective, the plants of a place can be interpreted
as a collective expression of landscape character. Different species
that grow in the same place often exhibit similarities in gesture.
These conformities, however, are superimposed on the unique morphology of each botanical species. Moreover, each plant, by virtue of
its species identity, will emphasize in its morphology a precise relationship to the polarity of light/dry and dark/moist. Some plants
will accentuate to various degrees light/dry qualities in their mor-

Figure 9.10. Leaf morphology of the white mulberry (from
a photograph of leaf presses by the author).

phology, while others will do likewise for dark/moist conditions. The
silver maple and scarlet oak (figure 9.8), for instance, are physio-
logically sensitive and responsive to moisture, soil chemistry, temperature, and illumination. Compared with the sugar maple and
swamp white oak (figure 9.8), light and dryness are expressed in the
leaf shapes of the silver maple and scarlet oak more evidently than
are the qualities of darkness and moisture. The sugar maple and
swamp white oak, in turn, are more expressive of air qualities than
either the American beech or eastern hophornbeam (figure 9.8). It
is as if each species, in its physiological constitution, is necessarily
receptive to the entire complex of environmental qualities but is capable of revealing, through its morphology, a picture of the activity
of only a limited few to which it is especially attuned.[3]

Finally, it seems appropriate to view the plant on the level of an
individual specimen reflecting temporal variations of its surroundings. Although most plants provide an integrated expression of
their varying environmental conditions, there are some that exist
in extreme environments and mirror changing ambient conditions
by displaying different kinds of foliage in different seasons. One example is the brittle bush, a shrublike composite of the Sonoran
Desert, which changes its leaves seasonally. In the rainy season, the
plant has large, soft leaves; in the dry season, smaller, hair-covered
foliage; and in continuing drought, new leaves are further contracted and densely covered with hairs (Walter, 1985). In this highly
responsive species, nature demonstrates how precisely the outer
conditions of a landscape are reflected in its flora, which exists in

unity with all the qualities of the place. A landscape's vegetation is, in a sense, in ceaseless dialogue with the ever-fluid qualities of its surroundings.

The Language of Animal Morphology

If plants are in harmony with the character of their surroundings, one may wonder if animals also give expression to a landscape's individuality. Many animals closely resemble features of their world (Portmann, 1959; Wickler, 1974). Some share the same colors and patterns of their immediate environment, while others also resemble the forms of objects in their surroundings. These phenomena of camouflage and mimicry, as they are respectively called, illustrate one way through which the physical landscape comes to expression through the form and coloration of animals. Following the approach of this essay, however, one can ask whether there are ways to recognize how more subtle, less tangible qualities of a landscape speak through the forms of its animal inhabitants. Can a reading of an animal's morphology uncover a deeper level of meaning of its world just as such a reading of plant form gives insights into the plant's surroundings?

Schad (1971) presents a method by which these questions can be addressed. By observing the forms and colorings of mammals as language, he identifies the signature of an underlying pattern (Riegner, 1985). Following a Goethean approach, he interprets each species as it both discloses its unique position among other mammals and also gives expression to a general unity that dwells among the diversity of forms. Here, I outline Schad's way of looking to illustrate how the intangible wholeness of a landscape becomes present through a reading of its mammalian fauna.

By first surveying mammals on the basis of their tooth morphology, Schad delineates three key groups, each distinguished by the accentuation of a particular tooth type: *rodents* have exaggerated incisors, the jaw's frontmost teeth; *carnivores* have pronounced canines, the middle, pointed teeth; and *ungulates* (hoofed mammals) have accentuated molars, the posterior, grinding teeth (figure 9.11). By extending his observations to encompass qualities of body form and coloration, Schad supports this threefold pattern by identifying how each group discloses its unique qualities in relation to those of the others. To provide a visible focus here, a North American mammal typical of each group is illustrated in figure 9.12. One

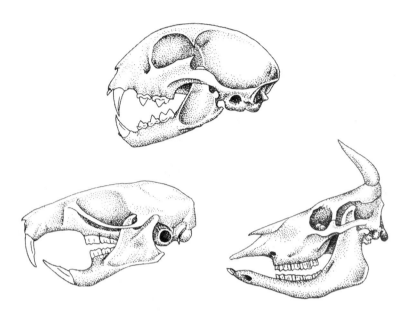

Figure 9.11. Skulls of a rodent (bottom left); ungulate (bottom right); carnivore (top) (drawings by F. A. Reid and used with permission).

Figure 9.12. Representative mammals: golden mouse—a rodent (bottom left); bison—an ungulate (bottom right); ocelot—a carnivore (top) (based on line drawings by F. A. Reid and originally published in *A Field Guide to Mammals Coloring Book*. Copyright © 1987 by Houghton Mifflin Company. Reprinted by permission of Houghton Mifflin Company).

finds that rodents—like the golden mouse shown—are relatively
small, exaggerated in their hindquarters, possess a lengthy tail
(which further accentuates their posterior), and typically have a fur
pattern with darker back and lighter undersides. In contrast, ungulates—such as the bison—are comparatively large, accentuated
in their forequarters, may have head protuberances (e.g., horns,
which further emphasize the anterior), and are colored uniformly.
Yet again, carnivores—represented in figure 9.12 by the ocelot—are
intermediate in size, have a balanced form, and often exhibit a spotted or striped fur pattern.

Although each of the three groups expresses a unique combination of qualities, these motifs are not exclusive to any one of the
three, as can be seen in figure 9.13. The short-tailed weasel, for example, is a carnivore, but exhibits "rodentlike" qualities in its small
size, quick and nervous movements, and sharply contrasting fur
pattern. The beaver, on the other hand, is a rodent that expresses
the "ungulate" motif: large size, uniform fur color, and a stolid tem-
perament if compared with rodents in general. Yet again, the
thirteen-lined ground squirrel is a rodent that embodies "carnivorous" characteristics; not only is it medium-sized, spotted, and
striped, but its diet includes insects, birds, and mice. Although they
are classified as ungulates and have hooves and well-developed molars, most species of wild pigs, including the introduced European
wild boar, show "carnivorous" traits in their balanced form, aggressive behavior, pronounced, tusklike canines, and tendency to eat
meat; furthermore, their young are spotted and striped. What at
first appear to be exceptions to Schad's general pattern actually
buttress his findings when the qualities of the three key groups are
interrelated in regard to particular mammals. What Schad's phenomenological approach reveals is that certain qualities tend to appear in combination, regardless of the kind of mammal that
embodies them.

How can this way of understanding animal form contribute to a
reading of the landscape in which animals live? In his discussions of
the three mammalian groups, Schad demonstrates that there is not
only a qualitative relationship between large size and uniform fur
color within the groups, but these qualities are often associated
with animals that tend to inhabit wetlands or aquatic environments. For example, within the rodent group, the beaver has a massive size, a uniformly dark coat, and is resident in ponds and
streams. Another large rodent, the muskrat, has an unpatterned
dark coat and is semiaquatic. Within the carnivores, otters are

Figure 9.13. (a) short-tailed weasel—a "rodentlike" carnivore; (b) beaver—an "ungulate-like" rodent; (c) thirteen-lined ground squirrel—a "carnivorelike" rodent; (d) wild boar—a "carnivorelike" ungulate (based on line drawings by F. A. Reid and originally published in *A Field Guide to Mammals Coloring Book*. Copyright © 1987 Houghton Mifflin Company. Reprinted by permission of Houghton Mifflin Company).

some of the largest members of the weasel family, are mostly colored uniformly, and inhabit freshwater and marine environments. Similarly among ungulates, the moose is the largest member of the deer family, has a uniform dark color, and is found in swamp and bog habitats.[4] Can a closer examination of the morphology of these animals reveal a correspondence between the nature of their form and the character of their environment? One way to address this question is to re-examine plant morphology in relation to watery landscapes.

How does a wetland landscape speak through the forms of its plants? Recall that plants of moist habitats, like the water lily, often have rounded, undivided, relatively undifferentiated leaves. The "watery" quality is thus revealed through the gesture of roundness and structural simplicity, epitomized in the form of a water droplet (Riegner, 1989; Riegner and Wilkes, 1988, 1989; Schwenk, 1965; Schwenk and Schwenk, 1989). Do animals of moist environments

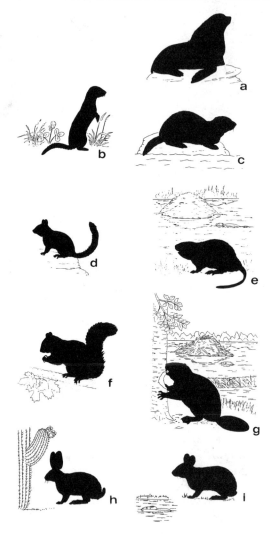

Figure 9.14. Mammals in left column inhabit terrestrial landscapes; those in right column live in wetlands or marine habitats: (a) northern sea lion; (b) short-tailed weasel; (c) sea otter; (d) cliff chipmunk; (e) muskrat; (f) eastern gray squirrel; (g) beaver; (h) desert cottontail; (i) marsh rabbit (based on line drawings by F. A. Reid and originally published in *A Field Guide to Mammals Coloring Book*. Copyright © 1987 Houghton Mifflin Company. Reprinted by permission of houghton Mifflin Company).

express this gesture? A reading of the animal's form provides an answer. Figure 9.14 illustrates members of various groups of mammals. Those mammals on the left are typical terrestrial group representatives, while those on the right are found in aquatic habitats. Note that, in general, the mammals on the right have more heavy-set bodies and less "refined" forms, as exemplified in the northern sea lion. The sea otter, for example, has a bulkier body and a blunter snout compared with the more delicately formed short-tailed weasel. Both the muskrat and beaver are portly rodents with foreshortened muzzles, compared with the cliff chipmunk and eastern gray squirrel. Even the marsh rabbit is stockier and not as delicately formed as its desert-dwelling counterpart, which has longer ears, legs, and tail. This relationship is also evident in the deer family (figure 9.15). A comparison of the moose with the white-tailed deer shows the former to be more massive and the latter to have more delicate features. These morphological tendencies are expressed even in the antlers of the two animals—those of the bull moose are broad and heavy, while those of the white-tailed deer buck are slender and branching.[5]

The reading of a mammal's form, therefore, discloses a correspondence between subtle features of its morphology and qualities of its landscape. Although both plants and animals have been shown to express "convergent" morphological features in their tendency toward simpler forms in watery environments, no speculation is

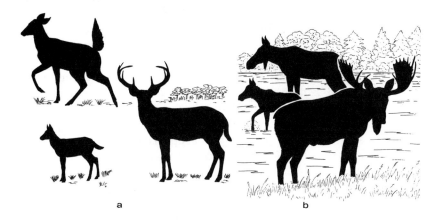

a   b

Figure 9.15.(a) White-tailed deer family; (b) moose family (based on line drawings by F. A. Reid and originally published in *A Field Guide to Mammals Coloring Book.* Copyright © 1987 by Houghton Mifflin Company. Reprinted by permission of Houghton Mifflin Company).

made here regarding causal factors. Rather, the emphasis is on descriptive interrelationships that suggest an underlying pattern.

The Animal in the Landscape

As with plants, one discovers that some animals at first appear not to fit the preceding generalizations. The woodchuck, for instance, is a rodent found in terrestrial landscapes—open woods, forest edges, brushy fields—yet it is large-bodied, uniformly colored, and has a foreshortened muzzle—all characteristics of an aquatic creature. This discrepency is less a contradiction, however, when one notes that the main life-realm of the woodchuck is the soil, the sphere where the watery quality is dominant. Accordingly, the woodchuck's unrefined form gives expression to the soil qualities of darkness and moisture, just as do the lowest leaves of a terrestrial plant, or a typical plant or animal of a watery landscape. Similarly, desert mammals such as the kangaroo rat (a compact-bodied rodent) and badger (a heavyset member of the weasel family) are not as delicately formed as might, at first, be expected. They occupy relatively humid subterranean burrows and emerge only at dusk under cover of darkness. Never exposed to sunlight or intense heat, they can be said to express qualities of the soil, especially darkness.

Another example of how an animal's morphology reflects the subtle qualities of its life-realm within a landscape is seen in a comparison of the white-footed mouse with the woodland vole (figure 9.16). Both rodents inhabit forests throughout the eastern United States, yet they occupy different niches within the forest environment. Their forms readily indicate which dwells underground and which typically in trees: the woodland vole burrows through the forest floor and seldom comes aboveground, while the white-footed mouse scampers through underbrush and trees, often making its home in a vacated bird's nest. Like the woodchuck, the vole expresses dark/moist qualities in its rounded proportions, while the mouse suggests light/dry traits as evidenced in its more graceful form.

A final example in which the polarity of light/dry and dark/moist qualities is expressed in mammals can be seen in a comparison of two closely related species: the raccoon and coati (figure 9.17). These medium-sized carnivores are found, in part, in North America. In general, the raccoon prefers woodlands along streams and lakes, while the coati favors arid terrain and open forests. These carnivores differ considerably in one aspect of their behavior:

Figure 9.16. (a) White-footed mouse at home in a tree; (b) woodland vole outside its underground burrow (based on line drawings by F. A. Reid and originally published in *A Field Guide to Mammals Coloring Book*. Copyright © 1987 by Houghton Mifflin Company. Reprinted by permission of Houghton Mifflin Company).

Figure 9.17. (a) Coati; (b) raccoon (based on line drawings by F. A. Reid and originally published in *A Field Guide to Mammals Coloring Book*. Copyright © 1987 by Houghton Mifflin Company. Reprinted by permission of Houghton Mifflin Company).

the raccoon is chiefly nocturnal; the coati is active primarily by day. In terms of the landscape, the raccoon can be considered to dwell in the "nightscape," whereas the coati exists in the "dayscape." An examination of their morphology provides evidence of this distinction in that the coati—with its relatively slender body, long, thin tail, and elongate snout—is more delicately formed and therefore more expressive of light/dry qualities, whereas in its more compact, rounder form, the raccoon reflects dark/moist characteristics.[6]

Toward a Phenomenological Ecology

Although the preceding sections deal separately with plants and animals, both should be considered together within the context of a landscape to approach more fully the character of a place. In fact, it is instructive to cultivate an attitude that the flora and fauna themselves constitute, in part, the landscape, which exists as an organic whole. An animal, for example, does not so much live *in* an environment as the environment is an extension of the animal. Conversely, the animal can be viewed as an extension of the environment. The two are reciprocally united. Thus, the wholeness of a place comes to expression *expansively* in the overall landscape and *focally* in the parts of the landscape.

To illustrate this distinction, consider the North American prairie, noted for its uniformity. As far as the eye can see, these grasslands extend uninterrupted with few distinctive topographic and biotic features. The quality of uniformity is therefore observed expansively on the scale of the landscape itself but is also encountered in the individual living components. For example, the dominant vegetation is represented by the grass family, which gives the impression of a homogeneous flora. Although composed of a variety of species, the separate forms are difficult to distinguish. Similarly, the typical bird fauna associated with the prairie includes various species of sparrows, whose likeness in morphology and coloration challenges the identification skills of even the expert birdwatcher. Thus, the prairie's quality of uniformity is expressed both expansively, in the overall landscape, and focally, in its vegetation and bird life.

The prairie example also illustrates how both plants and animals of a given landscape may embody similar qualities, as seen in the grasses and sparrows. The search for common motifs among apparently dissimilar life forms can lead to provocative discoveries. Using this approach, Popplebaum (Grohmann, 1974, p. 104) identifies an intriguing link between two life forms of the arid African steppes—the ostrich and a peculiar plant, *Welwitschia mirabilis*. In a sense, the ostrich can be seen as a perpetually youthful bird—a kind of giant chick that has reached reproductive maturity. The adult's plumage, for example, is composed of loose, downlike feathers, not unlike the feathers of many young birds. Additionally, the adult is flightless, like most chicks. This description gains significance when it is viewed in relation to qualities of Welwitschia, which shares much of the ostrich's geographic range. An unusual feature of Welwitschia is that it produces only two giant leaves. In one sense, this plant is like an oversized seedling, the two leaves analogous to a pair of seed leaves, or cotyledons. Just as the ostrich suggests an overgrown chick, Welwitschia suggests an overgrown seedling. Both organisms can be seen as youthful forms, in exaggerated size, occurring together over much of their range across the arid African steppes.

Further examples of apparently dissimilar life forms that express similar motifs can be seen in the parallel morphological developments of insects and herbaceous flowering plants. For example, Popplebaum (1961) and Riegner (1986) demonstrate that the stages of butterfly metamorphosis—egg-caterpillar-chrysalis-adult—are mirrored in plant development—seed-leaf-flower bud-corolla. In a parallel way, hummingbirds and sphinx moths show similar morphologies (figure 9.18). Some congruencies, however, require detailed examination of not only morphology, but also of

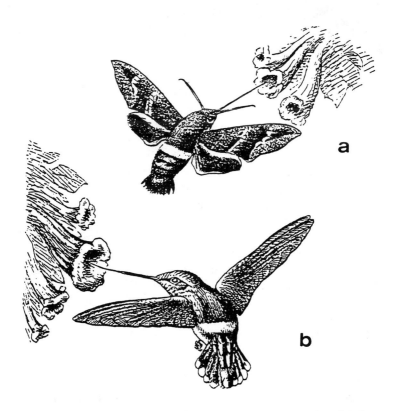

Figure 9.18. Similar morphology and behavior in (a) sphinx moth and (b) hummingbird (from Suchantke, 1982b, p. 215, and used with permission).

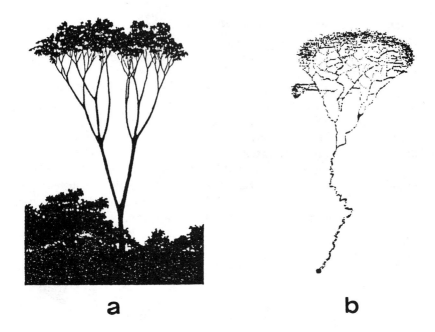

a   b

Figure 9.19. Branching architecture of tropical rain forest tree (a) resembles swarm pattern of army ants (b) found in those forests ([a] from Kricher, 1989, p. 32; [b] from Franks, 1989, p. 141, and used with permission).

behavioral phenomena. For instance, the typical branching architecture of tropical rain forest trees bears a strong resemblance to the swarm pattern of army ants found in those forests (figure 9.19).

If in a given environment unrelated organisms can be seen to reflect common motifs, is it possible to identify such similarities among organisms of separate, but corresponding, landscapes? According to the approach taken in this essay, geographic regions with similar physical elements should have life forms that exhibit parallel morphologies. A survey of the plant kingdom shows that this pattern is indeed the case. Many genetically unrelated species have adopted analogous life forms in similar habitats. The cactus (*Cactaceae*) and spurge (*Euphorbiaceae*) families, for example, have many strikingly similar forms in desert landscapes (figures 9.20a and 9.20b).

Animals also show this relationship of parallel morphologies between unrelated species. Among birds, the South American hummingbirds, toucans, and rheas have their respective counterparts in the African sunbirds, hornbills, and ostrich (figure 9.21). Perhaps

Figure 9.20a.

Figures 9.20a and 9.20b. Plants with parallel morphologies: (a) senita (*Lophocereus schottii*), cactus family, from Sonoran Desert, Arizona (upper photograph); and (b) cardon (*Euphorbia canariensis*), spurge family, from Tenerife, Canary Islands (lower photograph) (photographs by author).

Figure 9.21. Birds with parallel morphologies. Those in left column are South American; those in right, African counterparts: (a) hummingbird; (b) sunbird; (c) toucan; (d) hornbill; (e) rhea; (f) ostrich (drawings by author).

Figure 9.22. (a) American eastern meadowlark; (b) African yellow-throated long-claw (drawings by F. A. Reid and used with permission).

the most striking conformity between unrelated avian species is evidenced in the American eastern meadowlark and the African yellow-throated longclaw, both found in grasslands (figure 9.22). Mammals, too, exhibit striking resemblances between forms found on different continents (figure 9.23). At least in isolated instances, therefore, plants and animals have parallel forms in distant yet similar landscapes.

From a broader perspective, one can ask whether the entire flora and fauna of two distant, but climatically and geologically similar, environments are alike. Cody (1974) compares two geographically distinct Mediterranean scrub-type environments: the chaparral of California's Santa Monica Mountains and the matorral of Chile's coastal mountain range. Although composed of different species, the vegetation of the two areas exhibits a similar physiognomy, morphology, and flowering season (ibid., p. 189). Ecological comparisons between some twenty bird species in each environment show a remarkable correspondence between the avifaunas with some "near-perfect" matches (ibid., p. 194). Cody also finds parallels in size and morphology between the two bird communities, a fact particularly striking, since birds of the two landscapes are mostly unrelated (figure 9.24). Interpreted from the perspective of this essay, Cody's findings indicate that the chaparral and matorral landscapes disclose a similar wholeness in each, as revealed through their corresponding plants and animals. No two places, however, are ever identical, and parallels between their living components will never coincide exactly. Subtle differences between corresponding life forms, however, can be as revealing as their conformities in pointing to unique nuances of place character.

Figure 9.23. Mammals with parallel morphologies. Those in left column are African; those in right, South American counterparts: (a) pygmy hippopotamus; (b) capybara; (c) chevrotain; (d) paca; (e) royal antelope; (f) agouti; (g) duiker; (h) brocket deer; (i) pangolin; (j) giant armadillo (from Suchantke, 1982b, p. 389, and used with permission).

Figure 9.24. Birds of Californian chaparral (left) and Chilean matorral (right) (from Cody, 1974, p. 199, and used with permission).

A descriptive approach that strives to interpret patterns of relationships both within and among landscapes can be considered a *phenomenological ecology.* This way of approaching phenomena is not limited to the natural environment, but may also say much about the human landscape. Just as the individuality of a landscape comes to expression through its flora and fauna, so may it manifest through the architecture, art, and language of indigenous peoples (Mugerauer, 1985; Silko, 1987). Such accounts suggest that indigenous cultures often experience the wholeness that dwells in their land, and much that they produce bears its signature. In contrast, Western technological societies often have an undeveloped or contrived sense of the whole. Consequently, modern architecture, for example, may show little relationship to its surroundings and may seem out of context; the parts are not representative of the whole.

The approach outlined in this essay is an attempt to cultivate a way of seeing that seeks to experience the whole as it comes forth through the parts. By getting "in touch" with the wholeness that dwells in a place, its naturally occurring components take on new meaning. By grounding ourselves in that experience, the things we then create can support and extend that meaning. The task of a phenomenological ecology is not to discover new facts, but rather to permit phenomena to disclose themselves so that new meanings emerge. The parts become transparent to the whole. Those who participate in such a way of investigation are faced with the challenge of seeing the familiar through new eyes.

Notes

1. Here, I call the successive changes in leaf shape along the stem a "transformation" rather than a "metamorphosis." There has been some confusion in the literature concerning the equivalency of these terms. Following Adams and Whicher (1982), I reserve "metamorphosis" to indicate a different quality of change, such as that from leaf to flower.

2. As in patterns of leaf differentiation discussed earlier, there are exceptions to this generalization, and each one would likewise need to be observed in detail to uncover its relationship to the whole.

3. These differences in expressive tendencies are supported in a quantitative study by Canham (1988), who compared the growth rates of beech and sugar-maple saplings in dark and light areas. In the shade of a closed canopy, the beech seedlings grew faster than the maple, but in light gaps caused by fallen trees, the maples grew more quickly.

4. The cetaceans (whales and dolphins) are those mammals that particularly illustrate the relationship between large size and a marine environment.

5. The Florida key deer, a miniature race of white-tailed deer, is an apparent exception because its form is delicate, yet it lives in the aquatic en-

vironment of the everglades wetlands. This exception, however, may be so because this deer is expressive of the intense light qualities of its subtropical landscape, rather than of the watery element.

6. Similarly among birds, owls are nocturnal and have round, compact forms. Moreover, their eggs are nearly spherical—an uncommon feature in birds.

References

Adams, G., and Whicher, O. (1982). *The Plant Between Sun and Earth.* Boulder, Colorado: Shambhala Publishing.

Amrine, F. (1987). Goethean Method in the Work of Jochen Bockemuhl. In F. Amrine, F. Zucker, and H. Wheeler (eds.), *Goethe and the Sciences: A Reappraisal* (pp. 301–318). Dordrecht: D. Reidel Publishing.

Arber, A. (1950). *The Natural Philosophy of Plant Form.* Cambridge: Cambridge University Press.

Bockemuhl, J. (1981). *In Partnership with Nature.* Wyoming, Rhode Island: Bio-Dynamic Literature.

———. (1985). The Formative Movements of Plants. In J. Bockemuhl (Ed.), *Toward a Phenomenology of the Etheric World* (pp. 131–161). Spring Valley, New York: Anthroposophic Press.

———. (1986). *Dying Forests: A Crisis in Consciousness.* Stroud, United Kingdom: Hawthorn Press.

Bortoft, H. (1985). Counterfeit and Authentic Wholes: Finding a Means for Dwelling in Nature. In D. Seamon and R. Mugerauer (Eds.), *Dwelling, Place, and Environment: Towards a Phenomenology of Person and World* (pp. 281–302). New York: Columbia University Press.

———. (1986). *Goethe's Scientific Consciousness.* Nottingham, United Kingdom: Russell Press.

Brady, R. (1977). Goethe's Natural Science: Some Non-Cartesian Meditations. In K. Schaefer, H. Hensel, and R. Brady (Eds.), *Toward a Man-Centered Medical Science* (pp. 137–165). Mt. Kisco, New York: Futura Publishing.

———. (1987). Form and Cause in Goethe's Morphology. In F. Amrine, F. Zucker, and H. Wheeler (Eds.), *Goethe and the Sciences: A Reappraisal* (pp. 257–300). Dordrecht: D. Reidel.

Canham, C. (1988). Growth and Canopy Architecture of Shade-Tolerant Trees: Response to Canopy Gaps. *Ecology, 69,* 786–795.

Clausen, J., Keck, D., and Hiesey, W. (1948). Experimental Studies on the Nature of Species, III: Environmental Responses of Climatic Races of *Archillea*. *Carnegie Inst. Wash. Publ.*, *581*, 1–129.

Cody, M. (1974). *Competition and the Structure of Bird Communities*. Princeton: Princeton University Press.

Franks, N. (1989). Army Ants: A Collective Intelligence. *American Scientist, 77,* 139–145.

Goethe, J. W. von. (1974). *The Metamorphosis of Plants*. [Trans. of *Die Metamorphose der Pflanzen*, 1790]. Bio-Dynamic Farming and Gardening Association.

———. (1988). *Scientific Studies*, D. Miller (ed. and trans.). New York: Suhrkamp Publishers.

Grohmann, G. (1974). *The Plant*. London: Rudolf Steiner Press.

Hammond, D. (1941). The Expression of Genes for Leaf Shape in *Gossypium hersutum* L. and *Gossypium arboreum* L. I. *American Journal of Botany, 28,* 124–150.

Holdridge, L. R. (1947). Determination of World Plant Formations from Simple Climatic Data. *Science, 105,* 367–368.

Kricher, J. (1989). *A Neotropical Companion*. Princeton: Princeton University Press.

Larson, P. (1977). *A Sierra Club Naturalist's Guide to the Deserts of the Southwest*. San Francisco: Sierra Club Books.

Lehrs, E. (1958). *Man or Matter*. London: Faber and Faber Ltd.

Mugerauer, R. (1985). Language and the Emergence of the Environment. In D. Seamon and R. Mugerauer (eds.), *Dwelling, Place, and Environment: Towards a Phenomenology of Person and World* (pp. 51–70). New York: Columbia University Press.

Odum, E. (1971). *Fundamentals of Ecology*. Philadelphia: W. B. Sunders Co.

Popplebaum, H. (1961). *A New Zoology*. Dornach, Switzerland: Philosophic-Anthroposophic Press.

Portmann, A. (1959). *Animal Camouflage*. Ann Arbor: University of Michigan Press.

Relph, T. (1979). To See with the Soul of the Eye. *Landscape, 23,* 28–34.

Richards, P. (1981). *The Tropical Rain Forest*. Cambridge, United Kingdom: Cambridge University Press.

Riegner, M. (1985). Horns, Hooves, Spots, and Stripes: Form and Pattern in Mammals. *Orion Nature Quarterly, 4* (4), 22–35.

————. (1986). Blossoms and Butterflies: A New Look at Metamorphosis. *Orion Nature Quarterly, 5* (3), 30–39.

————. (1989). The Many Faces of Water. *Golden Blade, 41,* 21–32.

————, and Wilkes, J. (1988). Art in the Service of Nature: The Story of Flowforms. *Orion Nature Quarterly, 7* (1), 50–57.

————, and Wilkes, J. (1989). Flowforms and the Language of Water. *Towards, 3* (2), 4–9.

Schad, W. (1977). *Man and Mammals: Toward a Biology of Form.* Garden City, New York: Waldorf Press.

Schwenk, T. (1965). *Sensitive Chaos.* London: Rudolf Steiner Press.

————, and Schwenk, W. (1989). *Water: The Element of Life.* Hudson, New York: Anthroposophic Press.

Seamon, D. (1978). Goethe's Approach to the Natural World: Implications for Environmental Theory and Education. In D. Ley and M. Samuels (eds.), *Humanistic Geography* (pp. 238–250). Chicago: Maaroufa Press.

Silko, L. (1987). Landscape, History, and the Pueblo Imagination. In D. Halpern (ed.), *On Nature: Nature, Landscape, and Natural History* (pp. 83–94). San Francisco: North Point Press.

Sinnott, E. (1960). *Plant Morphogenesis.* New York: McGraw-Hill.

Steiner, R. (1968). *A Theory of Knowledge Implicit in Goethe's World Conception.* Spring Valley, New York: Anthroposophic Press.

————. (1985). *Goethe's World View.* Spring Valley, New York: Mercury Press.

————. (1988). *Goethean Science.* Spring Valley, New York: Mercury Press.

Suchantke, A. (1982a). Die Zeitgestalt der Pflanze. In W. Schad (ed.), *Goetheanistische Naturwissenschaft, Band 2, Botanik* (pp. 55–81). Stuttgart: Verlag Freies Geistesleben.

————. (1982b). *Der Kontinent der Kolibris.* Stuttgart: Verlag Freies Geistesleben.

Talbert, C., and Holch, A. (1957). A Study of the Lobing of Sun and Shade Leaves. *Ecology, 38,* 655–658.

Walter, H. (1985). *Vegetation of the Earth and Ecological Systems of the Geobiosphere.* New York: Springer-Verlag.

Wickler, W. (1974). *Mimicry in Plants and Animals.* New York: McGraw-Hill.

Part III

Living, Understanding, and Designing

Chapter 10

Different Worlds Coming Together: A Phenomenology of Relationship as Portrayed in Doris Lessing's *Diaries of Jane Somers*

◻

David Seamon

This article presents a phenomenology of *relationship,* which refers to the process whereby two worlds are drawn together in a lasting way. *World* relates to a person's sphere of action, recognition and experience, both firsthand and vicarious. Relationship involves the way that two people's separate worlds come together in a widening sphere of interaction, understanding and concern. Two worlds literally become one.

The real-world context for exploring relationship phenomenologically is British-African novelist Doris Lessing's *Diaries of Jane Somers* (Lessing, 1984). Set in present day London and written in the form of a diary, this novel describes the growing friendship between a stylish, middle-aged fashion editor, Jane Somers, and a proud, indigent ninety-year-old woman, Maudie Fowler, who eventually dies from stomach cancer. Lessing's presentation of these characters' radically different worlds and the way they gradually come together in friendship provides an empirical base for exploring the more general phenomena of relationships and separate worlds becoming one. Lessing's novel is the ground from which to identify steps in the process where two people of contrasting backgrounds and lifestyles come to care for each other and participate in each other's world.[1]

The pattern suggested by a phenomenological explication of Somers and Maudie's growing friendship in *Diaries* is the seven-stage *relationship cycle* of figure 10.1: dissatisfaction, asking, searching, trying to accept, accepting, understanding, and caring. These seven stages describe the experience that Somers and Maudie pass through as they become each other's friend; these

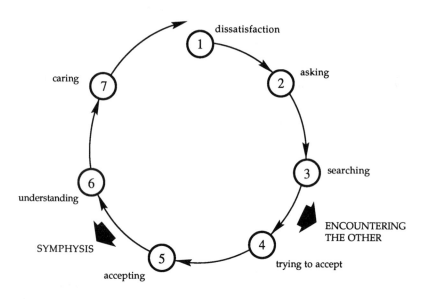

Figure 10.1. The Relationship Cycle.

stages happen largely *within* the women. At the same time, however, there are two other dimensions of the relationship—*encountering the other* and *symphysis*—that serve as spurs to move the relationship ahead and that require qualities *outside* the two women for the cycle to continue. In "encounter," this spur involves a right person that Somers feels comfortable with helping; in "symphysis," which literally means "growing together," this spur involves the gradual creation of a bond between the two women that eventually becomes as real as the two women themselves. Both encounter and symphysis involve a link in which what was unrelated before is now joined.

The nature of encounter and symphysis becomes more clear as the stages of the relationship cycle are explicated in detail below. This explication comprises the first section of the essay and is organized around the order of figure 10.1. Next, the essay considers the significance of the relationship cycle for social policy and environmental design. Particularly important in this discussion is the difference between relationship and what can be called *connection*—an arbitrary linkage between worlds that is susceptible to breakage when stressed or changed in any way. The argument is made that one reason social policy and environmental design often fail today is because they are founded in connection rather than relationship. With this recognition in mind, the essay last considers how the cycle of figure 10.1 might be used to explore other kinds of relationships, including those between student and teacher and client and architect. The essay concludes that a thorough understanding of the relationship process might be of value for thinking through situations where different worlds have the potential for coming together, be they in terms of planning and living, teaching and learning, or helping and being helped.

1. Dissatisfaction

For a relationship to form, there must first be the *dissatisfaction* of figure 10.1. The person feels a sense of confusion and incompleteness. One experiences a genuine need to reach out and become more, either in terms of seeing, understanding, doing, or helping. If one feels no need for change, extending one's world is not possible. For Jane Somers, this need to change comes gradually and painfully as she sees her weaknesses as a human being. She comes to realize that she is not as kind and good as she once thought.

Raised in a conventional middle-class London family that she describes as "heavy suburban respectable" (p. 7), Somers joins the staff of *Lilith,* a fashionable women's magazine, immediately after World War II upon graduating from high school. She eventually becomes assistant editor and then editor. As *Diaries* opens, Somers describes the preceding four years of her life. Her husband Freddie and her mother have both died of cancer within three years of each other. The shock of personal loss painfully confronts Somers with the awareness that her world may not be as successful or complete as she once thought. She has a strong need to find a fuller purpose in her life. She realizes that for some twenty years both her marriage and work lacked commitment and depth. In regard to Freddie, she says that "We did not have the sort of marriage where we talked about real things, I see that now. We were not really married. It was the marriage most people have these days, both sides trying for advantage. I always saw Freddie as one up" (p. 5). Until his death, she always thought of herself as a "nice person" (p. 5), but the shock of his passing makes her realize that "I know now that I did not ask myself what I was really like, but thought only about how other people judged me" (p. 5).

Freddie's death shakes Somers because she realizes that she acted selfishly and was not present to his suffering. Her mother

becomes ill and Somers must care for her. Though she feels remorse
in her behavior towards Freddie, she finds she can act little differently toward her mother:

> While mother was dying, I was doing my best, but not like Freddie
> where I simply didn't want to know . . . But I couldn't do it . . . I
> used to feel sick and panicky all the time . . . She used to look at
> me so straight and open. And I could hardly make myself meet her
> eyes. It wasn't that her look asked anything. But I was so ashamed
> of what I was feeling, in a panic for myself. No, I wasn't awful, as
> I was with Freddie. But it must have seemed to her that there was
> nothing much there—I mean, as if *I* was nothing much (p. 8).

After her mother dies, Somers realizes "how flimsy, I was, how
dependent" (p. 10). This shock is the confusion and incompleteness
of stage 1. This experience of inadequacy provides a powerful impulse that undermines Somers's former world. She realizes who she
is and can no longer be satisfied. She makes a decision that triggers
the rest of the relationship cycle: "I decided to learn something else"
(p. 11). It is the shock of what the old world is and a need for something else that provides the underlying motivation that extends
Jane Somers's strength as a person and eventually draws her to the
loneliness and helplessness of Maudie Fowler.

2. Asking

Her dissatisfaction leads Somers to a second stage in the relationship cycle—what figure 1 calls *asking*. Here, the person won-
ders how he or she can become different. This stage happens only
because of the vacuum created by the shock of stage 1. Lessing's
novel suggests that a person cannot begin real change in his or her
life if there is no dissatisfaction. This stage refers to a new kind of
awareness, which Somers calls *thinking*: "This way of thinking . . .
it is not so much thinking as holding things in your mind and letting them sort themselves out. If you really do that, slowly, surprising results emerge. For instance, that your ideas are different from
what you had believed they were" (p. 10).

This second stage involves asking who one is and what one
wants. Through this process, Somers discovers things about her life
that she had not realized before—that she has no home life, for example, and that the center of her world is her workplace: "I soon

saw that my life was entirely in the office. I had no life at home. *Home*. What a word! It was the place I prepared myself for the office, or rested after work. One of the things I am *thinking* is that if I lost my job, there wouldn't be much left of me" (p. 11).

Through this process of asking and thinking, Somers realizes that she had failed with Freddie and her mother because of a shallowness that awareness alone cannot change. She is who she is, and it is her lack of being—her inability to bear more difficult parts of life—that blocks her from acting in a way other than she does. She explains:

> What I was thinking most of all was that I had let Freddie down and had let my mother down *and that was what I was like*. If something else should turn up, something I had to cope with, like illness or death, if I had to say to myself, Now, you will behave like a human being and not a little girl—then I couldn't do it. It is not a question of will, but of what you are (p. 11).

This lack of being is crucial in understanding the relationship cycle because it says that *people can only do what they are*. A widely held assumption about human action today is that people make a decision and then carry it out in behavior. Somers's illumination here suggests that this assumption is sometimes an illusion—that the ability to change and act is intimately related to the strength of one's *being*, which here means *the amount that one can bear*. After Freddie's death and her sense of guilt, Somers tries to be more caring with her mother. She cannot really be different than she was with Freddie, however, because *she is who she is*—a limited, self-centered person. She phrases her dilemma as a question: "How did we get like this, so soft, so silly, so babyish? How?" (p. 82).

3. Searching

The thinking and realization of stage 2 leads Somers to a next stage—what figure 10.1 calls *searching*. This stage marks a shift from shock and confusion to active attempts at constructive change, some of which fail because they are poorly considered and superficial. For Somers, these attempts involve the effort to find someone whom she might help and thereby face the difficulties that she shunned with Freddie and her mother. Somers reads a newspaper advertisement that asks for volunteers to befriend old people. She answers the notice and through a social worker, Miss Snow, meets an old woman,Mrs. York, for tea. The meeting seemed "false and awful" (p. 11). Mrs. York didn't like Miss Snow, who was condescending but didn't know it: "I sat there and thought, what the hell am I doing here? What good does this do Mrs. York?"(p. 11). At the same time, Somers realizes that she might help her elderly nextdoor neighbor, Mrs. Penny, who is alone and "longing for me to befriend her" (ibid.). But Somers cannot help Mrs. Penny either because she is domineering: "She would take over my life. I feel smothered and panicky at the idea of being at her beck and call" (ibid.).

The key point here is that *not just anyone will do* in Somers's search for the right person to help. Somers cannot help Mrs. York and Mrs. Penny because in a sense they are just anyone. She becomes involved with them out of *connection*—an arbitrary linkage that is imposed from without, so that the situation has little chance to develop in its own way and time. In Somers's meeting with Mrs. York, this connection involves an impersonal agency that randomly links up availabilities; in Somers's link with Mrs. Penny, connection involves the older woman's just happening to be Somers's neighbor. Not just anyone will do in the establishment of a relationship. If it is to be genuine, the two people must fit. In time they become a part of each other, and this togetherness can arise only when *each is right for the other*. Otherwise, there is nothing but connection, and connection can not last because the two parts cannot hold. They fall back into separateness as soon as the artificial bond changes in some way.

Encountering the Other

At this stage in the cycle, the right person for a relationship must appear if the cycle is to continue. Without the right person, Somers's efforts cannot move ahead to stages 4 and 5. How do Somers and Maudie Fowler find each other? They meet coincidentally in the local pharmacy as they stand together in line. With her "fierce blue eyes . . . but something wonderfully sweet in them" (p. 12), Maudie asks Somers to get a prescription for her because Maudie cannot read the druggist's handwriting. In the moment that Somers takes the prescription, she realizes something else: "I liked her, for some reason, from that moment. I took the paper and knew I was taking much more than that" (p. 12).

Phenomenologically, there are two important aspects of this meeting. First, it is unplanned, happening by chance as the women carry out their everyday affairs—Maudie, getting medicine; Somers, buying cosmetics. Like so many events that truly matter in a person's life—for instance, finding a profession, making a friend, or meeting one's life partner—the first encounter is coincidental. Because Maudie and Somers just happen to patronize the same local pharmacy, they meet.

A second aspect of the encounter is the sense for both women that this meeting has a greater significance. In the moment of helping Maudie, Somers intuits that Maudie may somehow enter her life in a greater way. As she says, "I took the paper and knew I was taking much more than that." Somers also suggests that there is an equivalent sense of importance for Maudie: As they leave the shop and walk down the street, Somers notes that "she did not look at me, but there was an appeal there" (p. 13). "Appeal" is crucial because it suggests that Somers's sense of liking is answered by Maudie's sense of need. In a moment, there is a mutual bond of feeling: Somers's need to help someone; Maudie Fowler's need to be helped.

In one sense, it might be said that the two women choose each other in their moment of meeting, though "choose" is a poor word because neither woman wills the event or liking. Perhaps it is more accurate to say that because of need on both sides, the women come together, though it is important to emphasize that Maudie has no role in the process until Somers has already moved through stages 1–3. Like Somers, Maudie also has a strong need for change in her life because she is alone and longs for human companionship. By herself, however, she cannot initiate change because she is overwhelmed by her world. In this sense, Somers can be called the *active force* in the relationship because she initiates the cycle through her need to become a better person. On the other hand, Maudie can be called the *passive force,* since she receives Somer's help and in that sense reflects qualities of receptivity.

In a broader sense, however, *both* women are active and passive, depending on the situation. Maudie helps Somers become a better person just as Somers helps Maudie restore her sense of self-worth. Throughout the cycle, their efforts complement each other and together provide the force that eventually leads to friendship and love. Still, in her desire to grow as a human being, Somers activates the cycle and describes the experience in her diaries. Because the novel is written through Somers's eyes, her experience of the cycle is described more comprehensively. At the same time, however, Somers's diary entries say much about Maudie's experience of the relationship, and these descriptions are used to elucidate Maudie's sense of stages 4–7.

Ultimately, it can be said that both women work in different but complementary ways to make the relationship cycle successful. A relationship is possible between the two women because Somers has already moved past stages 1–3 that only involved herself. In her meeting Maudie, Somers's situation becomes radically different in that the wish for a person to help is now a reality. If Somers did not find the right person in Maudie, the cycle could not continue, since there would not be the other person with whom to attempt a relationship. In this sense, "encountering the other" is not just another stage in the relationship cycle but an essential outside spur that moves the cycle ahead. In the next two stages of the cycle, the women face a hazardous testing phase in which they work to accept each other.

4 and 5. Trying to Accept and Accepting

Stages 4 and 5 of the relationship cycle involve struggle and results. In trying to accept each other, Somers and Maudie Fowler eventually succeed, though they first face many obstacles, setbacks and denials. These two stages of the relationship cycle are not separate in time but swing back and forth in widening spheres of recognition and trust. Because of these intimate links, stages 4 and 5 are here discussed together. In the relationship cycle, however, it is important to identify them separately, since it is out of the effort to accept that acceptance is eventually possible. Without the attempt, there could be no result.

In these two stages of the cycle, there is no guarantee that a relationship will be forged. In trying to accept, there is hazard because misunderstanding or error may break bonds that are tentative and fragile. Somers's main effort in these two stages is to recognize the integrity of Maudie's world and, eventually through this awareness, to appreciate that world for what it is and not try to change it. Maudie's effort is to hold her pride in check and to accept Somers's growing liking for her. In this process, there is no one revelatory moment of acceptance but, rather, many small, incremental recognitions that give Somers and Maudie the will to keep trying with each other. Often, their efforts end in failure, but at other times they are successful and lead to moments of heartfelt contact. Three aspects of stages 4 and 5 are *realization, accepting responsibility,* and *dealing with physical difference.*

Realization

A first aspect of Somers's trying to accept is realization that worlds like Maudie's exist. As the two women walk toward Maudie's apartment after meeting in the pharmacy, Somers notices aspects of the world to which she was oblivious a moment before. She must walk slowly because of Maudie's infirmness and suddenly sees that "usually I fly along, but did not know it till then" (p. 13). Somers also realizes that she never before noticed the old people of her neighborhood: "Suddenly, I looked up and down the streets and saw—old women. Old men too, but mostly old women" (p. 13). And she realizes *why* she has not noticed them: "I had not seen them. That was because I was afraid of being like them. I was afraid, walking along there beside her. It was the smell of her, a sweet, sour, dusty sort of smell" (p. 13).

For Maudie, the effort to realize the nature of Somers's world is also difficult because it is in many ways so different from her lower-class London experience. As Somers buys her cosmetics in the pharmacy, Maudie stands by "watching, with a look I know now is so characteristic, a fierce pondering look that really wants to understand. Trying to grasp it all" (p. 13). Later, Somers describes her work with *Lilith* and Maudie responds "in that way of hers, as if she is trying to make things fit, make sense. 'Do you? And what do you . . . ' But she did not know what questions to ask" (p. 18).

After Somers visits her three times, Maudie asks if she is a good neighbor. Somers does not understand, and Maudie sees that she does not. Somers eventually learns that Good Neighbors are local people paid by the London social services to keep company with elderly people. Knowing that Somers is not such a person is crucial for Maudie's trying to accept her because "she wanted to believe I was not an official, paid person, but just a human being who likes her" (p. 20).

Accepting Responsibility

If one effort for both women in stages 4 and 5 is recognizing and accepting each other's differences, another effort is overcoming the fear that the other person might somehow interfere with her life. Throughout their getting to know each other, an attraction-avoidance tension exists: For Somers, the burden of responsibility; for Maudie, the blow to her pride of having to be helped. For Somers, this distress begins after her first visit with Maudie: "When I got home that evening I was in a panic. I had committed myself. I was full of revulsion" (p. 15). For almost a year, Somers faces a struggle between helping and avoiding Maudie. Much of Somers's denial involves the potential impact that caring for Maudie might have on her work: "I am sitting here, feeling quite wild, trapped is what I'm feeling . . . My life, my real life, is in the office, is at work . . . And I am not going to jeopardize what I really care about for the sake of Maudie Fowler" (p. 42).

At the same time, Maudie faces a struggle, though for her the effort is setting her pride aside and allowing Somers to enter her life. When they first meet, Somers explains that it is a difficult effort for Maudie to invite Somers into her unkept apartment: "She was ashamed, but wasn't going to apologize. She said in an offhand but appealing way, 'You go into my room, and find yourself a seat' " (p. 15). Somers's leaving at the end of this first visit is also difficult for Maudie because her pride will not allow her to say that she has enjoyed Somers's company and would like her to come again:

> And when I left she said, in her way of not looking at me, "I suppose I won't be seeing you again?" And I said, "Yes, if you'll ask me." Then she did look at me, and there was a small smile . . . "Oh, I would like, yes, I would." And there was a moment between us of intimacy: that is the word. And yet she was so full of pride and did not want to ask, and she turned away from me and began petting the cat (p. 14).

The moment of intimacy here is crucial because it is this kind of small reward arising out of the two women's efforts that provides the impetus to keep stages 4 and 5 alive. In the first several months that Somers visits Maudie, there is considerable confusion and tension as the relationship shifts back and forth between liking and disliking and other positive and negative feelings. Somers describes the fluctuations of a typical visit: "I could say, She was cross to begin with, then got her temper back, and we had a nice time drinking tea, and she told me about . . . But what about all the shifts of liking, anger, irritation—oh, so much anger, in both of us?" (p. 31).

Eventually, Somers sets herself to visit Maudie frequently. She does Maudie's shopping and nurses her in her bad times. In return, Maudie tells stories about her life: "She . . . entertains me. I did not realize it was that. Not until one day when she said, 'You do so much for me, and all I can do for you is to tell you my little stories, because you like that, don't you? Yes, I know you do'. And of course I do" (p. 87). Somers enjoys these stories because they give her a personal picture of London's everyday life in earlier times. Eventually, Somers uses Maudie's accounts as a basis for a romantic novel depicting the life of a London milliner—Maudie's work as a young woman.

Dealing with Physical Difference

Part of Somers's discomfort and fear in trying to accept Maudie's world relates to physical infirmness. Before meeting her, Somers took cleanliness, order, and style for granted: "For years of my life I cared so much about what I looked like that I was conscious if there was a strand or two less of thread on one button than on its neighbour" (p. 284). Her greatest daily pleasure is her bathroom and baths: "My bathroom is where I live . . . I bathe every morning, every night. I lie in the bath and soak for hours" (p. 23).

Maudie's world is infirm and decrepit, and an important effort for Somers in stages 4 and 5 is accepting this unpleasantness and recognizing that Maudie is no less a person because of it. When Somers enters Maudie's apartment for the first time, she is physically overwhelmed: "I went in with her, my heart quite sick, and my stomach sick too because of the smell . . . It was all so dirty and dingy and grim and awful" (pp. 13, 14). In drinking the tea that Maudie offers her, Somers explains that "It was the hardest thing I ever did, to drink out of the dirty cup" (p. 14).

This simple act of drinking is crucial in Somer's movement from stage 4 to 5 because it is in this gesture that Somers pulls away from her old world and first touches the otherness of Maudie's world physically. A large part of the struggle in stages 4 and 5 is Somers's letting go of her compulsion for order and cleanliness. By her fifth visit to Maudie's apartment, Somers can separate from her physical queasiness and set herself not to criticize: " . . . why do I go on about dirt like this? Why do we judge people like this? *She* was no worse off for the grime and the dust, and even the smells. I decided not to notice, if I could help it, not to keep judging her, which I was doing, by the sordidness" (p. 18).

In stages 4 and 5, Maudie must also make an effort in regard to this disorder. She must overcome her embarrassment and allow Somers into her apartment, no matter how unpleasant it may be physically. During one visit, Somers explains that Maudie does not want Somers in her bedroom, filled with "piles of rubbish, what looked like rags, bundles of newspapers, everything you can think of: this was what she did not want me to see" (p. 15). In getting beyond her shame and pride, Maudie makes a crucial effort for stages 4 and 5, since this effort allows Somers to enter her world and make her own effort to accept and help Maudie.

Symphysis

Out of the struggle in stages 4 and 5, the two women eventually begin to relate to each other in a more honest, deeper way. Whereas in the beginning the two women's worlds were distinctly different, there is a gradual coming together so that in time these two worlds draw close and what was two is now one. After considering such words as "union," "bond," "commitment," "blending," and "fusion," I call this situation of coming together *symphysis,* a word originally used as a medical term and meaning in Greek, "the state of growing together."[2] I choose this unusual word to emphasize that at this point in the women's relationship something happens that is not just another stage in the process. Rather, symphysis represents an entity that is as real as the two women themselves. In this sense, symphysis refers to the birth of a genuine bond between the two women. Once it is formed, the two women know without a doubt that they will be a part of each other's world until Maudie's death. The relationship is now secure and real.

Diaries provides no definitive single moment at which the women come together as one. As with trying to accept and accepting, there are a series of struggles and successes that draw the worlds more closely together. One of the first indications of symphysis is Somers's growing acceptance of Maudie's physical world. Over time, for example, she notes that "I have become used to drinking out of grimy cups" (p. 50). Somers also comes to realize that Maudie's dilapidated apartment is an integral part of her world. This recognition is crucial to Maudie because it means that Somers will support her wish to stay in her own apartment if the authorities insist that she move to housing that they consider better. When they first met, Somers assumes that Maudie would gladly change apartments, since hers seems so squalid to Somers. Over time, however, she realizes that the apartment is the central anchor of Maudie's life. As she tells Somers, "With your own place, you've got everything. Without it you're a dog. You are nothing. Have you got your own place?—and when I said yes, she said, nodding fiercely, angrily, 'That's right, and you hold on to it, then nothing can touch you' " (p. 19).

As Somers becomes more familiar with Maudie's situation, she realizes that the old woman is bound to her apartment and to move her to other housing would severely damage her sense of self. Though modern architectural and social criteria might argue that Maudie should be rehoused, Somers recognizes that material conditions are in the end irrelevant to Maudie, for whom physical difficulty has long been taken for granted: "By any current housing standard, [her apartment] should be condemned. By any human standard, she should stay where she is" (p. 103).[3] Somers understands that Maudie is immersed in her world and improvement in that world cannot be had by physical intervention alone:

> I've given up even thinking that she ought to agree to be 'rehoused;' I said it just once, and it took her three days to stop seeing me as an enemy . . . I *am* housed, says she, cough, cough, cough from having to go out at the back all weathers into the freezing lavatory, from standing to wash in the unheated kitchen. But why do I say that? Women of ninety who live in luxury cough and are frail (p. 86).

Perhaps the most decisive event for establishing the women's togetherness occurs several months after they first meet and involves intimate physical acceptance. Somers agrees to bathe Maudie when Maudie indirectly asks her. In touching and caring for Maudie in this direct way, Somers fully accepts Maudie for who and what she is: "So I see her now, I no longer *see* the old witch" (p. 56). As Somers bathes Maudie, she experiences two revelations. First, she realizes that Maudie's strength to live is coupled with her pride and anger, which Somers must not attack or undermine. Second, she understands the struggle and suffering of her mother and Freddie as they faced death:

> I slowly washed her top half, in plenty of soap and hot water, but the grime on her neck was thick, and to get that off would have meant rubbing at it, and it was too much. She was trembling with weakness. I was comparing this frail old body with my mother: but I had only caught glimpses of her sick body. She had washed herself—and only now was I wondering at what cost . . . Now I washed Maudie Fowler, and thought of Freddie, how his bones had seemed to sort of flatten and go thin under flesh that clung to them.

Maudie might be only skin and bones . . . She was chilly, she was
sick, she was weak—but I could feel the vitality beating there: life.
How strong it is, life. I had never thought that before, never felt life
in that way, as I did then, washing Maudie Fowler, a fierce, angry
old woman. Oh, how angry: it occurred to me that all her vitality is
in her anger, I must *not* resent it or want to hit back (pp. 51–52).

6 and 7. Understanding and Caring

Somers's bathing Maudie marks a turning point in the women's
relationship. After this event, Maudie enters Somers's life for good,
and their two worlds are now bound together. Somers will take care
of her until she dies a few years later. Practically, the relationship
maintains itself through Somers's visiting Maudie regularly:
"Nearly every evening after work I've been in to Maudie . . . It is a
routine now. I go in about seven, eight, after work, and bring in
what she has said she needs the night before . . . While I shop she
makes us tea" (p. 86). The relationship is now taken for granted and
as much an entity as Somers and Maudie themselves. The period of
trial and doubt is past.

With the establishment of the relationship's taken-for-
grantedness, the cycle of figure 1 moves into stages 6 and 7, which
are founded in *love*—"the delicate but total acknowledgement of
what is" (Lessing, 1969, p. 10). Love brings an important change in
the women's relationship—Somers moves from outside to *inside*
Maudie's world. She now realizes that Maudie's world *is as it is.* She
understands Maudie's need *to be herself,* regardless of how impov-
erished or unpleasant her life might seem to outsiders. At the same
time, Maudie allows Somers full entrance into her world. Somers
becomes the friend for whom she had hoped.

Like trying to accept and accepting, stages 6 and 7 are complementary, resonating in mutual meaning. Understanding leads to
deeper caring, which in turn supports deeper understanding. Like
trying to accept and accepting, however, these reciprocal stages incorporate important differences in that understanding involves
awareness whereas caring involves *commitment.* Ultimately, the relationship is successful because the two women commit themselves
to each other emotionally. This feeling of love draws two separate
worlds together, and the two women are now kin, at least in a figurative sense. As Somers explains several years after Maudie's
death when she reflects back on their experience: "she was in need

of help, I offered it, got in deeper than I had meant, and had ended by being something not far off a daughter to her . . ." (p. 407).

6. Understanding

A major part of Somers's understanding in stage 6 involves Maudie's physical deterioration, which makes her life so difficult: "I have realized how *heavy* everything is for her" (p. 104). "What makes poor Maudie labour and groan all through her day [is] the drudge and drag of *maintenance*" (p. 127). Somers gains one important insight about Maudie's physical situation shortly after she bathes her for the first time. She understands that the bodily unpleasantness is not really Maudie, who is "still there, alert, very much all there, on guard inside that old witch's appearance. *She* is still there, and everything has collapsed around her, it's too difficult, too much" (p. 55). Somers realizes how physical infirmness can impede a person's actions toward the world, and understanding replaces blame:

> I am thinking how Maudie Fowler one day could not trouble herself to clean out her front room, because there was so much junk in it, and then she left it and left it; going in sometimes, thinking, well, it's not so bad. Meanwhile, she was keeping the back room and the kitchen spotless. Even now she does her own chimney once a week, and then scraps the grate, brushes up the dust and cinders— though less and less thoroughly. She wasn't feeling well, and didn't bother, once, twice—and then her room was not really cleaned, only the floor in the middle of the room sometimes, and she learned not to look around the edges or under the bed. Her kitchen was last. She scrubbed it and washed shelves, but then things began to slide. But through it all she washed herself, standing at the kitchen table . . . Then she left longer and longer between washing her hair . . . and then she did not wash her clothes, only took out the cleanest ones there were, putting them back grubby, till they were the cleanest; and so it went on. And at last she was upright in her thick shell of black, her knickers not entirely clean, but not so bad, her neck dirty, but she did not think about it, her scalp unwashed (p. 55).

In time, Somers feels a need to learn about Maudie's world as thoroughly as possible. She writes that "I want to understand. I *do* understand a lot more about her, but is it true? I can only observe what I have experienced myself, heard her say, observed . . . But what else is there I cannot know about?" (p. 127). Out of her observations she eventually writes a diary entry entitled "Maudie's day" (pp. 113–123). This entry includes a picture of Maudie's typical morning and illustrates how Maudie's physical heaviness translates into problems with movement and toilet routines:

> Morning . . . oh, the difficulties of morning, of facing the day . . . each task such a weight to it . . . She sits there, thinking, I have to feed the cat . . . I have to . . . At last, she drags herself up, anxious, because her bowels are threatening again, and, holding on to door handles, chair backs, she gets herself into the kitchen. There is a tin of cat food, half empty. She tries to turn it on to a saucer, it won't come out. It means she has to get a spoon. A long way off, in the sink, are her spoons and forks, she hasn't washed up for days . . .
>
> . . . she has to let the cat out. She toils to the door, lets out the cat and stands with her back to the door, thinking. A general planning a campaign could not use more cleverness than Maudie does, as she outwits her weakness and her terrible tiredness. She is already at the back door: the toilet is five steps away; if she goes now it will save a journey later (pp. 116–117).

Maudie Fowler's understanding in stage 6 is considerably different from Somers's. Maudie never fully makes sense of Somers's world. In "Maudie's Day," Somers surmises that Maudie may in fact suspect Somers of certain falsehoods: "All her stories about her office, she is probably making it up, after all, how can she, a poor old woman, know better, if [Jane] chooses to embellish it all a little?" (p. 117). At the same time, Somers surmises that in some ways Maudie interprets the women's relationship unrealistically. Somers guesses that Maudie's most fervent wish is that Somers come live in Maudie's apartment: "She sits there, sometimes dozing, thinking of how [Jane] is living there, looking after her, and of how, when she wakes in the night, alone and frightened that she's in the grave, she can call out, and hear [Jane's] reply" (p. 117).

In considering the difference in understanding between the two women, the theme of active and passive forces is useful. For Somers, understanding is active in the sense that it leads to her acting more in harmony with Maudie, including acceptance of her unrealistic hopes. Maudie's understanding, in contrast, is passive in that it involves no deepening knowledge of Somers that could be had by looking actively. Instead, Maudie's understanding evolves within her world as it is; this understanding involves a growing trust founded

on the recognition that Somers is a faithful friend who understands
who she is.

Ultimately for Maudie, understanding requires the conveyance
to Somers of her importance in Maudie's life. In "Maudie's Day,"
Somers has Maudie think that "it was impossible the way that
[Jane] should fly into her life the way she did, who would ever have
thought of it?" (p. 116). Somers's presence is a godsend, and one day
Maudie expresses her gratitude aloud:

> She tells me about all the times in her life she was happy. She says
> she is happy now, *because of me* (and that is hard to accept, it
> makes me feel angry, that so little can change a life), and therefore
> she likes to think of happy times (p. 88).

7. Caring

In the last few years of their relationship, Somers takes full responsibility for Maudie. The relationship is unquestioned and now
solidly in stage 7. Somers washes Maudie regularly and does her
shopping. She takes Maudie to the doctor and to the park. Before
her final illness and stay in the hospital, Somers takes Maudie to
Sunday dinner with her sister and family, who think of Maudie as
"an eccentric, gone-to-nothing relation whom they wish they could
forget" (p. 208). They ask Somers if she is Maudie's Good Neighbor,
and she—determined that Maudie not be cheated out of a real
friend of her own—says, "No, I am not, I am Maudie's friend. We
have known each other for some time now" (p. 208).

The obvious irony here is that the very people who should tend
to Maudie's care have ignored her. Maudie is deeply hurt. She de-
teriorates rapidly afterwards and goes into the hospital. Somers is
confused and overwhelmed by the visit to Maudie's relatives. On one
hand, she realizes their callousness, but on the other hand, she realizes that life offers no guarantees. In her care and concern, she
has brightened Maudie's life. In her own life, she has moved beyond
the child-woman whose selfishness motivated her toward change at
the start of the relationship cycle. Her commentary on Maudie's situation reflects the maturity she has gained through becoming involved in the old woman's life:

> What I think when I sit there [in the hospital], holding Maudie's
> hand, that she ought to be in a large loving family like a rubber net
> that could stretch a little here and there to fit her in, is of course,
> nonsense. I am saying, as well, that she should have been an

intelligently loved child of sensible parents, and that her mother
should not have died when she was fifteen, and that she ought, *by
right,* to have been happy healthy wealthy and wise her whole long
life through. When I say what she, what an old woman, *ought* to
have by *right* as she dies, forbids hardship, suffering, injustice,
pain—denies, in short, the human condition (pp. 222–223).

Nearness, Connection and Relationship

In Somers's suggestion that one's sense of human dignity is not
necessarily guaranteed, what are we to conclude? That material
and economic inequity is an inescapable characteristic of human
life? That people will always be unequal? Are concerned people to
throw up their hands and say that social policy and environmental
design can do nothing?

Lessing's conclusion in *Diaries* is more optimistic, but it intimates the significant difference between connection and relationship. In the past, *Diaries* suggests, human relationship came about
largely through physical and familial *nearness*—that is, living as an
integral member of a place-based community that included blood
relatives. In *Diaries,* this traditional style of place and community is
symbolized by an Indian shopkeeper, Mr. Patel, who sells Maudie
her groceries. He cannot understand how Maudie's family would
not take care of her, yet he also tells Somers one evening as she
shops for Maudie that his own Indian traditions have begun to
erode in the same way: "Once, with us, we would not let one of our
old people come to such a life. But now—things are changing with
us" (p. 107). Somers replies that there can't be many Maudie Fowl-
ers left in the London neighborhood where they live, but he replies,
"I have six, seven, every day in my shop. All like her, with no one to
care for them. And I am only one shop" (p. 107). He looks at Somers,
who explains, "We are appalled, we are frightened, it is all too much
for us" (p. 107).

In the fact that it eases physical hardship and provides material convenience to large numbers of people, Western modernity is a
blessing. At the same time, however, modern transportation and
communication have weakened the significance of physical nearness as people with means live practically anywhere; they are no
longer necessarily bound to particular people and places. For less
fortunate individuals like Maudie Fowler, this loss of physical nearness has in some ways been a curse because it undermines one cru-

cial aspect of their identity as human beings: that they are part of a larger human community *just in the fact that other people are physically near.* Maudie can no longer trouble herself because there is *nothing to trouble herself for.* In the past, her family would be there, at least physically, because they would not have the technological means to be far away from her in the London suburbs. Through the taken-for-grantedness of nearness, she would have familiar people around her. She might not feel the painful loneliness she feels otherwise.

In this sense, nearness helps preserve human identity (Seamon 1991). Nearness joins people with a larger world, supporting relationship through kinship and shared location. In part because of nearness, people know their place, and this knowledge is unselfconscious because it is founded on blood ties and physical proximity. People automatically belong in their world because they arose in that world and are generally accepted without question, even in spite of idiosyncracies. Today, in contrast, weak and poor people often suffer because their identity is all they have, yet this identity is eroded as kinship and place diminish in importance. People like Maudie Fowler cannot buy identity as Jane Somers can through her lucrative job, fashionable clothes, and comfortable apartment. Nearness is crucial for people like Maudie because it automatically provides a world that includes other people and relationships.

How does modernity attempt to repair the loss of human identity due to the erosion of nearness? Modern solutions are founded on connection—the assumption that outside injections of monies, personnel and other resources will improve a person or group's well-being. In Maudie's case, the suggested cure was better housing, a larger pension, nursing, a home helper, and so forth. In some ways, of course, these benefits might help Maudie, but in the end they are founded in connection rather than relationship and miss Maudie's central need—the wish to be part of a larger human whole.

The significant point for policy and planning is that efforts to improve society today are too frequently grounded in connection rather than relationship. Relationship cannot readily happen because professional and client, politician and constituency, policymaker and people planned for—rarely do these people and groups have a real stake in each other. The result is that there can be no genuine change because these mutual parties never reach a sense of togetherness. In fact, much of the time, these connections never reach beyond encountering the other, since the other is not really seen or understood but force-fitted to meet the stereotype or convenience of the party in charge. If the outside injection of resources or personnel ends, the receiver's world falls back to the poverty or alienation that the external policy or plan was designed to change. In short, lasting change involves first of all a shift in human worlds rather than a redistribution of material resources.

Somers's extraordinary contribution to Maudie's world is that she returns to it *a certain kind of nearness*—the friendship of a person who likes Maudie for just being who she is. Somers becomes *close* to Maudie, and Maudie is no longer an isolated individual. Somers says, "Maudie, I like you as a person, I like knowing you," and through this respect restores Maudie's dignity as a human being. Maudie's family is doubly guilty because they not only ignore her presence but cut her presence down. From one perspective, Lessing's novel is a scathing indictment of all people who ignore their families and loved ones.

In terms of social policy and environmental design, therefore, Lessing's *Diaries* indirectly suggests at least two important points. The first point relates to connection versus relationship: that external injections of monies and other resources will not necessarily lead to societal improvement because they change material conditions but do not readily address deeper human needs of nearness and relationship. The significance of nearness points to a crucial value of environmental design: that it can provide a physical grounding for interpersonal relationships. Jane Somers meets Maudie Fowler because at least a portion of an older, humanly-scaled London neighborhood still survives and both women live there. Maudie's situation suggests that a diverse neighborhood providing a taken-for-granted mixture of different people and activities offers a better context for nearness and relationship to arise. Why? Because people of similar needs are more likely to come together if they are in spatial proximity and frequent the same places. A key design concern becomes the thorough understanding of ways in which the built environment can contribute to a sense of nearness, place and human togetherness.

This essay cannot suggest ways through which physical design can enhance nearness and relationship, since Lessing's *Diaries* offers no exact picture of the women's neighborhood or the kinds of human actions and activities it supports. The key point is that *Diaries* suggests that the physical neighborhood had a significant role in the possibility of Somers and Maudie's relationship. Future phenomenologies of place and relationship need to consider the links among physical nearness, diversity and people's coming together (Seamon, 1987).

Toward a Phenomenology of Relationship

The major question I have asked in this essay is how different worlds are drawn together in a lasting way. I have called this process of coming together *relationship,* and I have argued that a phenomenological explication of Lessing's *Diaries* suggests that the process unfolds in terms of the relationship cycle of figure 10.1. In summary form, this cycle includes three progressive phases that might be called a beginning, middle and end. In the beginning phase of the relationship (stages 1–3 in figure 10.1), the common thread is *search*—a sense that there is something more beyond who and what one is. In time, a situation in the world outside the person offers itself, which in Somers's case is the encounter with Maudie Fowler. The relationship then moves into a middle phase that might be called *trial* because it involves efforts of mutual acceptance (stages 4 and 5). The trial stage holds the greatest danger of failure because the two parties may not bond. If they do, a relationship results that is founded in the fact that two have become one. The third phase of the relationship (stages 6 and 7) might be called *fruition.* The relationship is now secure and as much an entity as the two participants, who feel mutual understanding and responsibility.

This phenomenology of relationship is based on only one descriptive text and is therefore tentative. The presentation in figure 10.1 needs confirmation and correction grounded in other contexts and situations. One potential avenue would be groups of interested individuals who share and explore relationships that they have known personally. The aim would be the description of underlying patterns, phases, and commonalities that identify relationship as a general process. Even in its preliminary form, however, the relationship cycle of figure 10.1 may offer some clues as to how other relationships unfold. Here, I examine two such possibilities with the hope that my interpretation might provide insights for future phenomenologies of relationship. I choose two relationship experiences with which I am familiar: the first, that of student and teacher; the second, that of client and architect. I examine both in terms of the relationship cycle of figure 10.1.

Learning and the Relationship Cycle

Figure 10.2 describes the student-teacher relationship, which I consider in terms of graduate education. Immediately notice that the graduate student takes the active position of Somers in the cycle. Sometime earlier in his or her life, the student realized a

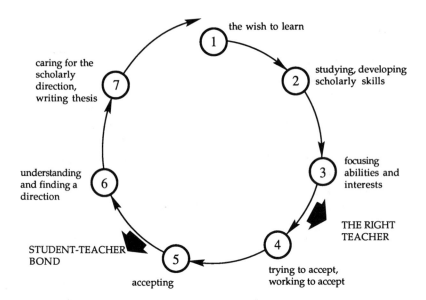

the wish to learn

caring for the
scholarly
direction,
writing thesis

studying, developing
scholarly skills

understanding
and finding a
direction

focusing
abilities and
interests

STUDENT-TEACHER
BOND

THE RIGHT
TEACHER

trying to accept,
working to accept

accepting

Figure 10.2. The Student-Teacher Relationship.

personal interest and aim related to intellectual ability, the pleasure of knowledge, the need to understand, and so forth (stage 1). Before finding "the right teacher," he or she has gone through a process that included mastery of intellectual and writing skills, choice of discipline, and sense of career direction (stages 2 and 3). Eventually, the student finds a professor who seems the right guide for the student's scholarly interests and aims (encountering the other). Once this "right person" appears, there is a testing period in which the student must demonstrate that he or she is worthy of the teacher's assistance (stages 4 and 5). The teacher is also on trial in the sense that the student determines whether the professor can or cannot provide the support or direction that he or she needs. Events of this trial stage include the mastery of the teacher's research tradition, the participation in his or her classes, assisting him or her with research, and so forth.

If student and teacher work well together, they eventually join in a kind of partnership (symphysis). This tie gives the student the force to conceptualize a dissertation topic and work toward its completion (stages 6 and 7). In this part of the cycle, there is fruition in the sense that the mutual understanding and love for the subject cements a bond between student and teacher that will carry over into the student's professional career.

In exploring the graduate student's experience in this way, one gains clues as to why graduate education so often goes awry today: students may not have a sincere wish to know, they may have chosen a field of study that is out of harmony with their personal intellectual needs, they may choose the wrong teacher, they may never establish a genuine bond with their teacher—so many problems like these touch graduate education today. At the same time, many professors have little sense of the student-teacher relationship and accept students they should not or reject students they should accept. In addition, graduate education is seen as a commodity and a means rather than as a quest and an ends. Many students are like sleepwalkers who move through the graduate experience physically but gain little intellectually or experientially. They experience connectedness with teacher and discipline but no relationship. In its recognition of search, trial and fruition, the relationship cycle gives insight into why there are these problems and failures. It also suggests ways in which a self-conscious understanding of relationship might help teachers and students to better carry out their mutual aims.

Designing and the Relationship Cycle

The client-architect relationship is illustrated in figure 10.3. Note that the client takes on a role similar to the student or Somers. There is a need for a house, office, or some other building (stage 1), and the client begins a search, first, in terms of a rough vision of what he or she needs; later, in terms of considering architects who can provide a satisfactory building (stages 2 and 3). In time, the client finds "the right architect," who must honestly judge whether he or she can provide the building the client needs (encountering the other).

Working together, client and architect move into a trial period (stages 4 and 5), which includes an exchange of understanding: the client must work to provide the architect with a clear picture of his or her needs; the architect must listen to these needs and translate them into design possibilities. At the same time, the architect must help the client become more sensitive to his or her needs and the way the built environment can support or stymie them. Over time and if properly done, this trial stage will lead to a "right design" (symphysis), which is then refined and finalized in the fruition part of the relationship (stages 6 and 7). At this stage, a series of new relationships begin—the architect's dealings with the contractor,

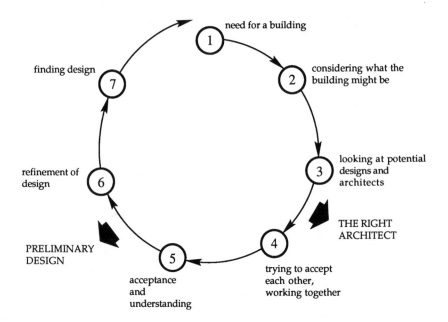

Figure 10.3. The Client-Architect Relationship.

the contractor's relationship with client, the client's relationship with the building, and so forth. Each of these relationships could be explored through figure 10.1.

Too often in architecture today, the relationship cycle is severely distorted, and figure 10.3 suggests possibilities as to why. One problem is that clients often have little sense of how important the built environment is to human livability. The result is that the client does not take the design process seriously. One way in which this lack of interest occurs is that the client supposes that the architect is the expert and holds all the answers. Alternately, the client supposes that any designer will do and carelessly chooses an architect whose abilities or design philosophy may be out of touch with the client's needs.

At the same time, the trial stage of the relationship is often dispensed with entirely as the client decides that he or she does not understand design and cannot, therefore, contribute to the design process. On the other hand, many architects have the dubious belief that they are creators and know what the clients need better than the clients themselves. The result is that the client-architect relationship is treated superficially, or there is no relationship at all.

Another problem is that many clients today are anonymous bureau-crats, committees, or corporate boards that have no direct interest or participation in the design process. The frequent result is build-ings that display the architect's ego rather than satisfy the need of the building's users.

Ideally, a phenomenology of the client-architect relationship might help clients understand that architecture is more than sim-ple building. Phenomenological insights might also sensitize the ar-chitect to the client's world that the building is meant to sustain. A self-conscious understanding of the relationship cycle might help both client and architect to move toward a more successful architecture.

Directions

These two examples of the relationship cycle are sketchy and incomplete, but they intimate a specific kind of coming-together process underlying particular relationships like friendship, learn-ing and designing. An explicit awareness of how a relationship comes to happen (or does not) might be useful in understanding particular situations where different worlds must meet and work together.

The above examples point to several dimensions of the relation-ship experience that need further exploration phenomenologically. One important question is whether relationship can involve part-nerships other than two people. For example, can relationship in-volve two groups, an individual and group, an individual and thing, an individual and idea, a group and thing, and so forth? The signif-icance of wish and need in the relationship cycle suggests that at least one of the members in the would-be relationship must be an individual or group, since only people can have a sense of aim and purpose. More than likely, the stronger this sense of aim and purpose is, the greater the chances that the relationship will be successful. From this perspective, large institutions are less able to involve themselves in relationship, since their direction is too of-ten determined by anonymous individuals, committees, or boards. Without individual commitment, no amount of technology, economic advantage, or political program can make lasting relationships happen because in the end relationship is much more than material change and improvement. The lack of human commitment is par-ticularly a problem for the client-architect relationship today, since both clients and designers are often employed by large firms that cannot provide the time and intimacy required for genuine cooperation.

Another intriguing aspect of the relationship cycle is its miraculous quality: How extraordinary that contrasting experiences and sensibilities can find each other and join in partnership! A more thorough understanding of the role of coincidence and seeming impossibility could be useful in that there might be indirect ways for creating a supportive context for their more likely occurrence. Conventional psychological and sociological conceptions of human action generally ignore events and situations that cannot be controlled directly. Yet our own personal experience as well as Somers and Maudie's situation illustrates that unexpected events are crucial in human life. Somers and Maudie's experience suggests that people cannot plan for such events directly because they are unpredictable. At the same time, however, Somers's determination, struggle and hope suggest that one can work with these coincidental happenings *indirectly,* through positive attitudinal qualities like wish, effort, and commitment. The indication is that need attracts results, though often these results are unpredictable and unexpected in their particular form.

In most general terms, a phenomenology of relationship is valuable because it helps people to understand more clearly the nature of everyday life, especially the forces of interaction and change. A central charge for policy and design is to make the world a better place in which to live. How can genuine improvement happen if there is no clear understanding of how worlds touch and change each other? Because we do not have a clear understanding of human experience and relationship, we often implement policies and designs that work against life rather than in harmony with it. A phenomenology of relationship provides a better understanding of how real change might be possible for individuals, groups, and society as a whole. In this sense, it is a tool for both personal and societal improvement.

Notes

1. *Diaries* has an intriguing publishing history. As an experiment to demonstrate the fickleness of critics, Lessing originally published *Diaries* as two separate novels, *The Diary of a Good Neighbour* (New York: Knopf, 1983) and *If the Old Could* ... (New York: Knopf, 1984), both under the

pseudonym of Jane Somers. Lessing's ruse gradually became known publicly, and in 1984 she republished the two novels as *The Diaries of Jane Somers,* using her own name. For Lessing's story of these events, see her "Preface" in *Diaries.* Also see Lessing, 1987, pp. 52–54.

The relationship between Somers and Maudie Fowler is described in *The Diary of a Good Neighbour,* and this essay draws most of its descriptive evidence from that novel. *If the Old Could . . . ,* however, is also used since it mentions Maudie Fowler in passing and describes Somers's efforts at helping another elderly woman, Annie Reeves. Useful introductions to Lessing's work include Draine, 1983; Fishburn, 1985; Rubenstein, 1979; Seligman, 1981; and Taylor, 1982. On phenomenology and imaginative literature, see Margolis, 1977; Pocock, 1988; Seamon, 1981, 1987. On the theory of quest, journey, and self-development in imaginative literature, see Stout, 1983.

2. I am grateful to Margaret Boschetti for suggesting this word.

3. An article in the *New York Times* (April 17, 1988, p. 11) explains that some one hundred relocated Ukranians, many of them elderly, have illegally returned to their former homes near Chernobyl, the site of the nuclear reactor explosion of April 1986: "most of those who returned are elderly and . . . many never adjusted to relocation." The human sciences are only beginning to understand the profound bonds that link people to their worlds, to such a degree in the case of Chernobyl, that these elderly Ukranians would risk the threat of radiation to be back in their former homes.

References

Draine, B. (1983). *Substance Under Pressure: Artistic Coherence and Evolving Form in the Novels of Doris Lessing.* Madison: University of Wisconsin Press.

Fishburn, K. (1985). *The Unexpected World of Doris Lessing: A Study in Narrative Technique.* Westport, Connecticut: Greenwood Press.

Lessing, D. (1969). *The Four-Gated City.* New York: Bantam.

——— . (1984). *The Diaries of Jane Somers.* New York: Vintage.

——— . (1987). *Prisons We Choose to Live Inside.* New York: Harper and Row.

Margolis, R. (1977). *Phenomenology and Literature.* West Lafayette, Indiana: Purdue University Press.

Pocock, D. C. D. (1988). Geography and Literature. *Progress in Human Geography, 12,* (1): 87–102.

Rubenstein, R. (1979). *The Novelistic Vision of Doris Lessing: Breaking the Forms of Consciousness.* Urbana: University of Illinois Press.

Seamon, D. (1981). Newcomers and Existential Outsideness: Their Portrayal in Two Books by Doris Lessing. In D. C. D. Pocock (Ed.), *Humanistic Geography and Literature* (pp. 85–100). London: Croom Helm.

———. (1987). Phenomenology and Environment-Behavior Research. In G. T. Moore and E. H. Zube (eds.). *Advances in Environment, Behavior, and Design,* vol. 1 (pp. 3–27). New York: Plenum.

———. (1991). Awareness and Reunion: A Phenomenology of the Person-Environment Relationship as Portrayed in the New York Photographs of André Kertész. In L. Zonn (ed.), *Place Images in the Media* (pp. 31–61). Savage, Maryland: Roman and Littlefield.

Seligman, D. (1981). *Doris Lessing: An Annotated Bibliography of Criticism.* Westport, Connecticut: Greenwood Press.

Stout, J. P. (1983). *The Journey Narrative in American Literature: Patterns and Departures.* Westport, Connecticut: Greenwood Press.

Taylor, J. (1982). *Notebooks/Memoirs/Archives: Reading and Rereading Doris Lessing.* London: Routledge and Kegan Paul.

Chapter 11

Putting Geometry in its Place: Toward a Phenomenology of the Design Process[1]

◙

Kimberly Dovey

Suddenly everybody expressed a feeling that they didn't like it . . . the plans looked alright, I mean plans always look alright, but a lot of people can't and I can't put a plan into bricks and stones.

————— Client's reaction to the beginning of a construction process (Dovey, 1987).

Phenomenology as applied to the physical environment has generally been concerned with a rigorous exploration and description of the environmental aspects of everyday experience. This essay extends the phenomenological approach to the design process. How are environmental design problems experienced by those who dwell in a place, and how is that experience shared with designers? How are proposed environmental changes experienced by designers and communicated to clients? How does one know that the agreed design proposal will deliver a better environment? How can designers avoid incidents where clients are surprised and disturbed when a design becomes reality?

My first concern is to reiterate some of the major tenets of the phenomenological approach to environmental studies, in particular, the distinction between lived and geometric modes of space. I then explore some aspects of the environmental design process from this point of view, particularly with regard to the kinds of translation required between space as geometry versus space as experience. A third aim is to identify several disjunctions that may prevent an effective transformation of the environment. Finally, I explore some strategies that can strengthen the environmental design process.

247

I believe that the lessons of phenomenology may be applied to all scales of environmental experience from room to building to city. My background, however, is in architecture along with my examples and my characterization of the design process. I trust that the reader may make connections with other examples and other kinds of process in the broader ecology of environmental transformation. My method is primarily one of interpretation, based on case studies and personal experience in research and practice. Much of the argument is a deductive exploration of the consequences of accepting the precepts of phenomenological philosophy for environmental design.

Lived-Space Versus Geometric Space

Phenomenological philosophy developed largely in opposition to the Cartesian world view and the perceived crises of understanding brought by the dominance of detached and supposedly value-free inquiry (Relph, 1970; Seamon, 1982). Phenomenology asserts the primacy of the lived-world of everyday experience (*lebenswelt*), as the field of scholarly inquiry. The lived-world is the pre-scientific experience of our world, before we have learned to detach ourselves from it and view it as having a separate objective existence. Thus, for Heidegger (1962), there is no 'being' apart from a 'world'; rather, there is first and only a 'Being-in-the-world'.

A reassessment of the concept of space is important to the application of phenomenology to the built environment. Norberg-Schulz (1971), Relph (1976) and others have characterized modes of spatial experience as aligned along a loose continuum ranging from the abstract, measured space of geometry to the concretely experienced space of everyday life. For purposes of simplicity, I call these poles "geometric space" and "lived-space". Plato declared in the *Timaeus* that geometry should be the science of space. Subsequent developments through Euclid have built geometric space into a powerful model for understanding the world. This model is so powerful that a geometric representation of the world is widely perceived as the one true arrangement, with people's various everyday experiences being more or less accurate in relation to it. The phenomenological perspective, in contrast, interprets geometric space as having a powerful predictive capacity rather than any superior claims to truth. From this view, the lived-space of the lifeworld is the primary spatial mode from which geometric space is abstracted (Bollnow, 1967). 'Being-in-the-world' is anchored in lived-space, thus lending it an ontological significance. This priority of experience inverts the conventional scientific notion that geometric space constitutes an absolute reality and can be used as an epistemological tool. Merleau-Ponty (1962, p. 243) asserts the priority of lived-space when he argues that:

> Space is not the setting (real or logical) in which things are arranged, but the means whereby the positing of things becomes possible. This means that instead of imagining [space] as a sort of ether in which all things float, or conceiving it abstractly as a characteristic that they all have in common, we must think of it as the universal power enabling them to be connected.

For Merleau-Ponty, lived-space is firmly anchored in the nature and structure of the human body and the potentialities for action. Space is not so much the arrangement of the physical world as it is:

> . . . a certain possession of the world by my body, a certain gearing of my body to the world . . . Between my body as the potentiality for certain movements . . . and the spectacle perceived as an invitation to the same movements and the scene of the same actions, a pact is concluded which gives me the enjoyment of space and gives to things their direct power over my body (1962, p. 250).

Interpreted in this manner, lived-space takes on a different character at different scales (Norberg-Schulz, 1971). At the level of small objects, it is centered around acts such as grasping and manipulating. At the level of furniture, people may be concerned with sitting, dining, talking and so forth. At the scale of a building, the concern may be with privacy, ease of access and visual form. At larger geographic scales, issues emerge such as landscape character and the sequences of various journeys. At such scales, space becomes increasingly conceived as well as perceived.

Schutz and Luckmann (1973) portray spatial experience in terms of primary and secondary zones of actual and potential reach. Sitting at my dining table, I feel the chair, smell the flowers in a vase, enjoy the sunlight and gaze out at the garden. This is the primary world within actual reach. Beyond this immediate context is a secondary world within restorable reach—the study with my books and papers, a university where work awaits me, the Melbourne and Australian landscapes complete with meanings and memories. There is a telephone and a television through which I can communicate over great distances and vicariously inhabit places I will never visit. Lived-space is infinitely complex, compounded by the fact that, like life itself, it is thoroughly socially and culturally conditioned. Chairs, gardens, studies, houses and landscapes are socio-cultural artifacts, and all interaction with the physical environment occurs within a social, political and economic context.

Geometric space, by contrast, is purged of social and cultural meaning; it is reduced to the coordinates of a map or the lines of a technical drawing. It achieves accuracy and predictability at the expense of experiential depth. Geometric space is a representation of a set of relationships among value-free locations. It is a representation of lived-space with the meanings and values extracted. Geometric space is a universal language of spatial representation and, therefore, has predictive value. The irony of geometric space is that it is the very elimination of human values that makes it useful.

The phenomenon of distance is fundamentally different in lived-space than in geometric space. Closeness as experienced depends on accessibility which, in turn, depends not only on the configuration of barriers and pathways but on social, cultural, economic, and technological factors. Since it is laden with meaning and memory, lived-space is more personal and idiosyncratic than geometric space. Lived-space, however, is shared to the extent that people share a common body structure, perceptual system and the intersubjectivity of a socio-culturally shared world view. Most importantly, lived-space is more than a mere setting to everyday life— it is an integral part of *being-in-the-world*. It is of the nature of human existence that we cannot inhabit geometric space and we cannot avoid lived-space.

Lived-space is the opportunity-laden setting for action in everyday life; it is the locale of human agency. As the structure of our language makes apparent, action *takes place*. Hence, the phenomenological concern with the concept of *place*. Place is a difficult concept, and I have defined it elsewhere as a *knot of meaning* in the fabric of human ecology. Places develop over time through human-environment interaction. They grow, are infused with life, may be healthy or unhealthy, and may die (Dovey, 1985). Place is to lived-space as location is to geometric space. Lived-space is experienced in everyday life with meanings and values intact. Its value is intrinsic as opposed to the predictive value of geometric space.

The Design Process as a Cycle of Lived-Space

Environmental change involves a transformation from one kind of place to another. It begins with a difference between the way a place is and the way it could or should be in someone's experience. This is the design problem and it is also an opportunity. The design and construction process begins and ends in lived-space, and its *raison d'etre* is the transformation of place experience. This transformation may or may not satisfy initial expectations or justify the expense. Geometric space is a means to improved lived-space, a shared language that contributes to a successful design process. This cycle from experience through geometric representation and back to a transformed experience I call the *cycle of lived-space*.

As the architect Charles Moore explains, "It is easy to see why we fail so often. For one thing we do not draw space, but rather plans and sections in which the space lurks" (Moore and Allen, 1976, p. 7). While it is not clear what Moore means by 'space', its use intimates what I see as a central dilemma for the design process. Only when desired qualities for a future environment are translated into geometric plans is it possible to undertake substantial changes to the built environment. Yet such a translation, of necessity, extracts everyday values and meanings as lived-space is transformed into geometric representation. It is the predictive value of geometric space that makes it essential to modern design. If the proposed design involves builders, contractors and local authorities, a shared spatial language with specific interpretation is essential. The measured simulations of space that geometry makes possible permeate the discourse and documentation of the professions of interior design, architecture, landscape architecture, urban design and environmental planning together with their governing regulations and codes. The problem, simply put, is that we design in one mode of space while living in the other. This problem is compounded by the fact that lived-space is essentially four-dimensional, involving sequences in time. In the design process, however, lived-space is generally reduced to two dimensions for purposes of design communication. There is an attempt to generate a four-dimensional simulation with a set of two-dimensional images. In sum, both geometric and lived-space are necessary yet insufficient for an effective design process.

The design process begins with a problem or opportunity in relation to the built environment of a person, family, corporation, government or community. The problem may be framed in terms of inadequate space for certain activities, the lack of certain formal or symbolic qualities in an existing place, or the opportunities afforded by the existing place together with available funding. In the conventional design process, this leads to a design program or brief in written form. The designer creates one or more proposals that are simulated, usually in the form of sketch plans. These simulations are presented to the client, who accepts or rejects them. If accepted, the proposal is simulated in the form of working drawings—i.e., specific geometric instructions to a builder who then transforms the built environment in accordance with the agreed plans. The new environment is occupied, and a new experience of place begins. Only then is an evaluation of the effectiveness of the entire design process possible.

The design process is described as 'cyclic' for two reasons: first, the process moves from the lived to the geometric and back to the lived; second, each design and construction process is only one cycle of change in what may be a long series in the history of a place. The process is a cycle of 'lived-space' because it is the experiences of lived-space that instigate and legitimate the cycle, provide the values that drive it, and, finally, determine its effectiveness. I now explore two major phases of this cycle—sketch planning and working drawings.

Sketch Planning

Most professional design proceeds through the phases of sketch planning (schematic design) and working drawings (documentation). Ideally, these two phases produce forms of communication that serve as a bridge between geometric and lived-space. Sketch plans are simulated versions of possible worlds. A major task of sketch planning is to capture the client's imagination and to lend a vicarious reality to what was formerly a nascent dream. Sketch plans, together with models and verbal or written explanations, are mediating tools between geometric space and lived-space. They are geometric inasmuch as they are a measured simulation of what is possible on a given site. In this sense, they have predictive value. At the same time, they are 'lived' inasmuch as they simulate through drawing the place as it will be experienced in everyday life. In one sense, sketch plans can be described as a series of questions that ask the clients, "Is this what you said you want?" Since clients may find it difficult to articulate their desired experiences, several iterations of this process are usually required.

Lived experience cannot be fully simulated as drawings. Yet effective sketch plans will enable clients to imagine themselves inside the proposed place, experiencing the sense of scale, the view from a window, the noise from the children's room, or the distance from the boss's office. Scale models add a third dimension to the simulation with the important effect of permitting a variety of perspective views. These models do not accurately simulate lived-space, however, since they induce a bird's eye view.

The aim of sketch planning is to evoke an experience akin to what Relph (1976) calls vicarious insideness—the manner in which we experience places secondhand through films, novels, poetry, travel brochures, photographs, and so forth. At the same time, the sketch plan partakes of a certain geometric objectivity which insures that the design can be built. The designer is a translater, speaking in two languages—lived-space with the client and geometric space with the builder. The designer must marry the imagined with the possible.

Working Drawings

Working drawings, in contrast to sketch plans, are entirely geometric representations of the proposed design. Everything from window frames to concealed structural members are drawn in the smallest detail. Working drawings are legal documents and their immediate concern is with 'facts', not 'values'. They do not deal in light, livability, views, or social interaction. Instead, they specify window size, ceiling height, and materials. The measurements shown in the working drawings are lived qualities translated into an abstract geometric mode. Working drawings and specifications are communications in the language of the construction industry, and they are not intended to be easily understood by the client. If the proposed transformation of the environment does not satisfy the client's program, this lack will not be immediately apparent to the client from the working drawings. A trained mind can decipher them to evoke an imagined lived-space, but this understanding can only be achieved with difficulty.

Under the designer's supervision, the builder constructs the full-scale version in accordance with the working drawings, thereby completing the cycle of lived-space. The builder has no access to sketch plans or to an understanding of the lived-experience that is the desired end of the process. Yet the builder inhabits the lived-space of the building site on a daily basis during construction, separated from the proposed lived-experience, yet most in touch with its emergence. Designer and builder have reciprocal roles, one translating client values into geometric plans and the other turning geometric plans into a livable place.

In a successful design process, the cycle of lived-space is integrated and the flow of communication from client to designer to builder is effective. This cycle of communication is more than a flow of explicit information. Ideally, there is a successful expression of symbolic meanings that relate to aesthetics, culture and personal or collective identity. Using the distinction argued by Langer (1953), one can say that such meaning is generated by symbols rather than signs. Symbols *connote* multiple, intangible meanings, while signs *denote* single, explicit meanings. Connotative symbolic meanings cannot be reduced to sets of instructions. When the designer captures the imagination of the client in the sketch-planning phase, it is primarily these symbolic meanings that are expressed. While the forms that generate such meaning can be encoded into the geometric instructions of working drawings, the meanings themselves cannot because they are a function of the relationship between the client and the proposed built form. Only when the construction process is complete and the transformed place is inhabited can the meanings emerge and grow.

Disjunctions in the Cycle of Lived-Space

The above discussion of the design process is simplified. In most design work, complexities and aberrations occur that may be the cause of disjunctions in the cycle of lived-space. I use the term 'disjunction' to refer broadly to ruptures or breaches in the cycle that produce a lack of integration. I will discuss three such disjunctions here—a conflict between the paying client and the user; miscommunication between designer and client; and a conflict of goals between designer and client.

Conflict Between Client and User

My use of "client" has so far included both those who are funding the proposed environmental transformation and those who will use the completed place. Yet the "client" is not always one single person or group, and the result is sometimes a conflict of values. Design problems arise from the desire for a more livable environment for the users, dominated by values such as convenience, privacy, access, beauty, safety, and so on. These values, however, may conflict with the desires of a non-user client for profit, status or political advantage. When user and client disagree, serious problems can result.

A first kind of discrepancy occurs when there is no current user, and a place is created for a particular market rather than for a person or group. In this case—for example, speculative housing or office development—the primary motive for environmental change is profit rather than livability, which become little more than a means to that end. Driving such activity is a potential market of users who value certain qualities of lived-space. That such a system responds to market pressure is both its strength and weakness. The strength is that unlivable places will not sell and, therefore, will not be produced. The weakness is that the system will not respond to pressure from those who are priced out of the market. Another problem here is that speculative construction deals primarily with classes of places. The model-house consumer, for instance, gets a choice of the "Pioneer" or the "Hollywood", which are essentially classes of lived-experience packaged for consumption in the form of cultural myths (Dovey, 1991). If the meaning of "place" embodies an element of uniqueness, it cannot be provided by such a process. The participation of the user in the design process is reduced to that of a consumption choice.

A second kind of conflict occurs under bureaucratic organizations where the user client is separated from an institutional client. Examples include housing, health, educational and corporate clients. In each case, there are several layers of bureaucratic decision-making interposed between designer and user. While it is the lived experiences of the users (students, residents, patients, employees and so forth) that constitute the foundation of the design program, the occupation by specific individuals may be short-term and their needs may be changeable. The role of bureaucrats as "surrogate clients" in this context can lead to bias that is thoroughly disruptive to the cycle of lived-space. The nature of bureaucratic organization, according to Weber (1978) involves a focus on rationality, objectivity, clear hierarchical relationships, and written rather than verbal discourse. Its success depends on "eliminating from official business love, hatred, and all purely personal, irrational and emotional elements which escape calculation" (Weber, 1978, p. 90). Bureaucratic procedures become biased towards those in charge, who tend to serve fellow bureaucrats rather than clients. In the case of the built environment, this pattern can lead to a situation where users become "invisible" (Grenell, 1972). The result is that the designers have no access to an understanding of the kind of lived-experience the built environment should support. The program is condensed and objectified into space standards based on stereotypes and framed in the geometric language of floor area per person. The symbolic meanings of the users will largely be eliminated in this process, but another kind of environmental symbolism often results. The 'institutional' character and negative meaning of many community service buildings and public housing projects is due to the fact that the institution and its bureaucratic representatives constituted the "real" client.

Miscommunication of Lived-Space

Assuming that the designer has access to both user and client, there are other disjunctions that may occur during sketch planning. These difficulties involve a miscommunication of the simulated environmental change such that clients do not fully understand the design before the process moves into construction. This is one of the most common disjunctions in the design process.

One cause of miscommunication relates to the professional context of design activity. Sketch planning for any project constitutes a certain percentage of budgeted time. In architecture, this phase may vary from about fifteen to twenty-five percent with working drawings, site inspection and management constituting the remainder. Sketch-planning is, however, the least predictable phase of the process because it relies on the agreement of the client. Furthermore, a good deal of sketch designing is often completed before the architect is hired, as a means of winning the commission. For these reasons, the relationship between designer and client at this stage is often cast in a selling mode. Profit for the designer is increased by reaching an early agreement on the design. The designer is under pressure to convince the client that the proposal will deliver an effective transformation of lived-space. The client is under pressure to trust the expert and to allow the project to get under way. The degree to which agreement is based on understanding rather than on faith is the degree to which the proposed change has been successfully and accurately simulated through sketch planning.

A particular kind of problem emerges from the fact that capacities for spatial abstraction vary widely. This is not a matter of intelligence, but of dominant modes of communication. Designers tend to be visually oriented, while clients may be verbal (Dovey, 1984). The inability to make the imaginative leap from the geometric image of a plan into an imaginary lived-space is widespread and is evident even in people looking at plans of the house they have lived in for many years.[2] This problem is further exacerbated by the assumed dominance of the geometric mode. The inability to make the leap becomes an implied disability, since the client is often expected to be able to deal in geometric space. The easy solution for the client is to feign understanding and place faith in the designer as expert. This may be precisely what the designer wants. Why undertake a series of perspective sketches or a model when agreement can be reached sooner without them? The designer may indeed understand the client's dreams and problems even if the proposal is not fully understood by the client, and the leap of faith may be justified, saving time and money. It may, as designers are wont to argue, produce something better than the client dreamed was possible. On the other hand, the designer's image may be different enough from the client's to make such faith dangerous.

Dominance of the Professional Cogniscenti

In addition to the designer's concerns with the representation of space to client and builder, there is another mode of spatial representation often directed at the designer's professional peer group. While professional design discourse is an important part of the generation and propagation of ideas, the dominance of such discourse can be disjunctive to the cycle of lived-space. Consider, for example, the case of Peter Eisenman, a well know architect whose reputation is partially based on sets of geometric drawings together with written theory. Neither Eisenman's drawings nor his ideas are intended to be understood by client or builder. Rather, in the early theory, there is an avowed aim to separate the form of the building from the program (Eisenman, 1973). The building forms are emptied of any meaning associated with function in favor of a "deep structure" that is to be unravelled by the viewer through a series of intellectual manipulations based on the drawings. The "deep structure" consists of two sets of formal systems, one of planes and volumes, the other of frontal and oblique relations. These formal systems are asserted to be universal.

There are two important points here. The first is that concern for dwelling in the building has been forgotten in favor of a formal geometric program that is autonomous. The viewer is expected to transcend the lived-experience and vicariously inhabit the abstract realm of geometric space. Instead of geometry as the means to a more livable environment, geometry has become an end in itself. The second point is that the drawings (and the buildings if they are built), are largely unintelligible and require the written theory as an adjunct. A few years ago during a lecture, I intentionally placed a cross-sectional drawing by Eisenman on an overhead projector upside down. The separation from lived-experience was sufficient that nobody noticed the difference. The rupture of buildings from use and the avowed unloading of traditional meanings entailed the eradication of people, room names and even the articulation of walls, windows, stairs and entries. While such designs may need the theory, they may not need to be built. Eisenman's reputation does not so much stem from his built work as from his published theories and especially drawings which now sell in boxed sets at high prices.

Eisenman is by no means alone in this retreat from lived-space. Current architectural representation abounds with fragmented plans, exploded views, and abstract figures emptied of human habitation. This "gallery architecture," as it is often called, represents an autonomous sub-cycle of design discourse that often acts against the cycle of lived-space. It is a cycle wherein the product of the design process is not a building but a drawing. Once again, the means has been confused with the end. The designer's aim is not so much to please the client or user of the building as to please the viewer of the drawing—the professional *cogniscenti* from whom approval is obtained or denied.

A personal anecdote illustrates the way that such peer pressure can disrupt the design process.[3] A housing authority decided to renovate the foyer area of a 1960s high-rise housing tower and engaged an architect who developed a design to working-drawing stage without consulting residents. The interior design included a skewed ceiling recess at the top of a column, marble inlay in the floor, a large block of concrete (not at sitting height), and a profuse use of industrial steel plate for seats, table and wall panelling. Outside, there was a two-story entry canopy of bright yellow steel I-beams. The Tenant's Council complained that what they wanted was not just a foyer but a meeting place where they could see the comings and goings of the foyer, stop for a chat, and share child care. The architect, under pressure from the housing authority, amended the plans to include a meeting room, but when the tenants had deciphered the working drawings they found it largely shut off from the foyer, destroying the social connections and passive surveillance useful for reducing vandalism. The project had been divided into two parts, one representing the architect's identity and the other representing the clients' identity. The residents won the battle to open up the meeting room to the foyer, but the entry canopy was built without the residents' proper understanding of what it would be like. At the opening party, residents were disparaging and nicknamed the canopy the "yellow peril."

In this case it is clear that the dominant client for the architect was the architectural *cogniscenti*—those who 'read' the building as a statement within an esoteric meaning system. The intended meanings were neither shared with nor 'read' by the residents of the building. Rather, these meanings emerged in lectures by the architect for other architects and students. The column with skewed ceiling recess was then drawn in perspective as a crucifix representing the possibility of 'redemption'. The large diagonal beams of the entry canopy were described as symbolic 'props' for the building and the problems of its low-income tenants. There were many other references to esoteric meanings built into the design, and it was successful in winning an award from the local institute of architects. The award stated: "The design has great power and depth, clearly working on many levels" (Thornton, 1987, p. 24). The experience of the users, however, was not one of those levels, and when the residents later gained the right to choose an architect for further projects, the prize-winning architect was not considered.

My argument is not whether such meanings are important in architecture, but whether they are shared by the dwellers and whether they displace other kinds of meaning. An entry canopy that is designed as a symbolic "prop" can become a "peril" in everyday life. I am certainly not opposing the introduction of novel and highly imaginative formal solutions in the design process. But it remains the task of the designer to capture the imagination of the clients and gain their commitment to the design based on thorough understanding. In terms of the cycle of lived-space, the dominance of esoteric disclosure introduces a counter-cycle whereby the sources of design do not originate with the client and the success of the design does not depend on the user's experience and indeed can interfere with it.

Heidegger's distinction between *zuhandenheit* and *vorhandenheit* as modes of being-in-the-world is relevant here (Heidegger, 1962; Relph, 1985). *Zuhandenheit* is a mode whereby we engage with the world in everyday life; the meaning comes from our living it. *Vorhandenheit,* on the other hand, is a mode whereby we reduce the world to an item for contemplation. We consider it and judge it without acting in or upon it. Both kinds of relationship are integral parts of human experience, but from a phenomenological point of view the former is more primary because it encompasses and arises from human intention and action. When the dominance of contemplation effects a separation between built form and everyday life, it can cause a major disjunction in the design process. This is true for both examples described above and for much of what passes for post-modernism in current design discourse. Inasmuch as post-modernism is a response to a perceived lack of meaning in the built environment, one result has been the reduction of environmental meaning to a set of formal references accessible only to the *cogniscenti* who understand the theories. The phenomenon is one of more and more meanings of less and less lived-significance.

Integrating the Cycle of Lived-Space

If one accepts the above commentary on the environmental design process, what proposals for change and improvement might be possible? Here, I propose four strategies that could enhance the quality of the built environment by strengthening the cycle of lived-space. The first strategy incorporates more user participation and less professional specialization. The second strategy focuses on the nature and techniques of design communication to ensure that the fullest and most accurate simulation of the proposed environment is achieved. The third strategy emphasizes a scale of design decision-making that is more piecemeal and manageable. The final strategy seeks to generate design information through post-occupancy evaluation. All of these strategies are concerned with integrating the cycle of lived-space as a flow of communication and, therefore, as a flow of meaning.

Elaborating the Designer's Role

I argued earlier that design begins and ends with the lived-experiences of the users for whom the place is being transformed. If, however, the design problem is framed in such a way as to prevent contact between designer and user, gaining access to such people is an essential first step. A schism between user and client is a classic problem of participatory design, and it is often not in the perceived interests of designers or funding clients to give such access. There is a political role for the designer here. This role may include the designer's redefining the problem and arguing for a different kind of design process rather than a different kind of form. The designer may "sell" this process to the funding client rather than "selling" the completed design ideas. In the case of an institutional client, a direct approach to the user group may be appropriate—for example, residents in the case of housing; neighbors in the case of a park; employees in the case of a corporate client or government agency; children and teachers in the case of a school. Designers must learn the language of the users, listen to their definition of the problem and elaborate possible designs from within that lived-context. Such participation requires a range of skills that are not in the traditional kit of the designer—for example, understanding of group dynamics, collective creativity and building consensus. Design education needs to be extended to ensure that designers are skilled in process facilitation as well as the generation of form.

Many of the disjunctions of the cycle of lived-space occur because of separations between designer, client and builder. It follows that the cycle can be integrated by strategies that begin to merge these roles. For example, in the case of the owner-builder-designer, the patterns of space usage and meaning that constitute the context of the design problem are also the everyday lived-world of the designer. Similarly, the lived-world of the construction site is also the lived-world of the client. The result is that a series of spatial communications and translations between lived-space and geometric space are eliminated from the design cycle. While such a merger of roles is difficult in most design contexts, a series of overlaps are possible. To the extent that clients actively participate in the design process, they become designers. To the extent that the designer or client becomes involved in the construction team, they become builders.

An integrated cycle of lived-space, however, is more than just the effective communication and simulation of a proposed environmental change. The cycle of lived-space also integrates a cycle of meaning. When the client becomes an active, creative participant in the design process, places gain meaning as the realization of creative action and the expression of personal and collective identity. This cycle of meaning is further enhanced when the client is involved in the task of construction. An integrated cycle of lived-space is a primary generator of environmental meaning.

Simulating Lived-Space

There is also a need to assess critically all documents produced as part of the design process in terms of what it is that they communicate, to whom, and in which spatial mode. While both geometric and lived-space modes are necessary, there is a need for some separation. Working drawings should not be used as surrogate sketch plans because the danger of the client's misunderstanding or pretending to understand is too great. Clients should not be expected to decipher complex geometric drawings any more than builders should be expected to construct on the basis of a perspective. As part of this reassessment of design documents, I do not see any role for drawings produced by and for designers to the exclusion of clients and builders. Design drawings are a means to an effective transformation of the physical environment. The elimination of drawings intended as an end in themselves would liberate considerable effort for the effective simulation of lived-space. After the place is transformed is the time to engage in critical professional debate about what has been achieved. Designers must learn to use the same visual language and system of meaning as those who will benefit or suffer from design decisions. The current postmodern retreat into a private architectural language may serve to shield the design professions behind a wall of mystique, but it will not serve the lay community in terms of a livable everyday environment.

There are many techniques that can expand the capacity to simulate lived-space. The use of scale models is one way of providing multiple lived-views of a proposed environment so long as the dominant bird's eye view that it induces can be overcome. The Environmental Simulation Laboratory at Berkeley (Appleyard, 1976; Bosselman, 1990) has developed techniques of modelling an entire cityscape, simulating the effects of planning controls, filming sequential eye-level views, and screening the results on television for public debate. Cuff and Hooper (1980) argue for the use of "conglomerate drawings," which incorporate multiple views of the most distinctive elements of places. The problem, however, is that although experience of place is multi-dimensional and may be most effectively represented in a "conglomerate drawing," it does not follow that an environment constructed from it will automatically achieve the experience that the drawing communicates. The danger is that the designer's concern to capture the intangibility of place experience in drawings may eliminate the necessary reliable connection between the drawing and the proposed experience that it simulates. One cannot disconnect lived-space entirely from geometric space without the risk that the sense of place will remain forever in the drawings only.

Inasmuch as the eye-level perspective simulates the lived-experience of the built environment, the translation from a geometric simulation to a lived-simulation can be largely computerized.

The rules of perspective constitute a mechanical translation from the geometric to the lived—a translation that is generally effected manually, with significant time delays and a severely limited number of views. Many design processes do not include perspectives at any stage of the process. With computers, the potential exists to effect translations from geometric plans, sections and elevations to perspective views of everything from building interiors and exteriors to streetscapes, open space and landscape designs. Imagine if the designer could generate not one or two but dozens of perspective views instantly as requested by a client. Imagine also if changes could be made and the lived-space effects immediately simulated. It is also possible to produce computer simulations of moving sequences on video, including the simulated experience of moving through a landscape, streetscape or building. Proposed changes can be superimposed on a video of an existing place to simulate the change in its visual context.

An added advantage of computer simulations of lived-space is that they cannot so easily be distorted to the advantage of certain groups and to the disadvantage of others. For example, large-scale commercial developments are often publicly communicated and politically sold on the evidence of an "artist's view of proposed development" that misrepresents the lived-experience. Computer simulations would offer a more readily verifiable connection between geometric space and lived-space. The practice of making large developments look smaller or fit better within their context may not stop, but computerization would make it easier to detect and provide a means of public accountability for professional simulations of lived-space.

There are dangers, however, regarding the use of computers. The first is that computer simulations produce cold and mechanical simulations of place, stripped of the art and craft of designer's drawings. Computers may enable a vast increase in communicability, but the loss of drawing quality must be addressed. Once the designer has been liberated from the time-consuming task of setting up each perspective, there should be more time to develop the character of the place, using computer drawings as a base. A second warning is that computers may be used either to generate interaction with clients or to destroy it. "It's on the computer" has become a new way of arguing that something cannot be changed or cannot be erroneous. Computers are most viable economically in the production and storage of working drawings. They may be used, however, to keep the design discourse within that geometric framework rather than to explore the more difficult task of effecting a proliferation of instant and accurate simulations of lived-space.

Another method of simulating lived-space is to build in some degree the proposed environmental change in full-scale mock-up. There are several cultures who traditionally build in this way (Lerup, 1977). Alexander (1979, 1985) has developed techniques using props to represent lived-space at full scale on site. The mock-up, like the sketch plan, is a heuristic method of test and adjustment. To be adaptable, the simulation must be minimal. Marking the building or landscape design out on the ground is not enough; vertical elements must be simulated to give a three-dimensional effect. The Laboratory for Architectural Experimentation at Lausanne has developed techniques for user participation in full-scale house mock-ups that include walls, doors and windows. Such a process achieves a significantly greater understanding of the proposed place at the same time as it liberates new design ideas from the users' experience (Lawrence, 1981).

The mock-up simulates the sense of spatial enclosure and can be used as a basis for evaluating the shape and size of indoor space. If the mock-up is on site, it also enables evaluation of the relationship between design and context. The usefulness of mock-ups relates to the general inability of many clients to understand the simulated plans in terms of lived-consequences. The mock-up still requires a certain leap of imagination by the client and the designer, but there is no leap of scale or any component of geometric space. In a sense the cycle of lived-space has been partially circumvented. At the same time, however, mock-ups have their drawbacks. A first problem is convincing both designer and client that the manipulation of boards or poles on site can be a more sophisticated form of professional design than the production of drawings. A second problem is that the leap of imagination from the mock-up to the imagined place may be significantly biased due to a lack of solid spatial boundaries. A third problem is that mock-ups are scale-dependent and become less possible with larger buildings. Yet in situations where perception of the scale of development is crucial in decision-making, it may well be worthwhile to experiment with balloons or similar aerial technology.

Piecemeal Change

A primary reason for a failed cycle of lived-space is that the scale and complexity of proposed changes to the physical environment commonly render a disjunctive process almost inevitable. The larger the scale of the project, the greater the gap between current and future lived-experiences and the greater the problems of simulation. Further, the greater the scale, the more likely is the split between user and client and the more difficult it is to gain access or even to discover who the possible user will be. In addition, the user group may be an unmanageably large size for participatory design and construction. The lack of human values in the environment may result more from poor problem definition that from poor solutions. An integrated design process is simply less possible as scale increases. Strategies for piecemeal change that break down the scale of environmental projects, that reduce the grain size of urban texture, and that limit the size of funding allocations would help to generate conditions necessary for a more successful design process.

Even after construction has begun, however, it is possible to make piecemeal changes that respond to the lived-experience revealed on site. At this stage, a series of unforeseen problems and opportunities may become apparent. During a school development process, for example, the architect had raised a classroom above the ground to get more light (Dovey, 1987). It became apparent to the client during construction that the scale would overwhelm young children at ground level. The design was adapted to include a series of stepped platforms that break down the scale and work as play places for the children. During the construction of another classroom, the builders had left a hole in the wall cladding which was seen by a teacher as an opportunity and turned into a window. Alexander (1979) argues that the most effective time to decide on the size, shape and placement of windows is during the wall-framing stage. Only then is it possible to make minor adjustments that achieve the best lived-experience in terms of view, light, privacy and sense of enclosure. Many of the complexities of lived-space—the multitudes of angles, views and sequences—cannot be perceived within the necessarily simplified simulations of sketch planning. The major problem with midstream changes is that they involve adjustments to construction drawings that constitute a legal contract. Legal "variations" are a significant source of profit for the builder, at significant cost to the client and, therefore, a major source of conflict between both builder and designer, and builder and client.[4] Strategies that break down this semi-competitive role system should make piecemeal design more possible.

Evaluating Places in Use

A final strategy for integration is completing the design cycle through the post-occupancy evaluation of places in use (Cooper

Marcus and Sarkissian, 1986). The argument is an old one, and in phenomenological terms it is that designers too seldom find out whether the users' lived-experience matches either their initial desires or their expectations engendered by the drawings. By expanding our knowledge of how certain kinds of design process and built form are associated with certain kinds of experience, we generate another means of integrating the cycle of lived-space. Evaluation entails research on how well a designed environment works for the users in relation to both the pre-design environment and the design and construction process.

The phenomenological perspective leads to evaluations that are significantly different from a measured account of behavior and attitudes using empirical methods (Seamon, 1987). Phenomenological evaluation seeks understanding rather than explanation of cause-effect relationships, and it rejects the notion of detached objectivity as both impossible and limiting. It aims for rigor in terms of depth of experience and meaning. Such research seeks an understanding of lived-experience in all its complexity yet aims to keep the intangible qualities of place experience at the center of the inquiry. Such an approach does not necessarily exclude more objective methods of inquiry. It is possible, for example, to use both in-depth interviews as well as questionnaire and observation to achieve both depth and breadth. If undertaken effectively, phenomenological post-occupancy evaluation has the potential to integrate the cycle of lived-space, particularly for those design projects that are most problematic—large-scale developments with institutional clients and unknown users.

Conclusion

Environmental design absorbs enormous amounts of money and resources, and once changed, the physical environment has a great deal of inertia. We have one chance to do the design well and when we fail, we generally adapt rather than demolish. Successful environmental design is driven by human values grounded in lived-experiences, whose meanings in turn are found in everyday life. Yet much of twentieth century design scars our landscapes and offends our aesthetic sensibilities. It is difficult to believe that we would have transformed our world in this manner if the consequences had been well simulated. There is an urgent need to ensure the integration of human values in the design process, and the lessons of phenomenology can guide us in this quest.

The rigorous application of a phenomenological perspective to the built environment entails a critical analysis of the design process to ensure that the primacy of experience is not lost to the complexities or scale of the development; to failures of communication; to the imperatives of capital development; or to the lure of geometry as an end in itself. In particular, phenomenology entails a critical distinction between lived-space and geometric space, between the experience of place and the geometric simulations which are a means to its effective transformation. If, as I have argued, the lived-experience of place both initiates and concludes the process of environmental change, then the task is largely one of putting geometry in its place. And the place of geometry is in the service of the lived. Geometric representation is abstracted from, subservient to, yet necessary to the design of livable places. It is a tool, a language and a technical means to a valued end. No more and no less.

Notes

1. I am grateful to Peter Downton and David Watson for critiques of earlier drafts of this paper.

2. This evidence comes from personal experience in a City Architect's office where I served people requesting plans of their house. When I asked them to confirm that I had the correct plans, many people could not do so. Admittedly these plans were working drawings, but they were generally simple and clearly drawn. I resolved the problem by asking a specific question about lived-experience, for example, "When you come through the front door, is there a closet on your left, a laundry straight ahead and a living room on your right?" Such questions were easily answered.

3. My role in this project was advisor to the Tenant's Association, which wanted help in communicating with architects. I was asked to do programming work and to decipher some of the architect's working drawings.

4. In Australia, builders often give low tender bids to secure a contract but count on design "variations" to increase profits during construction.

References

Alexander, C. (1979). *The Timeless Way of Building*. New York: Oxford University Press.

————. (1985). *The Production of Houses*. New York: Oxford University Press.

Appleyard, D. (1976). Understanding Professional Media. In I. Altman and J. Wohlwill (eds.) *Human Behavior and Environment* (pp. 43–87). New York: Plenum.

Bollnow, O. (1967). Lived-Space. In N. Lawrence and D. O'Connor (eds.) *Readings in Existential Phenomenology* (pp. 178–186). New Jersey: Prentice-Hall.

Bosselman, P. (1990). Dynamic Simulation of Urban Environments. Berkeley: University of California, IURD Working Paper no. 509.

Cooper Marcus, C. and Sarkissian, W. (1986). *Housing as if People Mattered*. Berkeley: University of California Press.

Cuff, D. and Hooper, K. (1980). Graphic and Mental Representation of Environments. In A. Seidel and S. Danford (eds.) *Environmental Design: Research, Theory and Application* (pp 10–17). EDRA 10 Proceedings, Washington.

Dovey, K. (1984). The Creation of a Sense of Place. *Places, 1* (2), 32–40.

————. (1987). A Place Biography: the Case of Arlington. Ph.D. Dissertation, University of California, Berkeley.

————. (1991). Model Houses and Housing Ideology in Australia, *Housing Studies*.

Eisenman, P. (1973). House I. In P. Eisenman, et al. (eds.). *Five Architects*. Cambridge: MIT Press.

Grenell, R. (1972). Planning for Invisible People: Some Consequences of Bureaucratic Values and Practices. In J. Turner and R. Fichter (eds.) *Freedom to Build* (pp. 95–121). New York: MacMillan.

Heidegger, M. (1962). *Being and Time*. New York: Harper and Row.

Langer, S. (1953). *Feeling and Form*. New York: Scribners.

Lawrence, R. (1981). Simulation Models in Architectural Design Process. *Architectural Science Review, 24,* 10–15.

Lerup, L. (1977). *Building the Unfinished: Architecture and Human Action*. Beverly Hills: Sage Publications.

Merleau-Ponty, M. (1962). *The Phenomenology of Perception*. New York: Humanities Press.

Moore, C. and Allen, G. (1976). *Dimensions: Space, Shape and Scale in Architecture*. New York: Architectural Record Books.

Norberg-Schulz, C. (1971). *Existence, Space and Architecture*. New York: Praeger.

Relph, E. (1970). An Enquiry into the Relations Between Phenomenology and Geography. *Canadian Geographer, 14,* 193–199.

———. (1976). *Place and Placelessness*. London: Pion.

———. (1985). Geographical Experiences and Being-in-the-World. In D. Seamon and R. Mugerauer (eds.) *Dwelling, Place and Environment* (pp. 15–32). New York: Columbia University Press.

Schutz, A. and Luckmann, T. (1973). *The Structures of the Lifeworld*. Evanston: Northwestern University Press.

Seamon, D. (1982). The Phenomenological Contribution to Environmental Psychology. *Journal of Environmental Psychology, 2,* 119–140.

———. (1987). Phenomenology and Environment-Behavior Research. In E. H. Zube and G. T. Moore (eds.). *Advances in Environment, Behavior and Design,* vol. 1 (pp. 3–27). New York: Plenum.

Thornton, F. (1987). Residential Award Citation, *Architect* (Victoria, Australia), July 27.

Weber, M. (1978). Essay on Bureaucracy, In F. E. Rourke (ed.) *Bureaucratic Power in National Politics,* (pp. 85–96). Boston: Little Brown.

Chapter 12

Sacred Structures and Everyday Life: A Return to Manteo, North Carolina

◻

Randolph T. Hester, Jr.

When a bridge was constructed to the North Carolina Outer Banks in the 1950s, highways built to facilitate travel to its beaches bypassed the island town of Manteo.[1] Within the next thirty years, the beaches grew and thrived as a summer playground for the metropolitan mid-Atlantic, but Manteo plummeted from being the region's primary trade center to a near ghost town. With unemployment and tax rates among the highest in the state, Manteo was typical of communities classified as depressed, high risk and desperate (Healy and Zorn, 1983).

In 1980 the townspeople of Manteo asked me, a community designer, to help them develop a plan that would bring new economic purpose and prosperity to the town, yet not sacrifice traditional lifestyles and valued landscapes (Hester, 1984; Hester, 1985). Today, much of this plan has been implemented. As a result of grassroots community development, Manteo has been revived. The town is home to a new state historical park and a reconstructed ship modeled after the vessel Sir Walter Raleigh's lost colonists arrived in, four hundred years ago. The ship was built on the Manteo waterfront at a boat-building center that builds wooden vessels and offers classes in traditional shipwright techniques. The increased tourism has restored failing indigenous industries and reduced unemployment. In some ways, Manteo's recovery is a familiar story: a small dying town reverses economic decline capitalizing on smallness, intimacy, natural beauty, village character, and a rural past (Kellogg, 1983; Richter, 1983). For many communities, however, this turnaround spells the eventual demise of existing community traditions, destruction of valued places, and an ingenuine folk culture's replacing the less-marketable indigenous one (Jordan, 1980). Recognizing the pitfalls associated with new development, Manteo took unusual steps to avoid a tourist takeover (Hester, 1985; Hester and McNally, 1983). As the town's community designer, I helped Manteo residents identify and preserve their valued lifestyles and landscapes in the face of change. Once identified, important social patterns and places—what came to be called the "Sacred Structure" by locals— inspired our plan for community revitalization.

Uncovering Valued Places

I was originally hired to redesign the village waterfront, but it took only a few days on site to realize that a waterfront park would merely be a cosmetic change. With more than twenty percent seasonal employment and a declining tax base, Manteo needed a new economy. On the day I discussed this with Mayor John Wilson, the hardware store downtown closed and moved to a nearby resort location. The mayor, a young architect and Manteo native, saw the town through the eyes of both professional designer and local insider. He loved the place. He wanted the town to recapture the spirit he had experienced as a child playing on busy docks. Not even nostalgic boyhood memories of a bustling waterfront, however, could deny the message of the hardware store. We agreed that day to expand our contract. I outlined a holistic community development process (Hester, 1984), and the Town Board approved the idea. I moved my office to Manteo. We began a community-wide discussion to design a strategy to overcome the problems besetting Manteo.

As I met with more community leaders, I realized that the people I talked to shared the mayor's passion for the place. I was struck not only by the emotion with which people talked about how special Manteo was, but also by how insightful they were about subtle qualities of the place. This was a happy coincidence for me. In my community design work, I search for social nuances to inspire form (Hester, 1975, 1978). I had just completed the design of a day-care center; I had used hypnosis to help the staff discover the spatial qualities they wanted in the facility (Hester, 1979). Startled that their hypnotic spatial preferences were so different from the questionnaire results, I read what I could find about spatial values and concluded that unconscious attachment to place might be a powerful factor in community planning. I felt that the concept of spatial values would be more useful to designers than our present idea of landscape aesthetics largely founded in visual and formal values.

I welcomed the opportunity to explore unconscious relationship to place in greater depth, but the problems confronting Manteo seemed to require economic development, not studies of emotional attachment to place. Through a community-goals survey involving a large number of Manteo residents, however, many of the same points articulated by the mayor and leaders resurfaced. When citizens randomly interviewed in their homes were asked what they liked most about their town, they often mentioned small-town qualities such as informal friendliness (fifty-one percent of one hundred citizens interviewed) and being able to walk almost everywhere in town (twenty-two percent). Places such as the waterfront, the village, and specific shops were mentioned as being important because they represented home or provided roots (Hester, 1980).

Residents wanted new economic development, but they also wanted the small town atmosphere preserved. My design team knew neighborhoods could be protected by zoning, facilities could be located compactly to reinforce walking, and a historic district could save venerable architecture. But that did not satisfy us. We felt we were missing the essence of what townspeople were saying. We undertook the task of finding out precisely what lifestyles and landscape features were essential for a continuation of the town's culture.

Behavior mapping gave us some important clues. For several weeks, we sat in various locations and recorded what people did, and where. The resulting maps showed us activity settings for the daily patterns of townspeople. When we put the rough sketches of our activity maps together, a deeper understanding of the town spontaneously emerged. Before us was a powerful cultural mosaic that illustrated not only how space related to the town's present social patterns but also suggested how collective memory had been invested in certain parts of the landscape. While people had described some of these places in the goals survey, most of what we observed had not been mentioned. Activities like exchanging gossip at the post office, hanging out at the docks, and going to the waterfront to check out the tides, shoreline, fishing catches and weather, recurred in the same places each day and likely had for years. Lifestyle and landscape were intertwined. Daily ritual was place-specific, and the cultural dependence on places seemed more widespread than people had reported in our interviews (figure 12.1).

Still, we were not certain which places were most essential to the life of the town. But we had hunches based on our knowledge of

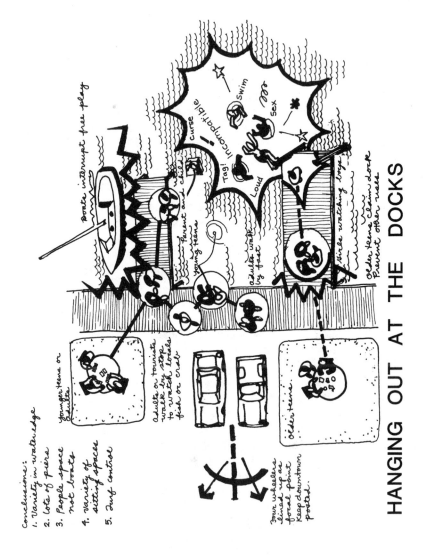

Figure 12.1. Hanging out at the docks: Activity mapping.

social patterns in other towns, the survey results, behavior mapping, and informal discussions with town leaders. Using these hunches, another community designer and I made a list of the places we thought were important to the town's social fabric—places where community and psychological values were concretized in the landscape. For example, we both thought the gravel parking lot near the waterfront was essential because it was the daily setting for checking out the water and special community festivals. Although it was an ordinary looking unpaved lot left over as the buildings on the abandoned waterfront were demolished, it embodied both everyday habits and special rituals essential to the town's sense of self. Similarly, we guessed that Jule's Park would be inviolable because the mayor had told us that Jule Burrus had built it from ruins as a labor of love for the town. When the high school that most Manteo residents had attended was demolished, Jule Burrus removed the rubble and built the park from it. The rubble evoked sentiment, representing high school days to nearly everyone. As the new park took shape, Jule's labor came to symbolize the value that Manteo citizens could build from ruins. We were right about these two places. We also thought actor Andy Griffith's house would be important because of the status he brought to the community. We were wrong.

We revised the list after checking it with several Town Board members. A newspaper questionnaire was developed for townspeople to rank these places in order of significance to them as individuals. We also asked residents to state which places they thought could be changed to accommodate tourism, and which places they were unwilling to sacrifice. We used historic tourism as a trade-off because that seemed the most viable economic development strategy. The questionnaire posed several specific trade-offs, such as whether the respondent agreed that it was more important to leave the Christmas tree in the gravel parking lot downtown than to use the space for parking. These responses provided a measurement for the intensity of attachment to places when weighed against the benefits of tourism, and allowed us to recheck the relative importance of places.[2]

This survey provided a ranked and weighted list of significant places. One resident, upon seeing how many places ranked higher than the local churches and cemetery, dubbed the list the "sacred structure," and thereafter the list was called the "Sacred Structure of Manteo." In further discussion, locals identified the cemetery and the high school as a cutoff for comparing special and less special

Figure 12.2. Jule's Park. Photographs by Randolph Hester, Jr.

places. Any place that locals rated higher than the cemetery and high school, we concluded, should not be negatively affected by new development. The places included the marshes surrounding the town, Jule's Park, a drugstore and soda fountain where local teens and the elderly were served freshly-squeezed lemonade and chicken salad sandwiches, the post office, churches, the Christmas Shop, front porches, the town launch, a statue of Sir Walter Raleigh, the Duchess Restaurant where locals gathered for morning coffee and political discussions, the town hall, locally made unreadable street signs, the town cemetery, the Christmas tree in the gravel parking lot, park post lamps placed there in memory of loved ones, and two historic sites (figures 12.2 and 12.3).

The local newspapers published the results. A map of the Sacred Structure was included with the inventory plans we prepared during the planning process for the town (figure 12.4). The map showed the places colored with varying intensities based on the questionnaire results. It looked similar to other land use maps. It was immediately clear that the "Sacred Structure" touched a sub-

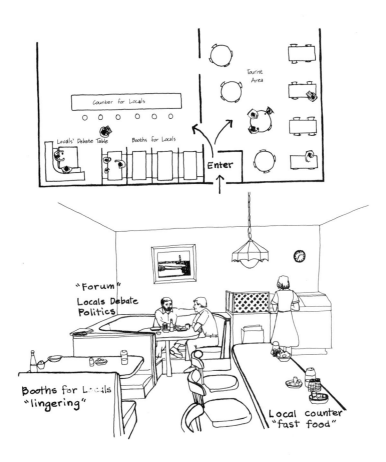

Figure 12.3. Duchess Restaurant: Activity mapping.

conscious nerve in the community. The residents wanted these places protected. One newspaper editor expressed concern that the identification of these places in the survey meant that the designers were considering changing the places to attract tourists. He carefully listed those places that must not be profaned for tourists, stating that they were "perfect jewels" the way they were (*Coastal Times*, 1981). His "perfect jewels" play on words referred directly to Jule's Park but also included the other most-valued places. Frequently during the subsequent planning process, the editor

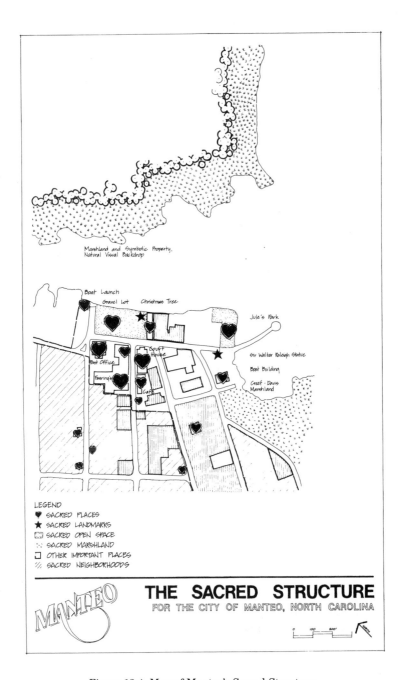

Figure 12.4. Map of Manteo's Sacred Structure.

reminded me that those places were sacred and that local people were willing to sacrifice economic gain to save them.

Sacred Places

What did people mean by the "Sacred Structure"? The concept of sacred place making, or a community sacred structure, is easy to accept in so-called primitive cultures. We smile knowingly at stories of tribes who proclaim their village square to be the center of the universe, who believe that passing through a doorway changes their state of mind, who designate twisted plants as magic trees or attribute dooryard gardens to the spontaneous generation of the earth, and who set aside these common landscape features as hallowed (Shepard, 1967; Stein, 1987). It is more difficult to comprehend that we, in our modern secular American society, hold any place necessary to our daily lives as sacred (Meinig, 1979). Yet our cultural preoccupation with placelessness and topophilia suggests that we do highly value some places (Gans, 1962; Relph, 1976; Tuan, 1974). In this context, perhaps a useful definition of sacred structure would be those places—buildings, outdoor spaces, and landscapes—that exemplify, typify, reinforce, and perhaps even extol the everyday life patterns and special rituals of community life. These places have become essential to the lives of the residents because of community use or symbolism. These places become synonymous with residents' concepts and use of their town. The loss of such places would reorder or destroy some social process familiar to the community's collective being.

For the most part, Manteo's Sacred Structure consists of seemingly mundane places that are the settings for the community's daily routine and embody the life of Manteo. While these places combine to express Manteo's uniqueness and probably structure residents' internal images of their town, none of these places is exotic. Yet all are eloquent in their context. They are typical and sometimes dilapidated features of what is commonly found along the Carolina coastal landscape. They are familiar, homey, and homely.

These places are almost universally unappealing to the trained professional eyes of an architect, historian, real estate developer, or upper-middle-class tourist. As a result, in Manteo only two places among the Sacred Structure were protected by historic preservation legislation. Only a few were protected by zoning laws and less than half were identified as significant in a Lynchian image survey

(Lynch, 1960). These discoveries were startling to us. They meant that the existing planning and design mechanisms developed precisely to preserve local cultural heritage ignored almost entirely the places most critical to the present lifestyles, most valued patterns, and local memory of Manteo. Decades of advances in local land-use controls had completely missed this essential point.

But the lack of planning and legal mechanisms to uncover and protect Manteo's sacred places was only part of the problem. Even to locals, the sacred places were outwardly taken for granted. This lack of self-consciousness partially explained why the planning and legal mechanisms ignored the sacred places. They were neither distant enough in history nor were they removed enough from daily life to be seen as special. Their value resided in the community's collective subconscious and loomed large in conscious minds of locals only after four stages of recognition—*threat, legitimization, collective awareness* and *consecration*. I should emphasize that these four steps in making conscious these unconsciously valued places seem essential only in retrospect. As we went through the design process, we were often uncertain about what to do because we knew of no precedents.

The residents' first stage of recognition involved the fact that the sacred places were threatened. As the town had declined, some of these sacred places, particularly the waterfront, had likewise suffered. Due to lack of maintenance and use, the waterfront was unrecognizable as the bustling wharf that many local people held in their memories. But gradual decline is difficult for most people to grasp as a threat. It was not until we began talking about the changes necessary for economic recovery that, first, town leaders, then, residents became aware that their community was in transition. The dramatic scope of our proposed plans to alter the town forced people to think about the social institutions and the environments that mattered most.

As townspeople pondered this threat, they faced a quandary. The places they most valued also held negative associations. The Sacred Structure was a repository of both love and embarrassment. Not one of the sacred places matched the popular media image of the "good environment"—the upper-middle-class suburb of residential areas neatly segregated from support facilities. In some cases the sacred places of Manteo seemed to be inconvenient anachronisms. To make matters worse, visitors came to Manteo expecting the town to be as quaint as Williamsburg. Such visitors were disappointed by the town's appearance and said so, making local people feel that the unpretentious places of Manteo were a bad reflection on the community. This created a psychological conflict whereby community members wanted to preserve their life patterns but felt they should remove these places because of their negative status with visitors. When we understood that local people were somewhat ashamed of the places to which they were so attached, we knew that we, as outside designers, needed to say that these places were fine and worthy of preservation. Our acceptance of the Sacred Structure was important in helping the community overcome negative media and visitor responses. We allowed, and possibly helped, the community to legitimize these sacred places.

Next, our design team presented a collective picture of the valued places to the community. Although each person might value and use many of the places, he or she likely did not know how much others valued the places or how the separate places created a collective framework—the mosaic of social activities and cherished rituals we had observed previously. The list of sacred places, the map, and the simple name "Sacred Structure" overcame this. The list and map provided the townspeople a gestalt of previously known but seemingly unrelated facts. The map turned special places into a pattern previously experienced but not grasped as a whole. The name, "Sacred Structure of Manteo," provided an understandable way of simplifying the whole. The Sacred Structure became part of the local vocabulary and was debated at the Duchess Restaurant and Betty's Country Kitchen, along with such topics as job opportunities and property tax benefits of tourism. The community's unconscious concern about special places had become part of a collective, self-conscious expression.

Finally, the places were consecrated, a process that required the residents to set aside the most important places from less valued ones. Residents did this systematically by responding to the newspaper survey and by refining their list of sacred places throughout the planning process. By the time our team had completed the design plans, residents were firm in their conviction that the most valued places be designated as inviolate and not be changed to accommodate new development.

At one point in the design process, for example, a plan was presented that would destroy significant parts of the Sacred Structure but produce some one million dollars more in annual commercial sales than the plan that preserved the Sacred Structure. In an act of collective sacrifice, the community voted for the Sacred Structure plan, thus downplaying economic potential but protecting the sacred places. In time, our design team estimated that preservation of the Sacred Structure would cost Manteo over half a million dollars in annual retail sales. This financial sacrifice was essential in residents' consecrating the sacred places, a fact confirmed when one newspaper editor repeatedly emphasized that these places had a higher value than dollars.

The Sacred Structure and Planning Decisions

After we presented the Sacred Structure map to the Planning Board, it became part of the formal discussion, influencing planning decisions in at least five ways. First, the Sacred Structure transformed the typically vague discussion about loss of valued lifestyles and landscapes into focused debate about what sites should be changed or kept to reap the benefits of tourism. The Sacred-Structure map depicted important social patterns and cultural settings more effectively than any other planning document.

Second, the Sacred-Structure inventory was used by residents to evaluate a specific plan in terms of impact on their lives. Townspeople could tell if a particular development violated places identified as sacred. For example, one plan was unacceptable because of proposed changes to Bicentennial Park, for which ninety-five percent of the survey respondents had indicated that changes, even minor ones to the Park's memorial lamp posts, were unacceptable. The Sacred Structure gave residents the rationale to articulate their intuitive responses to development plans and proposals.

Third, the Sacred Structure helped direct the final plan for Manteo's village center. Of seven prospective plans, townspeople chose one with somewhat less economic potential, specifically because the plan preserved more of the Sacred Structure and interrupted fewer of the townspeople's accustomed patterns and rituals. The Sacred Structure also inspired the weaving together of tourist and local places with a living-learning boardwalk. In addition, the Sacred Structure helped to preserve Jule's Park, the Creef-Davis boat works, the gravel parking lot and the Christmas tree for their existing uses. Even the visual quality of the new development was inspired by the Sacred Structure, inviting personal participation and interaction. The chosen plan had an unfinished appearance that made it open to community change. Locals would be able to add new touches. The feeling conveyed by the plan was warm and unpretentious.

Fourth, the Sacred Structure provided the basis for negotiation with outside developers who proposed desired but inappropriately scaled projects (Hester, 1981). Because the valued places were dispersed throughout the waterfront, their preservation precluded wholesale urban redevelopment. Developers balked at this limitation at first because it required small-parcel development. The town had several disappointing courtships with real estate developers because of the limitations of the Sacred Structure. After the plan was finalized, it was presented to one of the premier developers in the county, James Rouse, whose company then expressed an interest in the Manteo waterfront. After a Rouse Company affiliate developed a detailed plan, it was apparent that preserving the sacred places precluded the type of self-contained, large-scale waterfront development that Rouse normally undertook. When it became clear the town would not give up the sacred places, Rouse's interest waned. Several other national companies flirted with the town before a North Carolina firm finally undertook the development of the three dispersed parcels on the waterfront.

Last, the Sacred Structure provided the basis for ongoing citizen evaluation of zoning and building proposals. In a debate over the development of a new marina, residents pointed to the results of the Sacred Structure survey that showed that sixty-five percent of the townspeople preferred improved boat ramps and docks for locals over providing more docks for tourists. The private marina was delayed. Throughout the planning process, the Sacred Structure played a critical role. Because these sacred places embodied Manteo's existing social life, habits, rituals and institutions as well as its collective memory, the Sacred Structure was invaluable in describing the essence of life in Manteo in ways that were applicable to decision-making. The final plan that the Sacred Structure finally led to is illustrated in figure 12.5.

There were few precedents for legally preserving the Sacred Structure. The town formally adopted a "Guide for Development," which stated explicitly the intent to preserve the Sacred Structure. This guide was then incorporated into the local Coastal Area Management Plan to strengthen the Sacred Structure's legal status, but these actions were largely symbolic because the Sacred Structure was not specified by any of the appropriate state-enabling legislation. Of the seventeen most valued places, only five could be protected by existing legal mechanisms, using historic preservation and appearance legislation, the Coastal Act, or the local zoning ordinance. Had there been the slightest disagreement about the

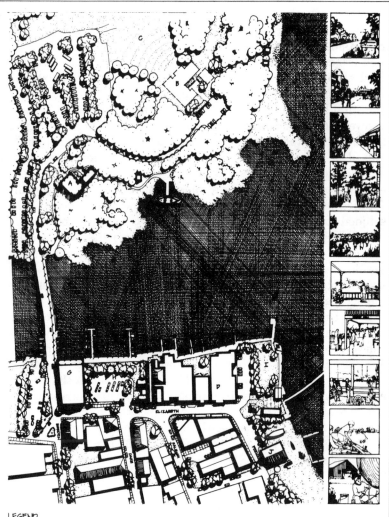

LEGEND

🛏 SACRED BUILDINGS		⌐ LIVING HISTORY EXHIBITS		E	ELIZABETHAN SHIP
▨ SACRED LANDMARKS		● LEARN BY DOING ATTRACTIONS		F	BEACH
⊟ REHAB BUILDINGS		A LIVING - LEARNING CENTER		G	INN
⬒ PROPOSED DEVELOPMENT		B PERFORMING ARTS CENTER		H	SACRED TREE
⌐⌐ FUTURE DEVELOPMENT		C ANGLO-AMERICAN FOLK FESTIVAL		I	JULE'S PARK
☐ EXISTING BUILDINGS		D NEW HOUSING/COMMERCIAL		J	BOAT BUILDING CENTER

THE VILLAGE PLAN
FOR THE CITY OF MANTEO, NORTH CAROLINA

Figure 12.5. Final plan for Manteo.

importance of the sacred places, their legal protection would have been jeopardized. The state legislature of North Carolina provided some legal help by passing historic-corridor legislation that protected the wilderness character of Manteo's main vehicular entrances and two of their valued sites. This corridor legislation also gave protection to Manteo's Fort Raleigh, a historic site, and for neighborhoods already somewhat protected by zoning. The legal mechanism that the town relied on most, however, was the creation of a village business district in which fourteen of the sacred places were located. A conditional use permit was required for all new development in the village business district. The conditions for receiving the use permit were articulated in the "Guide for Development." The guide mandated that any new development, rehabilitation, or change in the village must be assessed for impact on residents' use of the Sacred Structure and must protect or enhance local pedestrian access, parking, and visual access to sacred places (McNally, 1983). The builder must demonstrate that local access to the sacred places would not be negatively affected by the change before the conditional use was approved.

The Sacred Structure in 1988

During the winter of 1987–88, I spent two weeks visiting Manteo to examine how our community plan had fared over time. Was the Sacred Structure so much a part of Manteo's taken-for-grantedness that it would be soon forgotten and overrun by economic and legal pressures? To answer this question, I studied the town visually, interviewed some two dozen community leaders, and evaluated the results of a yearly resident survey that considered the impact of tourism on Manteo. In the last sections of this article, I overview the discoveries of my two weeks of study and discuss the successes and failures of our original plan.

The Visible Landscape

The entrance to Manteo from the east retains the wilderness character that citizens had wanted preserved at the beginning of our planning effort. Billboards have been removed along the highway leading into the town center, and an alley of recently planted oaks heighten a sense of processional passageway. In addition, a dozen new businesses have been built along the highway and several more are under construction. These buildings are all typical suburban-strip style, though their placement, massing and ornament is more environmentally and architecturally sensitive than in most suburban developments. The result is that strip development has been contained, and there is a clean edge between the town and its surrounding landscape.

In the village center itself, there has also been growth, but the sacred places are largely unchanged. The spartina marsh remains untouched, reminding me of how critical the water's edge was in defining Manteo's northern boundary. The town boat launch has been rebuilt in a new location with a new concrete launching pad. The Christmas tree retains its prime spot in the parking lot. Jule's Park, the homemade labor of love, houses a new playground, and the recycled brick rubble edges have been cemented in place. The park's old post lamps are still in use and the concrete cross that Jule Burrus found in the ruins of the high school remains the focal point of the waterfront. The overall quality of Jule's Park sets the style for the entire waterfront, as if any new development must pay respect in its design form to Jule's Park. Most new construction fits well into the fabric of the old town. Nearly all the new buildings are two and three stories, with facades built right to the sidewalk. Their fenestration and ornament echo the older buildings' architectural styles (figure 12.6).

One waterside project, however, seems glaringly wrong for Manteo. A mixed-use project containing shops, housing, and parking seems awkwardly out of scale and inappropriate in design. This project is one story higher and more massive than any of the other downtown buildings (figure 12.7). Conceived by outside developers and designed by outside architects, it does not adequately acknowledge either the street as a place for active public life or the water's edge as a public way. Instead, the design creates its own private "public space" in an interior court—a spatial configuration that has no local precedent. This project serves little purpose other than to divide public activities and thereby diminish the area's street life. A better solution would have been several narrow-fronted stores that break up the massiveness and support more visible public activity.

As I walked through the development, I recalled that it was one of the few projects that was too large for local contractors' bids. I wondered if there is a correlation between the size of projects that local contractors can manage and appropriate community scale. I also realized that the presence of this project represented a significant failure of our plan. This mixed development meets the letter of

Figure 12.6. Old buildings rehabilitated.

the law in our "Guide for Development" to preserve the Sacred Structure. It provides local parking to get to the water's edge, and is carefully contained by older buildings and a small open space. But the "Guide" did not adequately specify building height and degree of architectural massiveness. The result is that this project seems jarringly out of place.

Overall, Manteo looks healthier than at any time since I have known it (figure 12.8). Even on the bitter cold winter day when I first arrived for my return visit, the shops were bustling. There are few vacancies in the downtown where eight years ago twenty-five percent of all properties were empty. The streets are lively. People

Figure 12.7. The silhouette of the mixed-use project (left) contrasted with the silhouette of a typical older building (right). The new structure overwhelms the earlier buildings.

Figure 12.8. Manteo waterfront, 1988.

are out walking and shopping. An older couple pass on their daily exercise walk. There are people who appear to be locals and tourists, from lower-to middle-income levels. There are blacks as well as whites, and teenagers on bikes. Visitors stop by the statue of Sir Walter Raleigh and have their pictures taken. Across the street there was familiar congestion at the post office because people are lingering to greet friends and exchange news. There are several old men checking out the water level in the gravel parking lot. When they recognized me, they told me that local festivals are still held there. Teens are hanging out at the docks as always. After observing places in Manteo for several days, I concluded that life in town has changed very little. Manteo continues to have a strong sense of place (figures 12.9).

Responses from Interviews and Survey

As I looked at Manteo physically and observed downtown activity, I also interviewed community leaders to determine their viewpoints on the successes and failures of our Manteo plan. These individuals emphasized four issues that could not have been inferred only by visual study of the community: taxes, employment, housing

Figure 12.9. Manteo waterfront, 1988.

and political struggle. The City Clerk informed me that the plans
implementation had stimulated enough successful development so
that Manteo's tax rate, once among the highest in the state, was
now aproximately average. Unemployment, once depressingly high
at over twenty percent, had been halved countywide, but elected officials I spoke with were evenly divided over the cause. Some pointed
to the rosy national economy while others credited local efforts.

Jobs had been created in the building industry, tourism, other new businesses, the state park, and county government. Several community leaders noted that locals had gained employment from the implementation of our plan, except in several area projects so large that outside construction firms had been contracted, as with the mixed-use waterfront development described above.

One local official told me that the rising cost of housing was the biggest problem in town. Former Mayor Wilson proudly pointed out that one hundred units of subsidized housing had been completed, providing for elderly and moderate-income families who otherwise would be squeezed out as the town prospered. Other leaders feared that more lower-income housing would soon be needed. Although they did not blame the plan directly for rising housing costs, they pointed out that the success of the revitalization effort has been accompanied by an increase in property values and some gentrification. These trends could eventually force low-income people out of the community. Black leaders explained that the lower-income neighborhoods had received significant increases in public investments but were not yet being gentrified. These leaders pointed to paved streets and rehabilitated housing as the primary benefits. They were proud of the new park built around a historic church facade that commemorates important black history on Roanoke Island, but beneath the pride was a concern about rising housing costs. One black woman doubted that in five years her children would be able to purchase a home in Manteo.

Most people actively involved in our planning process explained that there had been much political struggle since the plan's completion. The Chair of the Planning Board described how control of the Town Board of Commissioners had seesawed between supporters and opponents of the plan. To her, the success of the project depended on "putting together a thousand-piece jigsaw puzzle, when some of the pieces were individuals who did not want the puzzle completed."

Members of the Town Board of Commissioners who conceived, designed and funded the first phases of the plan were reelected after it was adopted. At first, there was widespread community support for the plan in the hope that it would generate new life for the town. People felt they were part of a special process. Further, when the innovative idea of grassroots economic development through historic tourism and preservation of the Sacred Structure brought state and national attention to Manteo's plan, many previously uninvolved residents were caught up in the enthusiasm of the vision.

Several years of slow progress toward the plan's full implementation had worn on some community members. Eventually, several opponents were elected to the Town Board. The plan was debated anew. Projects were delayed. Charges of conflict of interest created dissent on the Board. In 1984, Mayor Wilson, whose foresight and energy had initiated the plan, resigned.

The new leadership berated the plan as too elaborate and sophisticated for a small town like Manteo. They opposed, for example, the development of a marina that had been approved as part of a private development for Manteo's harbor area. The leading opponent told me he feared the marina would undermine the preservation of the sacred places. The new leadership dismissed the city planning staff, and the Chair of the Planning Board resigned in protest. This Board had been central in developing and implementing the plan. With the loss of the Chair, the Board began to flounder, often meeting without a quorum. Only two of the six Town Board members who had approved the plan remained on the Board of Commissioners. They felt their vision was being dismantled.

Over time, however, this backlash to the plan ran its course. In the last two years, three supporters of the original plan were elected to the Town Board, joining with two remaining members to restore the plan as a basis for Manteo's development. Many people I interviewed described the recent events as "rekindling the dream." Both supporters and opponents of the plan noted that the preservation of the sacred places had been supported by all parties involved. This struck me as important because, in the face of change, the Sacred Structure had remained a constant, not only supporting the social life of the community but also providing a focus of community agreement in a time of political strife.

Local community actions confirmed the importance of the Sacred Structure (figure 12.10). For example, Fearing's Soda Shop was destroyed by fire in 1981. Defying economic projections, the owners rebuilt because they felt their shop provided a daily gathering spot essential to the town's life. Similarly, when renovations were made on the Duchess Restaurant, the owners considered removing a counter and circular table where locals had gathered every morning for years to have coffee and political discussions. The local architect and interior designer, well aware of the importance of the Sacred Structure to the life of the town, suggested an alternative renovation that preserved the traditional seating. My interviews indicated that community members have consistently taken similar conscious actions to save and enhance what they now call "Sacred Spots."

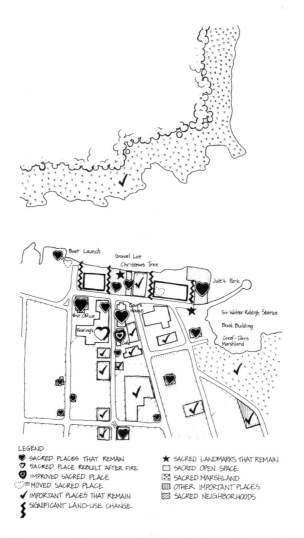

Figure 12.10. Map illustrating how Manteo's Sacred Structure has fared to 1988.

When consultants recently proposed an expansion of county facilities that would have altered three sacred places, many locals were opposed. As one resident I interviewed remarked, "Those consultants were from out of town; they just never heard of our 'Sacred Spots.' " The expansion plan was dropped, and the Town Board of Commissioners asked for alternative possibilities more in keeping with the original community design.

As part of our original plan, a survey is sent out each year by the Manteo Planning Board, asking citizens to evaluate the impact of tourism (School of Design, 1980; Town of Manteo, 1981, 1983, 1986). A review of these surveys reveals how citizen concerns have changed. Problems mentioned most often in 1980 and 1981—unemployment, the rundown waterfront, downtown business closing, and the need for sidewalks and street maintenance—declined in importance as these issues have been addressed. The surveys indicate that traffic congestion and lack of adequate parking remain the two most serious problems in spite of efforts to improve both. The increase in tourism has added to these two problems in spite of five hundred additional parking spaces located near the downtown visitor's center. Merchants, especially, complain about the lack of parking. Some local citizens have become increasingly concerned that the town is becoming too commercialized, although this issue is perceived to be a less serious problem than, for example, the quality of Manteo's drinking water.

During the time I visited Manteo, I was struck with the personal intimacy I felt as I conducted interviews and surveys. The interviews with people I had not known earlier were surprising because responses emphasized people, in spite of my more place-oriented questions. Respondents discussed the successes and failures of the plan in terms of how it affected people or in terms of what various people thought of the outcomes. I realized that any distractions from my predetermined questions were not a bother but, rather, the essence of the work in Manteo. It reminded me that I had not been so much a professional consultant as I had been a part of a community when I worked there. Our grassroots approach had succeeded in many ways. People remembered me more as a friend than as an outside professional, partly because I had helped them solve their problems by working and living with them rather than imposing an arbitrary, predetermined solution as an external "expert."

Conclusions

From the results of my visit to Manteo, it seems fair to conclude that the Sacred Structure remains fixed in the collective awareness of residents. In many ways, our original plan has been preserved and nurtured and figures in local decision-making. This result suggests that the Sacred Structure is one useful tool for cultural heritage preservation, which too often in the past has been based on principles too abstract for public discussion and community action (Richter, 1983). Local people in Manteo indicated that the Sacred Structure had allowed the town to benefit from growth without losing its sense of community. The Sacred Structure was a significant factor in the planning and design decisions in Manteo. The result was a community development plan that permitted the town to benefit from tourism and at the same time protect fragile place-related institutions from tourist encroachment. The plan has encouraged continuous local control and remains a part of the ongoing debate about community change.

The Sacred Structure represents a valuable tool in social design, particularly in reconciling tourism with existing community mores and rituals. The use of a Sacred Structure inventory could be an important mechanism for any neighborhood or city that wishes to maintain valued lifestyles and places. The Sacred Structure helps people to understand overpowering economic development in relation to a specific place context. By guiding change in increments around sacred places, the Sacred Structure can help disperse those changes throughout the community, thereby making their potentially negative impacts more manageable. In addition, because of their smaller size, the projects are more likely to benefit the local community in terms of financing, employment, and humanly-scaled environments.

In most general terms, the Sacred Structure can help a community maintain its identity as it changes. One striking characteristic about Manteo is that it is not as unified visually as most towns that incorporated tourism. There remains a healthy tension between the town's traditional aesthetics reflected in Jule's Park and the more ordered designs of new development, particularly along the waterfront. To the extent that the built environment can reflect values, Manteo of 1988 looks very much like what its residents set out to make, and certainly the Sacred Structure has contributed to this success.

My visit to Manteo also suggests that the process of community development has innumerable unforeseen aspects that influence any plan over time. Political uncertainty particularly stands out; how it is to be dealt with so that a plan can stay on course is a major issue that designers and planners need to understand in greater detail. Aspects of a plan itself create unexpected secondary effects. In Manteo our insistence upon preserving the Sacred Structure led to some buildings significantly out of scale with the sacred places themselves. More importantly, the success of the overall plan in attracting tourism has contributed to the possibility of another phenomenon—gentrification—that we did not foresee when we conceived the original plan. Because the town was so depressed, we never thought that gentrification could escalate housing prices and threaten the very residents for whom the "Sacred Structure" was preserved.

This dilemma raises a troublesome question about social preservation: Can the protection of valued places reinforce inequitable social patterns such as economic or racial segregation? In some cases this may no doubt happen, just as in some instances, zoning and historic preservation have led to economic and social selectivity. Though black leaders did not speak of unfairness in relation to Manteo's development, they did point out that new strip development along the highway outside of town is more racially and economically integrated than in the village, where most of the Sacred Structure is located.

In communities with widespread injustices, the preservation of a sacred structure would likely prolong inequities. And in places trying to overcome a troubled past, or in suburban communities suffering from environmental anomie, identification of a sacred structure might be a painful and divisive effort. For many communities facing economic transition, however, the identification and preservation of a network of valued places may be a practical key for change that builds on, rather than destroys, the existing sense of community and place.

Notes

1. Portions of this article are based on Hester, 1986. Much of my thinking about the underlying community structure of small towns has evolved through discussion with Ed Blakely, Ted Bradshaw, Marcia McNally, Brian Scott and Billie Harper. The use of the Sacred Structure as design inspiration is described in Hester, 1986. An earlier version of this article appears in *Small Town* (January–February 1990), pp. 5–21.

2. This technique was developed by Billie B. Harper under the direction of Henry Sanoff at North Carolina State University. Five percent of Manteo's residents returned responses via mail or at a questionnaire drop at the town hall. In general, the sample reflected the town's demographic characteristics, though a random sample would no doubt have provided more representative results.

References

Coastal Times (1981). Editorial, September 24.

Gans, H. (1962). *The Urban Villagers.* New York: The Free Press.

Healy, K. and E. Zorn. (1983). Taquile's Homespun Tourism. *Natural History,* November, pp. 80–89.

Hester, Jr., R. (1975). *Neighborhood Space.* Stroudsburg, Pennsylvania: Dowden, Hutchinson and Ross.

——— . (1978). Warning: Ivory Tower Designers May Be Hazardous to Your Neighborhood's Health. *Landscape Architecture, 68* (3), 296–303.

——— . (1979). A Womb with a View. *Landscape Architecture, 69* (4), 475–481.

——— . (1980). Survey of Townspeople: Public Report One. Raleigh: North Carolina State University.

——— . (1981). Guide for Development: Public Report Three. Town of Manteo, North Carolina.

——— . (1984). *Planning Neighborhood Space with People.* New York: Van Nostrand Reinhold.

——— . (1985). Selling Landstyle and Lifescape for Economic Recovery: *Landscape Architecture, 75* (1), 78–85.

——— . (1986). Subconscious Landscapes of the Heart. *Places, 2* (3), 10–22.

——— . and McNally, M. (1983). Manteo, North Carolina, Avoids the Perils of Boom-or-Bust Tourism. *Small Town, 14* (3), 4–11.

Jordan, W. (1980). The Summer People and the Natives: Some Effects of Tourism on a Vermont Vacation Village. *Annals of Tourism Research, 7* (1), 34–35.

Kellogg, M. A. (1983). Can Native People Save Their Lands? *International Wildlife, 13* (2), 18–23.

Lynch, K. (1960). *The Image of the City.* Cambridge, Massachusetts: MIT Press.

McNally, M. (1983). *Guide for Development.* Berkeley: University of California Press.

Meinig, D. W. (ed.) (1979). *The Interpretation of Ordinary Landscapes.* New York: Oxford University Press.

Relph, E. (1976). *Place and Placelessness.* London: Pion.

Richter, L. K. (1983). Political Implications of Chinese Tourism Policy. *Annals of Tourism Research, 10* (3), 395–413.

School of Design. (1980). Summary of Interviews with Town's People. Raleigh: North Carolina State University.

Shepard, P. (1967). *Man in the Landscape: A Historic View of the Aesthetics of Nature.* New York: Knopf.

Stein, A. (1987). Landscape Elements of the Makam: Sacred Places in Israel. *Landscape Journal, 6* (2), 123–131.

Town of Manteo. (1981). Annual Tourist Impact Survey.

Town of Manteo. (1983). Annual Tourist Impact Survey.

Town of Manteo. (1986). Annual Tourist Impact Survey.

Tuan, Y. (1974). *Topophilia: A Study of Environmental Perception, Attitudes, and Values.* New York: Columbia University Press.

Chapter 13

Designing for a Commitment to Place: Lessons from the Alternative Community *Findhorn*

◻

Clare Cooper Marcus

Situated on the coast of rural northeastern Scotland, Findhorn is a small alternative community founded in 1962 (figure 13.1). Despite its inauspicious beginnings and periodic financial problems, Findhorn has survived to become one of the most famous intentional communities in the world. How many of us, as professional designers, have consciously introduced into our plans measures which we predict will "foster neighborliness" and "enhance a sense of community"? It behooves us to look more closely at places like Findhorn where community-building has been remarkably successful, and to address three important questions, which are the focus of this article: First, what social and organizational practices have lead to group cohesion at Findhorn? Second, what has been the contribution of the physical and designed environment to that sense of community? Third, what lessons might be learned from the study of such a "self-conscious" community for the design and programming of more ordinary residential settings?

A critical question in studying alternative communities like Findhorn relates to a conceptual approach: What organizational criteria does one use to discover pointers or lessons that might be useful for more typical residential planning and design? My conceptual approach is provided by Rosabeth Moss Kanter's *Commitment and Community*, a sociological study of nineteenth century utopian communities (Kanter, 1973). In this work, Kanter argues that a strong sense of commitment was integral to the successful communities she studied: "The problem of commitment is crucial. Since the community represents an attempt to establish an ideal social order within the larger society, it must vie with the outside for members'

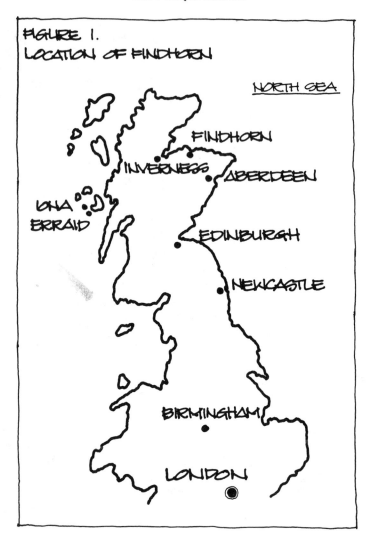

Figure 13.1. Location of Findhorn.

loyalty" (ibid., p. 65). Kanter argues that commitment forms the
crucial connection between self-interest and group-interest. She
identifies three crucial social structures that nurture and require
commitment: First, *retention of members* (people's willingness to
stay in the community); second, *group cohesiveness* (the ability of
people to develop collective strength and withstand threats to the
group's existence); and, third, *social control* (the readiness of people

to conform to the values and beliefs of the community). Through commitment, person and group become inextricably linked.

In her examination of several specific nineteenth century utopian communities, Kanter concludes that the success of those continuing for a long period of time required that abstract ideologies and visions be translated into everyday social patterns that solidified the strength and longevity of the community. These "commitment mechanisms," as she calls them, fostered community loyalty and, in general, were of six types:

1. Sacrifice, or giving up something valuable or pleasurable to belong to the group;

2. Investment, or commitment to the group;

3. Renunciation, or separation of oneself from outside society;

4. Communion, or sharing of work, decision-making and rituals;

5. Mortification, or submission to social control of the group;

6. Transcendence, or transference of decision-making to a power greater than one's self.

Here, I use Kanter's six mechanisms as a conceptual means for examining Findhorn's success as an alternative community. I am particularly interested in whether these mechanisms might relate to Findhorn's physical and designed environment, since such a connection might offer practical guidelines for more ordinary planning, particularly community design. The empirical evidence for my evaluating Findhorn on the basis of Kanter's six mechanisms comes from my own experiences with the community as well as from books and articles about Findhorn written by others (Caddy and Hollingshead, 1988; Doudna, 1987; Findhorn Community, 1975, 1980; Hall, 1987; Hawken, 1975; Inglis and Doudna, 1987; Slocombe, 1987).

I believe this evidence provides at least a preliminary base for considering Findhorn's twenty-five year success, particularly as this success may have policy and design implications. My personal familiarity with Findhorn extends over a ten-year period. I first visited for two weeks as a workshop guest in 1979. Returning over several summers, I eventually lived there with my two children for a year in 1983–1984. During that time, I worked and participated in the daily life of the community and eventually organized workshops and surveys on the future of Findhorn's housing and planning (Cooper

Marcus, 1984). I have returned every year since, and most recently coauthored a set of housing design guidelines for the community.

In this chapter, I first provide a background picture of Findhorn's evolution as an alternative community; second, I examine Findhorn in terms of Kanter's six commitment mechanisms; finally, I discuss lessons that Findhorn offers to community design, planning, and policy.

Findhorn, 1962–1988

Unlike many famous nineteenth century utopias, Findhorn was not consciously created but, rather, slowly evolved from simple, inauspicious beginnings. Three adults—Dorothy Maclean and Eileen and Peter Caddy—finding themselves unemployed in late 1962, moved with three small children to a mobile home, or "vacation caravan," near the Scottish fishing village of Findhorn. Despite poor sand-dune soils and lack of knowledge, the family planted a garden to raise food. For reasons that seemed inexplicable, given the circumstances, the garden flourished. For several years, they lived quietly, until news of the extraordinary garden spread. People began to visit, some wanting to stay to help expand the garden. The family served them meals in their already over-crowded caravan. Money was donated. Guest bungalows were erected and flower gardens planted. The Findhorn Community was born (figure 13.2).

As the Community grew, working groups, community finances and entry-procedures evolved. Soon, guests arrived who were at least as interested in experiencing the life of the Community as they were in helping with the original garden. Courses and workshops were offered. Findhorn evolved into an alternative educational setting, providing firsthand experience for approaching work, family, finances, health, and decision-making in new ways. Today, education is Findhorn's main function, and it takes place in two ways: first, as a place where new attitudes and lifestyles are demonstrated; second, as a center for more formal learning (Hall, 1987).

Guests were initially housed in rented caravans (figure 13.3), and classes were held in a nearby house. When the influx of visitors became too great for the caravan park, a large former hotel, renamed Cluny Hill College, was purchased in Forres, a town of about 7,000, four miles from the caravan park. Cluny has come to house short-term guests and young single members; private space is provided in bed-sitting rooms, while communal spaces include a dining

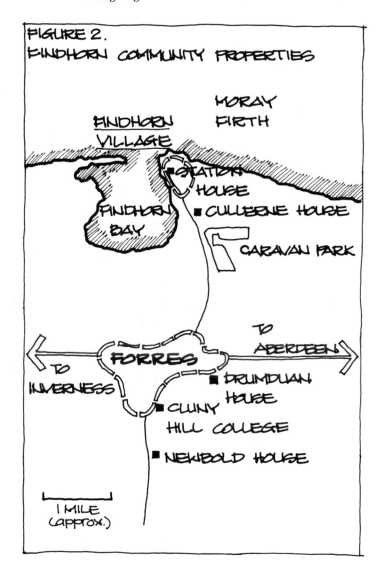

Figure 13.2. Findhorn community properties.

room, lounge, meditation sanctuary, sauna, library, bookshop, laundry, and meeting rooms. In contrast, the caravan park, now called "The Park," has come to house families and single middle-aged or elderly people, since the structures there have more private space than the hotel rooms at Cluny. Recently, the caravans are

Figure 13.3. Gardens flourish around the caravans that still form the heart of Find-horn, though these mobile homes are slowly being replaced by more permanent dwellings (see figure 13.4). Photographs by Clare Cooper Marcus.

being slowly replaced by more permanent dwellings, including some structures made from recycled whisky barrels (figure 13.4). Communal spaces at the Park include a community center, family house, laundry, bookshop, meeting rooms, café, apothecary, large auditorium, and two sanctuaries (figure 13.5).

As Findhorn grew, other properties within five miles of the park were purchased to provide for varying group size and privacy needs. Drumduan, an elegant mansion, provided bedroom spaces for eight singles or couples, plus shared kitchen, dining room and lounge; it has recently been converted into a school. Near the Park, the Station House, a former railway station and offices, houses fifteen adults and children in a number of semi-private flats, each with its own kitchen. Members who prefer a more typical housing situation tend to gravitate there. Further afield, Erraid, a small island off the west coast of Scotland, has been deeded to the community to manage, and up to fifteen adults and children live there in former lighthouse keepers' cottages.

Figure 13.4. New houses being built to replace mobile homes; building crew of community members and guests, summer 1990.

Figure 13.5. Annex to the Community Center completed in 1990; the structure includes a dining room and upper-level lounge.

Without any long-term plan specifically to create this situation, Findhorn has evolved into a multi-focused community, allowing members to seek out the most psychologically comfortable living situations and to move when circumstances change—for example, growing older, needing more time alone, or breaking up with a lover or spouse. Part of Findhorn's success no doubt stems from this diversity of accommodation, especially in contrast to some less successful communities documented by Kanter (1973). Findhorn today is in a period of rapid expansion; current groups, each known as a "family," are described in table 13.1. Permanent residents numbered 130 in April 1984; by 1988, membership had grown to 200. Asked to make an initial commitment of two years, members stay anywhere from two to ten years, with the mean stay presently being around four years. The demographic breakdown of membership in 1984 and 1988 is shown in table 13.2.

For people who want to experience Findhorn in a way other than full membership, other arrangements have evolved. People who want to stay longer than a one-week workshop but do not want

Table 13.1
"Families" within the Findhorn Community

Residence	Dwelling Type	Number Accommodated	Household Type	Date Acquired	Former Use
Caravan Park	Caravans and bungalows	150*	Singles, families, over-60s	1983	Originally a World War II Royal Airforce Base, then a tourist caravan park
Cluny Hill	Hotel/college dormitory	150*	Singles, couples	1975	Large vacation hotel and spa
Drumduan	Shared house	8	Singles, couples	1977	Private mansion
Cullerne	Shared house	6	Singles	1978	Private mansion
Newbold	Shared house	30	Singles couples, families	1980	Small hotel
Station House	Apartments	15	Singles, couples, families	1979	Railway station and offices
Island of Erraid	Row houses	10	Singles, couples, families	1978	Lighthouse keepers' cottages

*Members and guests at peak times

Table 13.2
Findhorn Membership, 1984 and 1988

	1984	1988
Single people (under sixty)	50%	34%
Two-parent families	29%	35%
Couples without children	8%	13%
Over sixty (singles and couples)	8%	7%
One-parent families	4%	10%

to commit themselves to membership are welcomed as "Living-in Community Guests." People who want to spend up to six months in the community doing research can do so as "Resident Scholars." A loose worldwide group of people who are committed Findhorn supporters and who work in academic, professional or activist settings are termed "Findhorn Fellows."

Findhorn's initial years were guided by the firm leadership of Peter Caddy, with many major decisions assisted by guidance that Eileen Caddy received during meditation (Caddy and Hollingshead, 1988). The governance of the community now rests in a nine-member "Core Group" that is composed of the managers, or "focalizers," of different work departments and living groups. Decision-making involves group consensus and requires family and community-wide meetings.

The most recent development in Findhorn's history is the gradual evolution of what might be called a "shadow" or satellite community around Findhorn proper. Possibly as many as two hundred people now live within a ten-mile radius. Originally invited as guests, some of these people want to share in certain community rituals such as meditation or shared meals, but do not want to make a full-time commitment. Others include long-time Findhorn members who decided they wanted more freedom, yet sought to remain within "calling distance" of the community. Many of these so-called "independent members" have established small businesses in construction, alternative technologies, computer programming, audio production, graphic design, wood carving, counseling and alternative health care. In 1987 these independent members formed their own loose-knit organization, "Open Forum," to foster mutual assistance, to maintain ties with the "mother" community, to debate how much they "owe" the community, what it should provide for them, and so on. The result is that the original distinctions between who is "in" and who is "out" of Findhorn have become less clear.

Writing of this new, potentially threatening situation, two long-time members and keen observers of the community note:

> The net consequence of this situation is that the community as a whole is experiencing not simply a renewed burst of energy, commitment and enthusiasm, but a virtual enactment of the creative tension between individuals and the collective, capitalism and communism which are in evidence in the world at large. Although these threatened for a period to divide the community no less than it has East and West, they also hold the potential and promise of enacting a creative synthesis between those essentially complementary polarities. (Inglis and Doudna, 1987).

Kanter's Commitment Mechanisms and Findhorn

I next want to consider Findhorn in relation to Kanter's six commitment mechanisms. In this way, one understands better the experiential and social structures that have allowed an alternative community like Findhorn to evolve and grow. I examine each mechanism in turn, first, in terms of its social and psychological aspects, then, in terms of the relationship between the mechanism and the physical environment.

Before analyzing Findhorn in relation to these six mechanisms, however, it is essential to be clear as to what kind of community Findhorn is. In considering alternative or intentional communities, Kanter made a useful distinction between *retreat* and *service* communities. A retreat community is one where members are drawn together principally by what they reject (urban life, technology, or the nuclear family, for example) rather then by a shared vision or ideology. Typically, such a community is rural, leaderless, lacking in formal structure, highly permeable as to its boundaries, and generally short-lived. It often resembles an extended family more than a utopian community, looks back nostalgically to a romanticized past, is anarchistic, easily dissolved, and predominantly youthful. In contrast, service communities are larger and more enduring; members are drawn to them because of shared ideological beliefs; the community provides some kind of service (therapeutic, educational, rehabilitative) to the wider society; their mission provides a focus around which to erect clear boundaries of membership; and they tend to have firm social structure of agreed-upon rules. Findhorn is clearly a service community, a fact that continually resurfaces as one examines Findhorn in terms of Kanter's six commitment mechanisms.

1. Sacrifice

As Kanter uses the term, sacrifice refers to the process of giving up something as a price of membership in a group; once a person has "sacrificed," the motivation to remain increases. An austere life style, devoid of the luxuries and comforts in the larger society, was often expected of those entering religious orders. In some successful nineteenth century utopias, severe forms of sacrifice were demanded in the form of abstinence—giving up luxuries, personal adornment, sexual relations, normal family life, and so on. Although the lifestyle at Findhorn may seem somewhat austere—and was much more so in the early years—no harsh rules exist. The only "rules" per se ban illegal drugs and smoking inside community buildings. Instead, Findhorn's primary form of sacrifice is financial. New members must pay 2,000 pounds for the first two years of residence. Subsequently selected as a Staff person, the member lives free and receives pocket money of seventy-five pounds per month. Staff now represent forty percent of the total resident membership. For many, the sacrifice of job security or a home sold to finance a stay at Findhorn is a real one. The sacrifice of not being paid directly for one's labor is weighed in people's minds against what they gain—membership in what they perceive as a supportive group with a powerful sense of vision.

Another significant form of sacrifice, experienced particularly by more mature members, is that of status or professional role. All members are expected to "start at the bottom," since work is perceived as an intrinsic part of spiritual learning. It is not unusual to find former professionals cleaning toilets or digging trenches. Members also give up a certain degree of privacy; at times, accommodation is so tight that members have to share rooms. Members also give up a certain amount of autonomy; for example, all agree to abide by community-determined work schedules. On the other hand, everything is "negotiable." In 1984, for example, the community decided to reduce the length of the work day from eight to seven hours in winter (when there are few guests), and to allow time off each week for creative work such as art, music and writing.

In turning to environmental aspects of sacrifice, one must look at Findhorn's residential accommodations. When asked in April 1984, "How satisfied are you with your current living situation?" those who regarded themselves as "very satisfied" ranged from eighty-eight percent on the Island of Erraid, to sixty-one percent of those living in large shared houses (Station House, Cullerne, Drumduan, Newbold), to thirty-eight percent of those living in hotel rooms at Cluny, to only eighteen percent of those living in caravans at the Park. The chief problems for both caravan and Cluny dwellers were lack of space, privacy and storage, and inadequate winter heating. Not only is the northern climate harsh, but space availability and indoor winter temperatures are below those expected by many residents, especially North Americans.

Although most members, according to the 1984 survey, feel that the advantages of the community far outweigh the difficult living conditions, one of the most salient aspects of sacrifice experienced today at Findhorn is the less-than-ideal living arrangements and frequent moves required of some members because of visitor accommodation needs during the spring and summer. Financial and architectural strategies to build for the future have met with resistance both from outside Findhorn (the fear of radical or "unseemly" designs) and from inside (the unwillingness to make further sacrifices of labor and money). People who leave to become "independent" members do so partially to regain financial independence but also to live in more comfortable settings. Ironically, the difficulties of building new and more comfortable accommodations *within* the Community may be in part fueled by a vague recognition that relative deprivation does seem to be a commitment-building mechanism.

Making a point relevant no doubt to Findhorn's future, Kanter notes that all the successful nineteenth century utopias she studied *did* construct their own buildings: "Not only do the struggles and austerity involved foster commitment, but at the end of the labor the community has physical symbols of its communal effort, structures invested with all that the members have given up to make them possible" (p. 79). Although most of the members' living accommodations at Findhorn have been purchased "as is"—that is, as caravans, hotels and other building types—several significant *communal* spaces were designed and built by community members: the Universal Hall (auditorium, café, sound and dance studios); the Family House (lounge space and kitchen that can be reserved for birthday parties and meetings); and the Community Center at the Park (dining and social space).

These building projects involved considerable sacrifice, and long-time members speak with mixed feelings about the drain on financial and human energy required by building the Universal Hall. At the same time, most members are immensely proud of the result. With its peaked, rock-covered roof, pentagonal footprint, and its outer stone walls that are mortarless, this building is a striking feature in the community landscape and, architecturally, is the heart of the community. The hall hosts community-wide meetings, concerts and film shows, and festivals open to the public. A smaller, twelve-sided, copper-roofed building for extra dining and social space was added to the Community Center in 1987–1988 (figure 13.5). The excitement that this building process engendered for builders and onlookers also confirms Kanter's observation that whatever sacrifice is involved in a community building is more than offset by the resulting sense of connection and commitment to the group.

2. Investment

Kanter points out that the investment of time, energy and money can also contribute to community commitment. In one sense, investment is closely related to sacrifice and is inextricably bound up with it. The more one sacrifices—in terms of comfort, privacy, labor, savings, and autonomy—the more one invests in a group and, therefore, the more bound to it he or she is likely to become. Some successful nineteenth century utopias demanded that new members transfer all property and savings to the group. Often, this investment was irreversible (Kanter, 1973).

No such rules exist at Findhorn; in fact, some members come with inherited wealth or a small private income and lead slightly more comfortable lives than others. Most members, however, see their investment in terms of time and energy rather than as a monetary commitment. Indeed, the word "energy" is used far more frequently in conversation at Findhorn than at any other place I have lived. The investment of energy in maintaining and extending the community has a powerful effect on group commitment, just as the investment of an individual or family in cleaning, maintaining, modifying, and personalizing a home is a physical token of commitment. In the case of both a community and single family, the fact that this labor and energy are unpaid monetarily points to further commitment.

In this regard, it is important to point out that daily cleaning at Findhorn is termed "housecare" rather than housework. In 1988, the term had shifted to "homecare." Guests, who often start their work experience in this department, are gently taught to see the cleaning of a bathtub or vacuuming of the dining room carpet as acts of loving care rather than as mindless repetitions of required work. Frequently emphasized at Findhorn is that "Work is love in action." In this respect, Findhorn's philosophy has much in common with the teachings of Zen Buddhism.

When one approaches physical labor in this way, the acts of cleaning and maintaining the environment become powerful connectors to community, both via the physical environment itself and via the camaraderie of work groups. On special days in the year, the whole community works on one task together—for example, preparing mailings, planting trees, or doing spring cleaning. From my observations at Findhorn, these events are probably the most group-enhancing experiences, recalling the barn-raisings of early frontier America.

3. Renunciation

Successful nineteenth century utopias such as Amana, Oneida, and the Shaker communities had relatively fixed or impermeable social and organizational boundaries. People were permitted to join if they espoused the belief of the group or met certain criteria for membership. The same is true at Findhorn. The only ways in which a visitor can "enter" the community are via a two-hour daily guided tour that was first offered in the early 1970s, or via "Findhorn Experience Week," a highly structured residential workshop of "initiation" first offered in 1974. Thereafter, a guest can participate in other workshops or become a temporary resident, or "Living-in Community Guest." Any person who then elects to become a permanent resident or "Family Member" must be approved by the Personnel Department and join a group of three new members for a two-month orientation program. Selection of new members involves a painstaking process of mutual evaluation in which the prospective member and long-term residents consider whether this step is beneficial for all. The new member must be deemed to have the "right" psychological and spiritual maturity, and must also have funds to pay for room and board for the first two years.

Though Findhorn does not ask new residents to cut their ties with the outside, membership does involve some level of "renunciation," especially in situations where family, friends or colleagues may express skepticism. Most successful utopian communities—

Findhorn included—insulate themselves from the outside by providing for almost every aspect of members' lives *within* the group.
Not only do Findhorn members work in and for the community, but
it also provides them with meals, entertainment, local transportation, spiritual teaching, and alternative medical services.

Another form of renunciation is ensuring that energy and work
are directed *to* the group rather than to a family or spouse. In many
nineteenth century utopias, two-person intimacy was seen to
present a threat to group cohesiveness, and it was discouraged by
either celibacy or group marriage. Neither is embraced at Findhorn, although couples experience subtle conflicts between the demands of the group and those of an intimate relationship. Many
members complain that there is not enough time for close friendships, due to the pressure of daily work schedules, the relative brev-
ity and noisiness of communal meals, and so forth. To find time to
be together, friends often leave the community temporarily, taking
a walk or going to a local pub or café.

Many of the successful nineteenth century utopias studied by
Kanter used special living arrangements to focus attention away
from the nuclear family to the community-as-family. The Shakers,
for example, had separate male and female households; at Oneida,
children were separated from parents. No such arrangements exist
or were ever contemplated at Findhorn. Single people have their
choice of living at Cluny, the Park or one of several large manor
houses where eight to twelve people create a "family unit." Married
couples are assigned larger rooms at Cluny or can live in a caravan
at the Park. Couples with children occupy caravans or bungalows at
the Park or reside in an apartment at Station House. Each couple
has a space that is private from other families or single people,
though it is generally limited in size and comfort. If anything, families seem to welcome the attention both demanded of and given by
the group; it is often the isolation of the family in the outside world
which has "pushed" them towards Findhorn in the first place. Undoubtedly, one of the benefits at Findhorn is the *variety* of living arrangements. As circumstances change, one can, within reason, find
an alternate living situation somewhere else in the community.

The practice of rearing children separately to foster group loyalty, embraced by many successful nineteenth century utopias and
some modern communities and kibbutzim, has never been part of
life at Findhorn. When a couple has a child, the community supports one parent's staying at home during the child's infancy.
Though in earlier years the woman stayed home, now the respon-

sibilities of child rearing are generally shared by both parents. Although a community pre-school exists for children between three and five, child care for smaller children is less well organized at Findhorn than in many ordinary communities. Since, however, many of the tasks normally performed by parents are carried out by the community—food purchasing, cooking, maintenance, transportation—the task of child rearing is considerably eased, especially for the single parent. In addition, the facts that few people own automobiles and that everyone knows everyone else is conducive to childrens' safety and to their exploring the environment on their own at an early age.

In terms of the outside world, successful utopias of the past were frequently located in remote settings to minimize contact with the larger society, which was sometimes viewed as contaminating. Though no one at Findhorn regards the "outside world" as something to be shunned, most members regard Findhorn's remote location as fortuitous, since people must make considerable effort to get there. It may well be that such a radical social experiment, even in the mid-twentieth century, can only survive through a fair degree of geographic isolation.

In regard to Findhorn's relationship with the local Scottish community, the boundary between "inside" and "outside" was bolstered in the early years by the introversion of Findhorn and the suspiciousness of locals. Over time, social boundaries have relaxed as local people are invited to Findhorn events and as Findhorn members become familiar to locals through the businesses they have set up in the community, personal relationships, and so forth. Two important factors for intra-community trust are a Findhorn-run Rudolf Steiner school located in Forres and welcoming all children; and the Youth Project, which involves teenagers from both Findhorn and the Scottish Community.

4. Communion

Communion, as Kanter defines it, refers to the formal and informal means by which members increasingly feel a sense of togetherness. For a group to coalesce there is first some commonality in shared values. At Findhorn this commonality is present, since people are drawn to the community rather than recruited, and potential members are rejected if they seem out of harmony with Findhorn's underlying philosophy. Without planning it to be, the community has evolved as predominantly white and middle-class, although Findhorn's members vary widely in age, educational level, nationality, and life experience. What links members together sociologically is a relative disinterest in material wealth or possessions, and a compelling concern for spiritual exploration and "world service."

Shared work is another important experience of "groupness" at Findhorn. The community is divided into work departments (kitchen, garden, maintenance, personnel, and so on), each with a manager, or "focalizer." The work day runs from nine in the morning to five in the evening, and work assignments are rotated— frequently for guests so that they can get an experience of many aspects of the community and less often for members who direct the long-term aims of work departments. Job rotation largely eliminates the concept of status or career, and allows members to expand their experience in jobs they might not encounter otherwise. In addition to work, many regular occurrences reinforce a sense of group—regular dining together in the community center; voluntary daily meditations in the sanctuary attended by approximately one-third of Findhorn members; weekly community meetings that discuss future policy and planning; and Friday night talent shows or "sharings." There are also special ceremonies to celebrate marriages, equinoxes and solstices, and special dates in community or national history—for example, Guy Fawkes Day, the Fourth of July, and the November founding of Findhorn. Collective participation in these events also fosters a sense of community (figure 13.6).

Writing of the role of the arts in the community, a long-time member who is a playwright, script-writer, and actor, notes that a vital function is to "mirror [Findhorn's] follies and fear. Pride, self-righteousness, and fascism are among the greatest threats to any spiritual community and one way that these negative forces can be successfully defused is by the ability of any community to laugh at itself. There is a strong and healthy tradition at Findhorn of self-mockery through skits and satires." In an annual play, "the sacred cows and concerns of the years are put up for public ridicule" (Slocombe, 1987). Though Findhorn is an international and polyglot community, this particular use of humor as a community-enhancing medium is very much rooted in British culture.

In regard to the physical environment, an important part of communion is the ways that Findhorn members encounter each other informally. Do frequent, casual meetings nurture Findhorn's sense of community, and are they enhanced by a relatively dense, pedestrian environment? In my community-wide survey of April

Figure 13.6. Celebrating the autumn equinox with sacred dances and group meditation.

1984, I asked members who lived or worked in the Park where they most frequently "bumped into" other Findhorn members and stopped to chat (table 13.3). The building most prominent in responses was the Community Center, which houses the community dining room and a small lounge. Respondents also mentioned the importance of such activities as social events at Universal Hall, picking up mail and messages in a small reception building, getting food at the foodshed, looking for secondhand clothes at "the Boutique," or just "walking around the neighborhood."

Ironically, the amount of contact generated by these numerous casual encounters is not always reinforced by adequate private space where friendships can be pursued more directly. Rooms and caravans are barely adequate for day-to-day living, let alone entertaining. When asked, "Where/how do you get together with special friends," forty-five percent of the respondents said "At my house, or in my room," but the remaining fifty-five percent mentioned other ways of meeting, such as "a drink at the pub" (twenty-six percent), "going for a walk" (seventeen percent"), or "at work," "at classes," "theater rehearsals", "on the bus," and "at the sauna" (the remaining

Table 13.3
Where Do You Most Frequently "Bump Into"
People and Stop for a Brief Chat?

Location	Percentage who responded Often	Sometimes
Communal meals at the Community Center	86	13
Communal lounge at the Community Center	63	32
Social events at Universal Hall	60	30
Reception building (mail, messages, phone)	57	33
Entrance to Community Center	56	41
Walking around neighborhood	54	43
At work	51	28
Foodshed or boutique	41	34
Community bookshop	32	52
Community laundry	4	22

twelve percent). Of those respondents who did invite friends home, most lived in caravans or bungalows, and fifty-three percent rated their space as "barely adequate" or "quite inadequate" for entertaining. As one respondent described the situation in 1984, "I would like our lifestyle to change so there is more time to nourish relationships. My greatest social contact is either on paths to and from work, at work, or eating at the Community Center. . . . I would like part of the dining room to be a place where people could choose to eat in silence; and another part to be a more comfortable lounge, where social contact can take place." Such a lounge was completed in 1988.

As Hayden (1976) explained in her study of successful nineteenth century utopias, the right balance of shared and private spaces is critical to the success of community. Findhorn is slowly discovering that crucial balance. Because the community began, incongruously, in a caravan park, the original dwellings in what is still the heart of the community are mobile homes, some enlarged to bungalows. In the early years, meals were prepared by the Caddy family and served to residents and guests. As numbers grew, the Community Center was built, and the tradition of eating meals together continued. As table 13.3 indicates, the Community Center is still the most highly communal space at the Caravan Park.

In terms of members' needs to have privacy at the Park in the midst of Findhorn's communal atmosphere, three mechanisms are important: First, each caravan or bungalow has a kitchen, and breakfast—perhaps the most "private" meal of the day—is eaten at home; second, those members who eat community-prepared food but prefer to dine privately may take food home from the Community Center; and third, those members, mostly elderly, who never eat communally, may obtain foodstuffs from the community's food shed to do their own cooking. For Findhorn, such options for maintaining privacy are crucial, since differing psyches, changes in mood, and the needs of age lead to differing degrees of tolerance for "togetherness."

Findhorn also provide options regarding ownership. Kanter points out that in all successful nineteenth century utopias, property was held in common. This approach is the case for all the community buildings and most of the living accommodations at Findhorn. As in earlier communities, the assumption is that members will have more time for spiritual growth when most of their material welfare is taken care of by the group. As with communal meals, however, there are options, thus many older members own their own bungalows, while some families with children own cottages in the nearby village of Findhorn. Though it might have threatened the cohesion of Oneida or the Shaker communities, this flexibility in regard to property ownership seems appropriate for the late-twentieth century. It suggests that the Findhorn community can attune itself to the times, recognizing the value of new and different forms of commitment to the group.

5. Mortification

To enhance group purity and cohesiveness, members of many nineteenth century religious communities were expected to confess their "sins," sometimes in the form of mutual criticism. In modern-day alternative communities like Findhorn, such coercive rituals generally do not exist, but there are still subtle means by which separate, private unconnected egos are directed toward group norms. Many people are drawn to Findhorn because they feel their lives to be lacking and their selves to be only partially evolved. The mortification that they experience through identity change is now termed "personal growth." At Findhorn, psychological and communal issues are discussed in a variety of ways. One context is weekly meetings called "attunements," which are organized in terms of each work department. There are also community-sponsored workshops on such topics as dream interpretation, masculine-feminine energies, and spiritual healing. Last, there is "The Game of Transformation," an intense, esoteric board game that confronts players with lifelong patterns of relating to others, the world and their higher selves. Though such activities might be criticized for being narcissistic, they assure the individual that the group cares about his or her thoughts and feelings. These group experiences facilitate an openness and trust among group members that enables the individual to contemplate discarding old patterns and to seek a stronger, more holistic image of self. Many members and guests move out from the community after profound personal experiences, often seeking ways through social activism and environmental politics to foster transformation at a societal or global scale.

Environmentally, this commitment-building process of self-discovery is enhanced by the many small meeting rooms at Cluny, where work departments ranging in size from four to twelve people can meet regularly with some degree of privacy. Also important are larger meeting rooms at Cluny and The Park for classes and group experiences. Finally, there are four meditation sanctuaries, each with seating circles focused on a low central table on which there are flowers and a single candle. Three times a day, these sanctuaries house non-verbal group meditations that are often powerful collective experiences.

For some people, solitude is the best way to deal with personal and spiritual needs. There are several solitary places nearby: next to Cluny is a beautiful pine and beech forest with many trails; within walking distance of the Park are the tidal shores of Findhorn Bay and ocean beaches on the Moray Firth; a weekly community bus service takes members and guests to a retreat house on the remote island of Iona on the west coast of Scotland, or to the nearby community-managed island of Erraid where visitors can rest or join in farming tasks at their own pace. This pattern of distant retreat from Findhorn echoes an observation of Hayden (1976), who points out that successful nineteenth century utopias sometimes sanctioned vacations and retreats to distant community properties. Oneida, for example, maintained a sloop on the Hudson River and a cottage on Long Island (ibid., p. 61).

While processes encouraging critical self-reflection characterized successful nineteenth century utopias, as they do Findhorn today, another set of behaviors—Kanter terms them "de-individuation mechanisms"—encourages the relinquishing of self-interest by removing differences among people and eliminating "the loneliness of individual separateness" (Kanter, 1973, p. 110). Although members were necessarily required in Findhorn's early days to live in close proximity and to eat meals communally, these practices continue today because they enhance a sense of community. Independent members, when negotiating with the community about their continued connections, often choose to come to a certain number of meals at the Community Center. The noise and lack of privacy at group mealtime is seen as one sacrifice for the benefits of group membership. For many Findhorn residents, excessive privacy in the form of isolation, alienation, or lack of family was the very thing that drew them toward community life in the first place.

6. Transcendence

Martin Buber (1958) defined transcendence as "the need of man to feel his own house as a room in some greater, all-embracing structure in which he is at home, to feel that the other inhabitants of it with whom he lives and works are all acknowledging and confirming his individual existence" (p. 140). If mortification involves "detaching," or a submission to a power greater than self, transcendence involves "attaching," or transferring some decision-making to a power greater than the self. Buber argues that the utopian impulse inevitably involves transcendence—"a longing for that rightness which, in religious and philosophical vision, is experienced as revelation or idea, and which of its very nature cannot be realized in the individual, but only in human community" (ibid., p. 147). Transcendence becomes manifest by some sense of power, meaning or awe residing in a community and often recognized via special qualities in its founders.

Many successful communities of the past have had charismatic leaders who engendered a sense of transcendence: for example, Ann Lee of the Shakers or George Rapp of Harmony. At Findhorn, a sense of charisma was associated with the three original founders and the garden. Eileen Caddy was the receiver of inner guidance; Dorothy Maclean was in tune with the spirits of nature; and Peter Caddy was the person of organization and action, without whom the community could never have been built. In 1970, the arrival of David Spangler, a charismatic intellectual leader, prompted a sudden growth in the community. By the end of his three-year stay, the community had expanded to close to 120 members.

As Kanter points out, some nineteenth century communities disintegrated as soon as the original founder left or died, but this has not happened at Findhorn. David Spangler left in 1973 to continue his work in the United States; Dorothy Maclean left in 1975 to continue her spiritual work in her native Canada; and Peter Caddy, who separated from Eileen in 1980, now resides in Germany. Though Eileen continues to live at Findhorn and is a much respected figure, she has little to do with the day-to-day running of the community, which is now delegated to a "Core Group," as it is called. In short, Findhorn has a life and structure of its own which seems to continue without the presence of charismatic leaders. To a large extent, the transcendence experienced in the early years through contact with the community's founders, is now experienced through transformative workshops and group experiences.

Writing of the process of psychological growth and change that seems to happen to many Findhorn visitors and residents, a long-time member described the community as "a place where the soul may be experienced" (Doudna, 1987, p. 12). After "Findhorn Experience Week," a structured introduction to the community, people almost uniformly feel themselves to be "transformed . . . They experience themselves as part of a group wherein the sense of separate self is fused with something greater than themselves whose welfare is integrally linked with their own . . . they seem to have been touched by a kind of spiritual power . . . this process has been characterized as a "soul awakening' . . ." (ibid.)

This experience, which echoes Buber's definition of transcendence, is one which seems to heighten an awareness of—and commitment to—both personal and societal change. Although Findhorn adheres to no central teaching, dogma or philosophy, a perusal of titles in Findhorn's two community bookstores leaves a visitor with no doubts about the shared ideology at Findhorn. These beliefs embrace mysticism, feminism, ecology, community, Eastern philosophies, personal growth, alternative economics, holistic health, organic gardening, alternative technology and spiritual exploration rather than specific spiritual doctrines or traditions. Overall, members seek a more holistic view of self, society, and the environment.

Intrinsic to a comprehension of the place called "Findhorn" is an understanding of its interconnections with a global network of individuals, groups, communities, and growth centers that has emerged in the last two decades to espouse a similar holistic philosophy of life and evolution, loosely termed "New Age." Not grounded in any organization, creed or political party, the New-Age movement is united principally by common attitudes and values. Russell (1982) has identified four recurring themes in New Age thinking: first, the existence of human potentials beyond those people generally use; second, the recognition that humanity and the environment are one interconnected system; third, the understanding that current ways of living mistreat both people and their surroundings; forth, an optimistic belief that humanity *can* change for the better. Requiring a profound shift in the human sense of self, this new world view is "holistic, non-exploitative, ecologically sound, long-term, global, peaceful, humane and cooperative" (ibid., p. 115). This new world view also requires a deep and widespread shift in consciousness, and New-Age proponents such as Russell (1982), Thompson (1973, 1978) and Capra (1982) believe that communities such as Findhorn play a crucial part in kindling and strengthening this new perspective.

All the successful communities that Kanter studied had shared ideologies, and all legitimated demands made on members by reference to some higher principle such as justice, the will of the people, the will of nature, or the will of God (Kanter, 1973, p. 115). Findhorn began with a small group who were all long-time students of meditation. Startled during meditation by apparent "messages" from plants struggling in the group's meager, recently planted sand-dune garden, Peter, Eileen and Dorothy did what the messages asked them, and the garden flourished. These events set the stage for seeking guidance through individual and group meditations—a practice that continues at Findhorn today. Members' opinions vary widely as to whether the meditative guidance is common sense, inspiration, intuition, or the word of God; all members would probably agree that personal and group decisions empowered by intuitive guidance create more successful outcomes than those emanating solely from linear thinking grounded in the ego. This belief is another aspect of Findhorn's holistic approach: to make decisions *only* via rational deduction is to use only half of one's capabilities. Reason and intuition need to be balanced.

Although successful nineteenth century utopian communities undoubtedly evoked a sense of charisma once established, Findhorn is unusual in that it was the place itself which seemingly "called" the group into being. Virtually everyone who visits the community has heard of the "Findhorn Garden." Though it no longer produces the forty-pound cabbages that brought attention to the community in its early days, the garden still has a magical quality of peace and attunement with nature. As I studied the "sacred places" within the community, virtually everyone I interviewed named "the original garden" as a space that must never be altered, despite the fact that it now produces a very small proportion of the community's food and is squeezed among various community buildings.

Findhorn is unique among former or present-day utopias, in that its birth came about through an intense, intuitive interaction between people and place. Unlike some nineteenth century utopian communities like the Shakers', Findhorn has no desire to proselytize or create similar communities, though a few have evolved, including Chinook and Sirius in the United States; and Homeland in Australia. Though these communities have each been successful in its own way, none has the charisma of Findhorn. A significant reason is the transcendence inherent in Findhorn *as a place*. Some believe its location on a peninsula surrounded on three sides by water, and the consequent proliferation of negative ions in the air, may have something to do with the benign experience of place. Others consider the long history of meditation and communication with nature in this location to have somehow created a tangible presence or "spirit of place" which a newcomer can experience. Whatever the reason, more than three thousand guests come to Findhorn each year, most having seen a television program or having read a book or article about the community. Perhaps having made personal sacrifices to come, a guest's first sight of the gardens and caravan park can be akin to a spiritual experience in itself. Such is the transcendent quality attached to this community.

Lessons for Environmental Design

Having discussed Findhorn in relation to Kanter's six commitment-building mechanisms, I next want to ask what lessons might be learned for the programming and design of more ordinary residential environments. Table 13.4 summarizes the six mechanisms as they apply to Findhorn in regard to social-psychological and environmental aspects. I argue that many of these characteristics also describe successful pre-planned residential settings in the everyday world. To illustrate this argument, I first consider one specific residential setting—St. Francis Square in San Francisco. I compare this community with Findhorn and then offer some general guidelines.

Sponsored in the late 1950s by the International Longshore Workers Union, St. Francis Square is a moderate-income cooperative of 300 units, comprising part of a redevelopment area in San Francisco known as the Western Addition (Cooper Marcus and Hackett, 1968). Apartments are in three-story buildings arranged around three landscaped courtyards, which turn their backs on the adjacent busy streets. Residents are heterogeneous by age, family structure, and ethnic background, but homogeneous in terms of a lifestyle embracing urban living and neighborly co-operation. St. Francis Square has very low turnover; new members are selected according to financial viability and ethnic background. There is an informal "quota" system to maintain an approximate balance among white, black and Asian residents. By all accounts—resident satisfaction, financial viability, longevity of tenure, design awards—this is a successful community (Cooper Marcus, 1971).

When one looks at the success of both Findhorn and St. Francis Square, there are some remarkable parallels, especially in terms of environmental aspects. Many residents at St. Francis Square consider their apartments as less than ideal, but feel the total community environment—especially the lush landscaping—more than makes up for small kitchens, lack of dining rooms, and lack of private garages (Cooper Marcus, 1971). In addition, a variety of unit sizes allow residents to move as family composition changes. The pedestrian scale of St. Francis Square is also important to its success, since frequent casual encounters occur in the laundries, play areas, parking lots, and so on. Banning cars to the periphery helps to create a safe environment for children; in fact, one of the goals of the client was to create a setting for raising children that was an alternative to suburbia. The on-site manager's office provides a convenient setting for frequent co-op committee meetings, and an adjacent elementary school provides auditorium space for large resident meetings. Residents participate in most management and maintenance decisions, and the gardeners and maintenance personnel employed by the co-op are frequently residents. Since all residents are part-owners, there is a strong commitment to maintaining the environment; the efforts of "The Yard Birds," a volunteer group of St. Francis Square residents, have resulted in numerous improvements to the landscaping, play equipment, fencing, and other parts of the physical environment.

In comparing Findhorn and St. Francis Square in terms of Kanter's six commitment mechanisms, one notes immediately that mortification and transcendence are not applicable, since St. Francis Square as a community does not involve personal growth or spiritual values. In considering, however, the environmental aspects of Kanter's other four mechanisms—sacrifice, investment, renunciation and communion—one notes a series of parallels: volunteer efforts strengthening a sense of togetherness; individual ownership supporting a sense of attachment; a variety of settings ameliorating other less attractive environmental features; a pedestrian-scaled

Table 13.4
Kanter's Six Commitment Mechanisms Applied to Findhorn

Mechanism	Social-Psychological Aspects	Environmental Aspects
1. Sacrifice	• Austerity • Use of savings • Loss of status	• Less-than-ideal living conditions enhance unity through shared adversity • Unpaid labor for constructing buildings reinforces commitment • No personal equity in property strengthens attachment to group
2. Investment	• Labor • Energy • Savings	• Cleaning and maintaining environment enhances a strong sense of care • "Barn-raising" efforts strengthen group-consciousness • Personalizing private space allows individuals to retain a sense of uniqueness
3. Renunciation	• Commitment to membership and group • Institutional completeness	• Variety of settings permits choice of living arrangements • Lack of traffic and communal lifestyle promotes relative ease of child rearing • Maintenance of symbolic boundaries reinforces a sense of inside and outside • Remote location insures that only committed individuals arrive and stay

4. Communion	• Homogeneity of values • Shared work • Group meditations • Shared meals • Community meetings • Weekly "Sharing"	• Buildings and meeting spaces support group experiences (eating, decision-making, meditation, entertainment, celebration) • Movement based largely on walking; community-run bus service facilitates many casual encounters • Meeting spaces enhance work of personal growth in groups • Purpose-built sanctuaries support group meditations
5. Mortification	• Commitment to personal and spiritual growth	• Natural settings inspire contemplative walking • Accessibility to remote retreats allows for periodic "escape" from community
6. Transcendence	• Charisma of original founders • Connections to worldwide movement for personal and societal changes	• Charisma of "Findhorn Garden" still prevails • Special attractions of environmental setting inspirational to many

place facilitating informal interaction; and a built environment supporting community experiences.

There are also several parallels relating to the negative aspects of each place: conflict over philosophical direction and financial policies; subtle tensions between family and group loyalties; a relative lack of privacy; a degree of envy or suspicion aroused in neighbors by the tight introversion of the group setting; conflicts over group control of equity-labor investment. In both cases, however, the positive aspects of community living appear to outweigh the negatives. Just as important, if residents of either community are not satisfied, they have the freedom to leave.

What can clients and designers of new residential settings learn from Findhorn as I have interpreted it in terms of Kanter's six commitment mechanisms? I believe that my interpretation offers some general guidelines that should serve as a foundation for preliminary planning and design. They are:

1. A community has to have some degree of shared values.

2. Residents may accept dwellings that are less than ideal (in terms of space, privacy, and amenities) if, in return, they have access to quality communal facilities for play, recreation, entertainment, and so forth.

3. A stake in management decisions and in the maintenance of the environment may enhance a sense of community commitment.

4. A pedestrian-oriented environment enhances child rearing and has the potential to facilitate casual social encounters.

5. Environmental and organizational boundaries foster a sense of membership in the group.

6. A diversity of living arrangements enhances people's ability to stay in the community as family circumstances change.

7. A variety of meeting spaces provides convenient settings for different aspects of group decision making.

8. A beautiful setting—especially in terms of nature and landscape—has the potential for fostering affection and pride among residents.

If one could weigh them in balance, the social, psychological, and organizational components of Findhorn no doubt have more impact on its palpable sense of community than does its physical environment, and the same could probably be said of St. Francis Square. This relative worth, however, does not deny the significance of the physical environment, especially in the ways it subtly or directly enhances the social purposes of the group.

This essay has considered one modern alternative community in terms of those components that prompted success in other earlier utopian communities. Then I briefly looked at one urban, non-alternative community in terms of social and environmental parallels with Findhorn. The next step would be to consider a greater range of alternative and non-alternative communities to verify, correct and hone the environmental components that support and strengthen a successful sense of community. By being aware of these components *before* programming and design, policy-makers, planners, and designers would have available a sphere of possibilities well tested in the successes and failures of real-world communities, both ordinary and alternative.

References

Buber, M. (1958). *Paths in Utopias,* trans. R. F. C. Hull. Boston: Beacon Press.

Caddy, E. and L. Hollingshead (1988). *Flight into Freedom.* Shaftesbury, U.K.: Element Books, Ltd.

Capra, F. (1982). *The Turning Point.* New York: Simon and Schuster.

Cooper Marcus, C. (1971). St. Francis Square: Attitudes of its Residents, *AIA Journal,* December.

————. (1984). Visions for the Future: Housing and Planning at Findhorn—Results of a Membership Survey, unpublished mimeo.

Cooper Marcus, C. and Hackett, P. (1968). Analysis of the Design Process at Two Moderate Income Housing Developments. Working Paper No. 80, Center for Planning and Development Research. Berkeley: University of California.

Doudna, R. (1987). Psychology, Human Growth and Change at Findhorn, *Findhorn Today,* paper prepared for New Synthesis Think Tank Conference, New York City, October 1987.

Findhorn Community (1975). *The Findhorn Garden: Pioneering a New Vision of Man and Nature in Cooperation.* New York: Harper and Row.

———— (1980). *Faces of Findhorn: Images of a Planetary Family.* New York: Harper and Row.

Hall, C. (1987). Education at Findhorn, a paper prepared for the New Synthesis Think Tank Conference, New York City, October.

Hayden, D. (1976). *Seven American Utopias: The Architecture of Communitarian Socialism, 1790–1975.* Cambridge Massachusetts: MIT Press.

Hawken, P. (1975). *The Magic of Findhorn.* New York: Harper and Row.

Inglis, M. and R. Doudna, (1987). Work and Vocation, a paper prepared for the New Synthesis Think Tank Conference, New York City, October.

Kanter, R. M. (1973). *Commitment and Community: Communes and Utopias in Sociological Perspective.* Cambridge, Massachusetts: Harvard University Press.

Russell, P. (1982). *The Awakening Earth: The Global Brain.* London: Routledge and Kegan Paul.

Slater, P. (1970). *The Pursuit of Loneliness.* Boston: Beacon Press.

Slocombe, J. (1987). The Plausible Impossible: The Arts as Community Oracle, a paper prepared for the New Synthesis Think Tank Conference, New York City, October.

Thompson, W. I. (1973). *Passages About Earth.* New York: Harper and Row.

Thompson, W. I. (1987). *Darkness and Scattered Light.* New York: Anchor/Doubleday.

Chapter 14

Promoting a Foundational Ecology Practically Through Christopher Alexander's Pattern Language: The Example of Meadowcreek[1]

◻

Gary J. Coates
and
David Seamon

Phenomenology is a critical, descriptive science, the heart of which is concern, perseverance, and clear seeing (Spiegelberg, 1982). A primary focus of phenomenological work is a description of human experience and behavior *as they are lived.* The belief is that careful, extended looking at everyday meanings and events as people live and experience them leads to a more lucid picture of who and what we are as human beings. In this way, the theories, models, and concepts of social and behavioral science may become more in touch with human meanings, actions, and experiences as they are in the world of everyday life (Polkinghorne, 1983). One value of phenomenological insights to the designer is that through them he or she may become more sensitive to human environmental experience and therefore create buildings and places more in tune with the essential nature of our humanness (Norberg-Schulz, 1985).

In the last decade, phenomenological research particularly useful for design has focused on the topics of environmental ethics and environmental behavior (Seamon, 1982; Seamon and Mugerauer, 1985; Seamon, 1987). Largely basing their work on the German phenomenological philosopher Martin Heidegger (1971), scholars such as Relph (1976, 1981), Zimmerman (1983, 1985) and Grange (1977) have asked how people can understand and act toward the environment in a more caring, respectful way (also see Evernden, 1985; Foltz, 1984; Norberg-Schulz, 1985).

Foundational ecology is the term that Grange (1977) gives this concernful attitude toward the environment. In the last two

decades our treatment of the environment has clearly improved, but
Grange argues that this better treatment is founded on a *dividend
ecology*—an environmental attitude of fear which worries that if
we do not repair the environment, it will eventually be destroyed,
and with it, ourselves. Dividend ecology, Grange believes, will eventually fail in saving the environment because it springs from the
same selfish impulse which brought on the ecological crisis in the
first place. The need is to promote a foundational ecology that fosters love and concern in relation to creatures, objects, places and
environments.

This article argues that one significant means for creating a
foundational ecology practically, especially in regard to environmental design, is Christopher Alexander's Pattern Language (Alexander, 1975, 1977, 1979, 1980, 1983–84, 1984a, 1984b, 1985, 1987;
Alexander et al., 1977; Coates et al., 1987). As Alexander defines
them, patterns are particular aspects of the physical environment
that assist in a specific experience or activity: "every place is given
its character by certain patterns of events that keep happening
there" (Alexander et al., 1977, p. 55). In *Pattern Language,* the master volume of his design approach, Alexander (Alexander et al.,
1977) identifies 253 patterns, arranged from larger to smaller environmental scale and including such design elements as *independent regions* (no. 1), *identifiable neighborhood* (14), *main gateways*
(53), *high places* (62), *intimacy gradient* (127), *windows overlooking
life* (192), and so forth. Pattern Language seeks to identify and design physical elements often present in beautiful, humane environments, and therefore helps foster a sense of place (Relph, 1981). In
that its underlying motivational force is a sense of environmental
care and concern grounded in a positive emotional impulse, Pattern
Language offers one practical means for translating feeling into action and environmental concern into environmental design.[2]

This essay examines Pattern Language's ability to join understanding and practice by presenting its use in an upper-level architectural studio at Kansas State University co-taught by the two
authors and involving ten advanced architecture students. The studio focus was the *Meadowcreek Project,* a multi-disciplinary
environmental-education center on a 1500-acre valley site in the
Ozarks region of Arkansas (figure 14.1). Now several years old,
Meadowcreek is a learning community that is also a living laboratory for the practice of "right livelihood." Meadowcreek hopes eventually to support itself economically through a balanced mix of
tuition, farming, and renewable-energy businesses, including a
sawmill and woodshop. A resident community of some fifty student

Figure 14.1. View of Meadowcreek Valley from the south looking north.

interns and fifteen permanent staff will engage in a balanced multi-disciplinary program of research, teaching and learning. As with similar experimental communities, a major aim is nurturing personal and community growth within a context of regional responsibility and sustenance (Coates, 1980).

In one sense, a foundational ecology is Meadowcreek's primary aim, and, in creating a master design for Meadowcreek, it was essential that the studio work be grounded in a set of underlying philosophical assumptions which arose from and supported a foundation ecology for the Meadowcreek site itself as well as for the larger Ozark region. At the same time, students in the studio might become more aware of a design approach that treated ecological and human needs holistically. This essay overviews the results of the Meadowcreek studio, both in terms of design and educational results. First, we discuss the design approach and resulting design proposals. Second, we examine the learning value of the studio based on students' written evaluations at the end of the semester.[3]

Meadowcreek and Pattern Language

Given the attitude of foundational ecology underlying the Meadowcreek Project, we believed that Pattern Language would be more appropriate for the studio than conventional planning methods, which typically use an aggregate, quantitative approach to implement piecemeal changes often not integrated in terms of the larger environment or place (Sieverts, 1982). Rather than a "Master Plan" established at one point in time and then "finished" in the future, Pattern Language prescribes an on-going design process in which users participate by drawing on their lived experiences and knowledge of patterns that they have helped develop as desirable for their place (Alexander, 1975, 1985). Master planning by outside "experts" is replaced by the self-conscious awareness and concern of users themselves. The designer becomes a facilitator and, ideally, the built environment eventually reflects the guiding Pattern Language agreed upon by the users (Alexander, 1975, chap. 2). To facilitate user participation in our studio, we visited Meadowcreek at the start of the term; students involved directors and staff in lengthy discussion of Meadowcreek's aims and design needs. Throughout the semester, we kept the Meadowcreek directors informed of our progress. Near the end of the term, one of the directors spent three days visiting us and reviewing student work. The design proposals overviewed here incorporate his criticisms and suggestions.

Before writing an actual Pattern Language for Meadowcreek, however, it was important to clarify the underlying philosophical assumptions of Meadowcreek, so that we could create a set of design patterns in tune with these deeper aims. Using Alexander's idea of patterns as a guide, we identified, described and symbolized Meadowcreek's essential aims, which we termed *meta-patterns*. Following the format of Pattern Language, we first established a problem statement, then provided a solution indicating practical consequences. After considerable studio discussion and debate, we arrived at the six meta-patterns described in figure 14.2: *stewardship ethic, sustainability, sense of place and region, community commitment, place as process,* and *connective education.*

As we later proceeded with actual design work, these meta-patterns were invaluable, since they provided a sighting device which kept our specific patterns in touch with the essential aims and needs of Meadowcreek. For example, sense of place and region required design patterns that incorporate the culture and ecology of the Ozarks, while community commitment suggested physical design that supports and enhances a sense of sociability and group, especially for Meadowcreek residents and staff. The meta-patterns were also valuable in that they clarified the concernful attitude of

Meadowcreek's Philosophical Foundations
Six Meta-Patterns

THE STEWARDSHIP ETHIC
Mistakenly assuming that nature is indestructible and peripheral to human existence, people often act in ways that cause irreparable damage to the environment.

Therefore: Teach people to value the land, not as a commodity, but as a community of which they are a part and for which they are responsible. Cultivate an attitude of care and restraint. Act in ways that are compatible with nature and avoid actions that are detrimental to the health of the land. Use technology to go forward, but with measured steps, so that mistakes are recognized and corrected before major damage is done.

SUSTAINABILITY
The quality of human life depends on the discovery of solutions to the global ecological crisis. Though the size of environmental problems may seem insurmountable, people can contribute to at least a partial solution by working at the local level.

Therefore: Seek to create a sustainable society that balances the needs of culture and nature. Make Meadowcreek a living demonstration of a sustainable society.

SENSE OF PLACE AND REGION
Today, few people feel a sense of place or region. They often move from place to place and have little sense of belonging or identity beyond the individual dwelling unit in which they live. People often feel alienated and homeless.

Therefore: Emphasize a sense of place and region at Meadowcreek. Establish a feeling of insideness through activities and events that foster an active community participation. Work for sensitive architectural design that strengthens a sense of belonging and rootedness. Strengthen a sense of region through programs that emphasize the Ozark's natural and cultural worlds and through environmental design that reflects the regional landscape.

COMMUNITY COMMITMENT
Participants at Meadowcreek arrive as individuals. Though drawn to Meadowcreek by common interests and goals, these participants may experience barriers that prevent them from involving themselves in the community.

Therefore: Plan Meadowcreek in a participatory way, using an approach that invites change grounded in the contributions and interests of individuals. For example, encourage participation in the design and construction of Meadowcreek.

PLACE AS PROCESS
The timeless quality of place involves a unique balance between continuity and change. Isolation of self and community can result in parochialism, while too much involvement with the outside world can undermine community coherence.

Therefore: Allow for a process of incremental change and growth at Meadowcreek. On the one hand, maintain a clear sense of community identity and purpose. On the other hand, keep open communication channels with the larger world and make use of developments that assist the aims of Meadowcreek.

CONNECTIVE EDUCATION
Modern education too often involves a fragmented and specialized knowledge that disconnects students from nature. They feel morally and emotionally apathetic toward the environment.

Therefore: Develop an educational curriculum that is interdisciplinary and multidimensional. Include programs that involve "hands-on" experience. Work to foster a harmonization between feeling and thinking, theory and practice, and life and learning.

Figure 14.2. Meta-Patterns for Meadowcreek.

foundational ecology in relation to specific themes such as self-sufficiency and environmental education.

A Pattern Language for Meadowcreek

Alexander argues that each place requires its own Pattern Language (Alexander et al., 1977, p. xxxviii). Our next task, therefore, was to generate a list of patterns for Meadowcreek, continuously making sure that they were in harmony with the meta-patterns. Our first step was to identify particular areas of the Meadowcreek site that most urgently required detailed planning. We identified four such areas: first, the "site as a whole," which needed to be considered in terms of such uses as circulation, agriculture, recreation, and environmental education; second, the "bench area," site of the conference center and the hub of Meadowcreek as a place for connective education; third, the "micro-industrial area," which would be Meadowcreek's center in terms of sustainability and self-reliance; and, fourth, "staff housing," which would provide residential space for Meadowcreek personnel and visitors.

After over a week of discussion, argument and compromise, members of the design studio generated a list of forty-nine patterns, listed in Table 14.1. The first several patterns guided design largely in terms of the site as a whole, while later patterns related to bench, micro-industrial, and housing requirements. In this article, we discuss the patterns and designs for the site as a whole, the bench, and the micro-industrial area. Housing designs are not presented, since four students from the studio continued work on residential planning after the semester ended and considerably modified the original studio proposals.[4]

1. Site Patterns

Located in the Boston Mountains of the Ozark region approximately one-hundred miles north of Little Rock, the Meadowcreek site is a three-mile valley running north to south. Its bottom lands have traditionally been used for mixed farming, while surrounding bluffs are covered with a mixed pine-hardwood forest. This site offers a variety of scenery and landforms, several of which are striking and inspirational—for example, the creek itself and the Chimneys and Pinnacle Point, both high rock structures providing scenic views of the valley. The primary patterns used to guide site design

Table 14.1.
Patterns Used for Meadowcreek

1. Degrees of Human Impact*	26. Main Building
2. Sacred Sites	27. Positive Outdoor Space
3. Site Repair	28. Building Complex
4. Activity Nodes	29. Connection to Earth
5. Hierarchy of Paths*	30. Building Edge
6. Identifiable Edges*	31. Main Entrance
7. Degrees of Publicness*	32. Quiet Back
8. Small Learning Groups	33. Entrance Transition
9. Circulation Realms	34. Edible Landscape*
10. Work Community	35. Outdoor Rooms
11. Self-Governing Groups	36. Communal Eating
12. Main Gateways	37. Small Parking Lots
13. Paths and Goals	38. Garden Growing Wild
14. Access to Water	39. Tree Places
15. Pools and Streams	40. Fruit Trees
16. High Places	41. Meditation Places*
17. Terraced Slopes	42. Master and Apprentices
18. Path Shape	43. Small Meeting Places
19. Path and Rest*	44. Small Work Groups
20. Looped Local Roads	45. Bulk Storage
21. Green Streets	46. Seat Spots
22. Something Near the Middle	47. Stair Seats
23. Activity Pockets	48. Sitting Walls
24. Shielded Parking	49. Garden Seats
25. South Facing Outdoors	

*Not originally in *Pattern Language* and written especially for Meadowcreek.

are shown in figure 14.3. These patterns preserve and strengthen the site's character by limiting and concentrating development as well as by identifying and enhancing natural features such as water, slope, and vegetation. The largest pattern, *degrees of human impact,* requires that development be concentrated around existing places and paths. This pattern is extended and clarified by others such as *sacred sites* and *site repair,* which advocate protection of special areas and construction of new structures in areas which are least pleasant and beautiful or already occupied.

To understand better the spatial significance of these eleven site patterns, a "site-design group" of four students brought the site patterns together on maps of the Meadowcreek property. This group located major new construction on the northern part of the site, an area already housing several farm buildings and dwellings. A country road paralleling the east side of Meadowcreek was marked as the major pedestrian and vehicle path for the site, and several nodes along it were chosen for various sorts of development—for

Patterns for Site

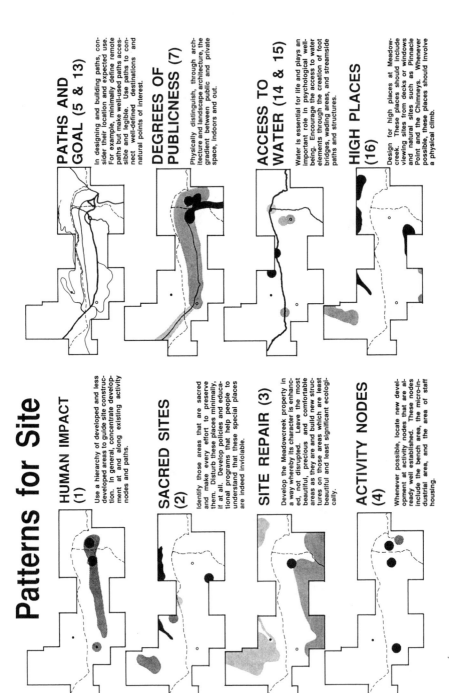

HUMAN IMPACT (1)

Use a hierarchy of developed and less developed areas to guide site construction. In general, concentrate development at and along existing activity nodes and paths.

SACRED SITES (2)

Identify those areas that are sacred and make every effort to preserve them. Disturb these places minimally, if at all. Develop policies and educational programs that help people to understand that these special places are indeed inviolable.

SITE REPAIR (3)

Develop the Meadowcreek property in a way whereby its character is enhanced, not disrupted. Leave the most beautiful, precious and comfortable areas as they are and build new structures on those areas which are least beautiful and least significant ecologically.

ACTIVITY NODES (4)

Whenever possible, locate new development at activity nodes that are already well established. These nodes include the bench area, the micro-industrial area, and the area of staff housing.

PATHS AND GOAL (5 & 13)

In designing and building paths, consider their location and expected use. For example, minimally define remote paths but make well-used paths accessible and legible. Use paths to connect well-defined destinations and natural points of interest.

DEGREES OF PUBLICNESS (7)

Physically distinguish, through architecture and landscape architecture, the gradient between public and private space, indoors and out.

ACCESS TO WATER (14 & 15)

Water is essential for life and plays an important role in psychological well-being. Encourage the access to water elements through the creation of foot bridges, wading areas, and streamside paths and structures.

HIGH PLACES (16)

Design for high places at Meadowcreek. These places should include viewing sites from decks or windows and natural sites such as Pinnacle Point and the Chimneys. Whenever possible, these places should involve a physical climb.

Figure 14.3. Key Patterns for the Meadowcreek Site Design.

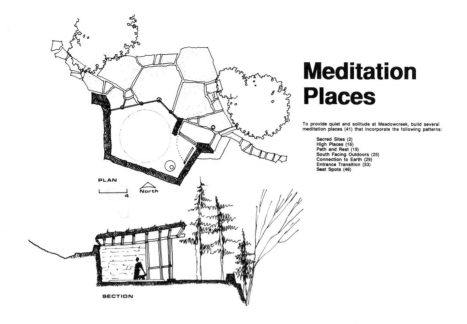

Meditation Places

To provide quiet and solitude at Meadowcreek, build several meditation places (41) that incorporate the following patterns:

Sacred Sites (2)
High Places (16)
Path and Rest (19)
South Facing Outdoors (25)
Connection to Earth (29)
Entrance Transition (33)
Seat Spots (46)

PLAN   North

SECTION

Figure 14.5. Design for a Meditation Space at Meadowcreek.

example, staff housing and recreation points. Unspoiled natural areas such as Bee Bluff, Pinnacle Point, Chimney Bluffs, Rocky Bluffs and Whipple Ridge would be disturbed as little as possible.

To illustrate how the pattern language could guide specific site development, the group designed a path to Whipple Ridge (figure 14.4). Making use of both larger and smaller patterns, this design works to create a series of places as the hiker moves up the steep slope to a lookout point at the top. Qualities of both movement and rest are enhanced through physical design to give a sense of tranquility and nature. For example, one smaller pattern is *meditation place,* which led to the design illustrated in figure 14.5. Built into the hillside and covered by an earth-covered roof, this structure is a small one- or two-person sun trap where people can collect their thoughts in the midst of nature.

2. The Bench

Located in the northern part of the site near the major road entrance to the property, the bench is the heart of Meadowcreek. It is

A Path to Whipple Ridge

DEGREES OF HUMAN IMPACT (1)
Direct development along existing areas—in this case, the old logging path to Whipple Ridge.

TREE PLACES (39)
Use trees to create enclosures, avenues, squares, and groves.

SOUTH FACING OUTDOORS (25)
Place buildings and plantings on the north side of natural open spaces.

MEDITATION PLACES (41)
Make at least one area where people can reflect and meditate.

DEGREES OF PUBLICNESS (7)
Use a spatial gradient to provide various degrees of privacy and publicness.

IDENTIFIABLE EDGES (6)
Use plantings and building elements to provide orientation and a sense of enclosure.

MAIN GATEWAYS (12)
Use plantings and building elements to reinforce transitions.

QUIET BACK (32)
Provide quiet areas apart from the trail.

HIERARCHY OF PATHS (5)
Keep the more remote parts of the trail less defined and less developed.

EDIBLE LANDSCAPE (34)
Create a landscape that works ecologically, aesthetically, and practically.

GARDEN GROWING WILD (38)
As much as possible, use plantings native to the Meadowcreek region.

PATHS AND GOALS (13)
Design new sections of the trail so that they connect natural points of interest.

SEAT SPOTS (46)
Use climate and view to position seating.

PATH SHAPE (18)
Widen the trail at various points to provide places where people can linger and rest.

HIGH PLACES (16)
Establish Whipple Ridge as a high place where newcomers, especially, can experience Meadowcreek as a whole.

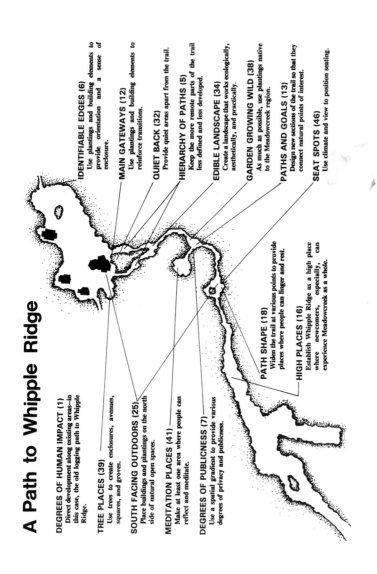

Figure 14.4. Patterns Used in Designing a Path to Ripple Ridge.

the center of educational and conference activities; existing facilities include two dormitories and conference center. The master design for the bench is shown in figure 14.6 and incorporates several goals and patterns. The first goal for the bench design was to create a network of paths that connect buildings and activities, provide vehicular access and parking, and give clear definition to a central common area. Important patterns in achieving this goal include *identifiable edges, hierarchy of paths, activity nodes, path and rest,* and *shielded parking. Identifiable edges,* for example, uses natural and human-made elements to give the bench a distinctive boundary and a sense of closure. *Path and rest* creates places along passageways to allow people to pause, taking advantage of views, breezes, sun and shade. The major aim of all patterns associated with the first goal was to unify the bench's existing and future features into a comprehensive visual and experiential whole.

A second goal of the bench design was to develop the south side of the conference center to provide more usable outdoor space and to integrate building and landscape. *South facing outdoors* is the starting point for developing this area. *Positive outdoor space* directs the use of *sitting walls* to define the space as an *outdoor room. Raised flowers, fruit trees* and *edible landscape* define edges and provide shade. Spaces formed by the *sitting walls* and *terraced slope* are directly adjacent to the conference center's indoor dining area, and they suggest the pattern of *street café,* which leads to an *outdoor amphitheater* with stage and fire pit. The amphitheater melts into the swale formed by the removal of an existing dirt pile and provides a view of the entire valley. *Connection to earth, site repair,* and *degrees of human impact* are patterns completed by the amphitheater, beyond which is an *accessible green* bounded by the forest to form an identifiable edge to the bench as a whole and complete *hierarchy of open spaces.*

The third goal guiding bench design was to improve circulation in the area. Major movement patterns run among dormitories and conference center, thus paths were laid out to connect building entrances most directly (*paths and goals*), while respecting *site repair* and *degrees of human impact.* The area between these buildings was given a spatial focus by designing a central court with sitting walls to provide an *activity node.* Running from the conference center is a pathway with two design elements to facilitate open space and sitting. First, just outside the main door, is an *outdoor entrance room* to provide sitting. Second, further along the path, is a larger open space (*outdoor room* with *sitting walls*) to provide a place for

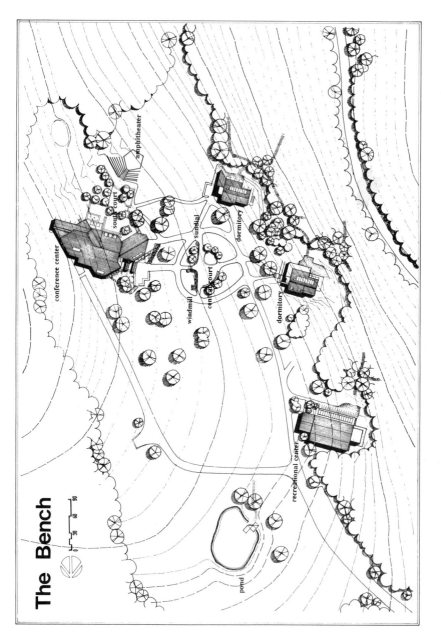

Figure 14.6. Site Plan for Meadowcreek Bench and Conference Area.

breaks from indoor activity. Vine covered structures (*trellised walk*) signal the entry to the conference center (*main entrance*) and mark transition through enclosure and texture (*entrance transition*). In accordance with *hierarchy of paths*, other walkways running from the conference center are less marked, as, for example, the woodchip path running from the rear of the conference center to the *high place* of Whipple Ridge above the bench.

3. The Micro-Industrial Area

The micro-industrial area is a central component of Meadowcreek's interest in an environmental education that is experiential. The design of this area was largely based on the two metapatterns of *sustainability* and *connective education,* as well as the pattern *work community,* which suggests that a sense of group for the micro-industrial area can be encouraged by small workplaces that have a common courtyard as their shared focus. Eventually, these workplaces will include a saw mill, woodworking shop, machine shop, granary, sorghum mill, and facilities for lumber drying and storage.

In the early stages of designing for the micro-industrial area, students made use of patterns drawn from the original set of forty-nine. After consultation with the Meadowcreek directors, however, students realized that these patterns did not consider several functional and mechanical needs. Students therefore constructed a specific pattern language for the micro-industrial area, which includes several new patterns (Table 14.2). As students refined the design, these new patterns were kept in mind but sometimes modified or bracketed because of functional or mechanical requirements. For example, *small public square* could not be developed to its full extent because of the need to run vehicular paths through the courtyard for the sorghum and saw mills. A conflict also arose with *small public square, positive outdoor space* and *south facing outdoors.* Practically, it was useful to cluster buildings around the steam tractor, since it would be the major source of rotational power for the micro-industrial area. This clustering strengthened *positive outdoor space* but hindered *south facing outdoors* and broke the courtyard into smaller, fragmented spaces lacking a sense of unity. Even with the refined pattern language for the micro-industrial area, the result was that too often functional and mechanical needs were designed without an adequate framework of patterns. Eventually, the micro-industrial group concluded that the pattern language needed

Table 14.2.
Patterns Used for Micro-Industrial Area

Self-Governing Workshops	Sheltering Roofs
Identifiable Edges	Building Edge
Main Gateway	Arcades
Entrance Transition	Edible Landscape
Master and Apprentice	Garden Growing Wild
Positive Outdoor Space	Sitting Wall
South Facing Outdoors	Access to Water
Small Public Square	Accessible Green
Courtyards That Live	Connection to Earth
Hierarchy of Space	Small Parking Lots
Activity Pockets	Shielded Parking

further refinement, incorporating technical and practical requirements as much as possible. As it was, many of these requirements were designed without supportive patterns.

In spite of these difficulties, however, Pattern Language was useful for designing the micro-industrial area in that the patterns provided a general field of guidance for planning decisions (figure 14.7). As indicated above, a primary aim of the design was to provide for vehicular circulation and power supply. This aim was satisfied by integrating vehicular traffic with the central courtyard and using the steam tractor as a building focus. A second aim was to create an environment which would support connective education. Again, the clustering of activities was an important means for achieving this second aim, since the common courtyard would provide an informal meeting place. A final goal was to provide easy accessibility to activities and machinery. This aim was achieved by providing as many buildings as possible with access to the central courtyard, which allows for convenient physical and visual access.

The Meadowcreek Studio as a Learning Experience

If a foundational ecology involves a concerned environmental sensitivity, then the designs above are one kind of evidence indicating that students developed a stronger awareness of ecological, human and place needs. Through efforts to achieve a holistic understanding of the design context, students gained a thorough picture of Meadowcreek's needs and developed the various design foci in light of that larger picture. In this regard, Pattern Language played a crucial role, since it broached the gap between the broad, philo-

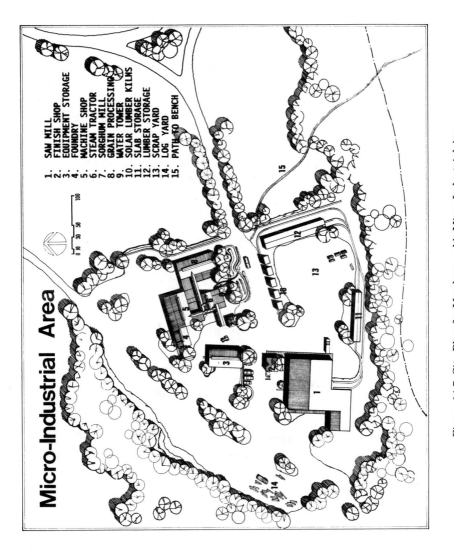

Micro-Industrial Area

1. SAW MILL
2. FINISH SHOP
3. EQUIPMENT STORAGE
4. FOUNDRY
5. MACHINE SHOP
6. STEAM TRACTOR
7. SORGHUM MILL
8. GRAIN PROCESSING
9. WATER TOWER
10. SOLAR LUMBER KILNS
11. SLAB STORAGE
12. LUMBER STORAGE
13. SCRAP YARD
14. LOG YARD
15. PATH TO BENCH

0 10 30 50 100

Figure 14.7. Site Plan for Meadowcreek's Micro-Industrial Area.

sophical qualities of foundational ecology, on the one hand, and the practical need for real-world design, on the other. Pattern Language helped the studio transcribe a wish to safeguard the environment into practical understanding which, in turn, was transcribed into design. In short, Pattern Language provides one useful means to heal the schism between theory and practice, and research and design.

This healing process is also illustrated when one examines student evaluations of the Meadowcreek studio. These reports indicate that, in terms of both substantive understanding and personal growth, the studio worked well, especially in fostering the concernful environmental sensitivity which is the heart of a foundational ecology.[5] General descriptions of the studio experience emphasized a better sense of design needs, a heightened awareness of the difficulty in harmonizing ideas and real-world needs, and a stronger ability to organize and actualize a master design. The following written observations provide an overview:

- "This studio provided me an awakening to the sensitivities of designing and how this awareness makes a space or place special."

- "This studio has provided the kind of input that I've needed to grow, not only as a designer but as a person."

- "From this studio, I've come to realize that answers can't always be found right away, and that raising questions over and over is a good way to find the right answers."

- "This studio has been an advantage to my education ... It helped me to realize how difficult it is to design for reality. I saw that complexity in a design often has to be toned down, and, most importantly, that communication is a virtue of existence."

The emphasis on communication in the last report indicates one of the most frequently mentioned value of the semester: cooperative group work. In the typical undergraduate design studio, students often work independently and competitively; each student attempts to create the best design. For most of the ten students in the studio, the Meadowcreek exercise was the first time they had shared their design efforts toward a larger end. The following reports indicate the value of cooperative efforts in the studio:

- "Being small and being together as individuals has been one of the most memorable experiences of my undergraduate education. I am sure that no other group could have done what we did in the way we did."

- "The freedom allowed to the group and the outline of the class was unlike any I had experienced in any other studio. The freedom was very nice. It made us feel like adults, put on our own to learn what we wanted and have an input as to what we wanted to do."

In terms of substantive knowledge and awareness, many themes were mentioned in the evaluations, including practice in writing, working with a real client, and becoming more sensitive to "sense of place." The work with Pattern Language was emphasized in the evaluations as a useful tool for facilitating more sensitive design. Some students did not feel completely satisfied with the approach, but all participants felt they had received some benefit:

- "As far as using the patterns, I felt our design became much richer; we seemed to become more aware of the environment and making things more human."

- "I have begun to see more pattern-related parts of buildings and that has enriched my appreciation of buildings which I had taken for granted before."

- "It wasn't until I could identify an actual design goal and formulate it clearly that I felt at all comfortable in using the patterns. Without a specific goal, they can all be considered as attractive ideas but are without practical reason."

- "Choosing and writing patterns for Meadowcreek was very productive and important work. The patterns helped us to begin and refine our design."

- "The patterns seem to have become so engrained in our thinking that we can't shut them off. Hopefully, this means we've become more in tune with what's happening around us."

- "I now catch myself doing patterns without thinking consciously about their names or what they mean."

- "The patterns were self-consciously helping each group design better than if we hadn't known the patterns at all.

In a similar way, the exercise of writing meta-patterns for Meadowcreek was mentioned as a valuable task, since it provided one means for grasping quickly the essential aims and purpose of Meadowcreek:

- "I feel the meta-pattern exercise definitely helped the group gain a feel for the underlying philosophy and ideals of Meadowcreek. I

believe that the process of finding these meta-patterns for ourselves was a large part of the profit and that if another group were
to do this task again, there might be some interesting results.
Would the patterns be the same? Would the students believe that
there is something like a meta-pattern? Would it be beneficial to
look at our meta-patterns first, or set ours aside until afterwards?"

• "Writing the meta-patterns was an important part of the semester. This task nailed down exactly Meadowcreek's ideals and goals,
which helped in programming the rest of the work. It helped me to
see what was necessary to reach the project's ideal state of
completion."

• "Working out the meta-pattern provided an anchor for making
secure the beliefs and intentions of Meadowcreek and gave us a
point of departure for design."

• "Trying to write the meta-patterns helped me to understand
Meadowcreek's goals, but I was bothered by a feeling that we were
only projecting our beliefs onto theirs, or acting as imperfect
translators. When I brought this worry up, however, it was pointed
out (rightfully) that this is all we can ever do in interpreting a client's desire."

All of the student evaluations included problems and weaknesses of the studio—its non-typical emphasis on written as well as
graphic presentation; the difficulty of our Kansas State studio's being far from the design site; the need for better site documentation;
frequent disharmony between theoretical knowledge and practical
design; occasional lack of clear direction. Some students found that
in the early part of the semester, their expectations of the studio
were much different than the actual work; they therefore had to
break out of their negative attitude, and this task took energy away
from their work.

Overall, however, the evaluations indicate that the students
gained in both knowledge and sensitivity and came to realize more
deeply the difficulty of programming for and designing effective
places. As one student explained, "I came out of this studio more
aware, more sensitive, and somewhat confused." The evaluations indicate that Pattern Language was a valuable means for balancing
thinking and doing, and designing and building. At the same time,
Pattern Language appears to have fostered a greater sensitivity for
environmental concerns, both at a local and regional level. These
conclusions support the contention that Pattern Language can be a
significant tool in promoting a foundational ecology practically.

Conclusion

The above design experience indicates that a Pattern Language approach can play a significant role in transcribing the philosophical ideals of a community into practical design requirements. Specifically, the advantages of Pattern Language are at least three. First, it allows environmental order to grow out of a series of small-scale, incremental design changes guided by a holistic planning framework. Second, Pattern Language is an approach that makes design more accessible to laypeople, allowing non-designers to participate meaningfully in shaping their built environment. Third, and in a related way, Pattern Language transforms design into a shared learning process, thereby allowing environmental design and management to become an ongoing part of the Meadowcreek curriculum. The directors of Meadowcreek acknowledged the value Pattern Language can have for clients when they wrote in an introduction to the studio's master design that the students' work:

> helped us to clarify our values, goals, assumptions, and design strategies. Their work culminated in three volumes of design materials: (1) "A Pattern Language for Meadowcreek"; (2) "The Meadowcreek Micro-Industrial Area: A Design Proposal"; and (3) "Designing for a Sense of Place: A Pattern Language for Meadowcreek." The class also prepared four physical models of the project and specific areas. To say that they sharpened our thinking is a large understatement. We hope they benefited nearly as much as we did (*Meadowcreek Notes*, 1984, p. 1).

Perhaps the major value of Pattern Language is the healing action described above: theory and practice, research and design, client and architect, natural and built environments are brought together through a sensitive tool of conceptualization. A supportive reciprocity is established between landscape and built environment and understanding and designing. In this sense, Grabow (1983) is correct when he suggests that Pattern Language marks a radically new architectural paradigm that has the potential to harmonize thinking and doing, conceptualizing and building.

In an essay discussing the practical significance of Heidegger's notion of dwelling, philosopher Michael Zimmerman (1985) argues that a foundational ecology must not be taken too easily. He suggests that Heidegger's emphasis on "letting beings be" (Heidegger, 1971) can too readily become:

a slogan to guide our planning and organizing in ways that de-
crease the impact of human activity on the biosphere. We even try
to design houses in line with what Heidegger supposedly means by
true 'dwelling' (Zimmerman, 1985, p. 247).

We must not, Zimmerman suggests here, take Heidegger's philosophy too superficially, particularly in regard to the nature of
dwelling. What is required "is more profound understanding of who
we are, so that we can behave more appropriately on earth" (ibid.,
p. 255). Alexander's Pattern Language is significant in this regard
because it founds real-world design on a deepened sensitivity of who
people are in relation to particular landscapes, environments, and
human needs. Alexander argues that we must understand how people and place mutually relate in both constructive and destructive
ways. By understanding this people-place reciprocity, the schisms
between conception and design, design and construction, thought
and practice, people and nature, expert and layperson, and so forth,
move toward harmonization. There arises a virtuous circle grounded
in balanced thinking and doing.

The design scheme for Meadowcreek provides one real-world illustration of how Pattern Language might practically contribute to
this virtuous circle. Though at the present time little of our master
design has been implemented at Meadowcreek, partly because of
funding problems, we believe strongly that our work has sensitized
the Meadowcreek staff to the crucial contribution that a plan
grounded in a foundational ecology can offer the community. At the
same time, we have come to appreciate the many practical advantages of Pattern Language, particularly its valuable facility at
keeping general aims in mind as one actualizes specific design details. In its ability to integrate philosophical and practical needs,
Pattern Language offers a powerful conceptual tool for designing
environments that both arise from and sustain a foundational
ecology.

Notes

1. We would like to express our grateful appreciation to David and Wilson Orr, the founders and the first directors of the Meadowcreek Project, for
allowing us opportunity to contribute to Meadowcreek and use the site as a
design focus. For more information, write *The Meadowcreek Project,* Fox,
Arkansas 72051. The authors would also like to thank the ten Kansas State

University students who participated in the Meadowcreek studio. These people are: Steven Hackman and Steven Lafferty, who were responsible for the site design; Stan Koehn, Tom Larson, Mark Nelson, and Daryl Rantis, responsible for the bench design; Doug Pierce and Steve Downen, responsible for the micro-industrial design; Linda Hall and Lois Justyna, responsible for bench and housing design. Without these students' interest, determination and professionalism, this article could not have been written.

2. Useful discussions of Pattern Language and its application to real-world design include Canine (1987), Carpenter (1987), Davis (1982), Filler (1983), Fromm and Bosselman (1983–84), Gallagher (1986), Grabow (1983), Mulfinger (1984, 1987), Retondo (1984), Shipsky (1984), Krakauer (1985), Fischer and Viladas (1986), Fromm (1986), Jackson (1986), Spencer (1986), Fallon and Edrington (1986–87).

3. The original plan for the Meadowcreek studio is described in Coates and Seamon, 1984b.

4. Unlike the master design for Meadowcreek, this housing has actually been constructed, and the four students participated as designer-builders, using a Pattern Language approach. A description of this housing and the students' experience as designer-builders can be found in *Meadowcreek Notes,* summer 1985, p. l0; and Downen et al., 1986, 1987.

5. Positivist evaluations of learning attempt to measure it empirically and use such devices as standardized examinations and questionnaires, control groups, predetermined statistical techniques, and so forth. From a phenomenological perspective, such exact determination of learning is impossible, since learning is multifaceted and difficult to define and describe precisely. For example, frequently, a person recognizes the full value of a learning experience only several months or years after the learning experience takes place. Here, we make use of written evaluations provided by students to identify strengths and weaknesses of the studio experience. These evaluations should not be seen as only subjective, anecdotal accounts but, rather, as a kind of descriptive "text" that can be explicated to identify more general characteristics of the studio learning process. On a phenomenology of learning, see Colaizzi, 1973.

References

Alexander, C. (1975). *The Oregon Experiment.* New York: Oxford University Press.

———. (1977). Value. *Concrete* [newsletter of the College of Environmental Design, University of California, Berkeley], *1,* 3–4, 15, (November 15).

————. (1979). *The Timeless Way of Building*. New York: Oxford University Press.

————. (1981). *The Linz Café*. New York: Oxford University Press.

————. (1983–84). Mexicali Revisited. *Places, 1*, 76–77.

————. (1985a). *The Production of Houses*. New York: Oxford University Press.

————. (1985b). Construction of the New Eishin Campus. *The Japan Architect, 340* (August): 15–35.

————. (1987). *A New Theory of Urban Design*. New York: Oxford University Press.

————, Ishikawa, S., and Silverstein, M. (1977). *A Pattern Language*. New York: Oxford University Press.

Canine, C. (1987). Building by the Book. *Harrowsmith, 3,* (March) 51–59.

Carpenter, P. (1987). Pattern Planning. *Building Ideas, 5,* (summer) 104–112.

Coates, G. J. (Ed.). (1980). *Resettling America: Energy, Ecology and Community*. Andover, Massachussetts, 1981.

Coates, G. J. and Seamon, D. (1984a). Design Plans for Meadowcreek: Promoting a Foundational Ecology Practically through Christopher Alexander's Pattern Language, *Meadowcreek Notes, 7* (summer 1984), Fox, Arkansas: Meadowcreek Project.

Coates, G. J. and Seamon, D. (1984b). Toward a Phenomenology of Place and Place Making: Interpreting Landscape, Lifeworld and Aesthetics. *Oz, 6,* 6–9.

Coates, G. J., Siepl, S. and Seamon, D. (1987). Christopher Alexander and the Nature of Architecture. *Orion Nature Quarterly, 6* (spring), 20–33.

Colaizzi, P. F. (1973). *Reflection and Research in Psychology: A Phenomenological Study of Learning*. Dubuque: Kendall/Hunt.

Davis, H. (1982). Individual Houses in Groups: The Pattern Language in a Teaching Studio. *Journal of Architectural Education, 36,* 14–19.

Downen, S., Koehn, S., Pierce, D., and Rantis, D. (1986). Architecture as Place Making: A Sustainable Farmstead and Staff Housing. *Oz, 8,* 48–51.

————. (1987). Homework in the Ozarks: Four Architecture Students Design and Build a Solar Farmhouse. *Fine Homebuilding, 37,* 70–75.

Evernden, N. (1985). *The Natural Alien*. Toronto: University of Toronto Press.

Fallon, R. and Edrington, D. (1986–87). Working with *A Pattern Language, Fine Homebuilding, 36,* 51–55.

Filler, M. (1983). Zen and the Art of Building Design. *TWA Ambassador, 9,* 53–63.

Fischer, T. and Viladas, P. (1986). Harmony and Wholeness: Christopher Alexander, *Progressive Architecture* (June), 92–103.

Foltz, B. V. (1984). On Heidegger and the Interpretation of Environmental Crisis. *Environmental Ethics, 6,* 321–338.

Fromm, D. (1986). An Approach to Wholeness. *Architectural Review, 181,* 24–32.

——— and Bosselman, P. (1983–84). Mexicali Revisited: Seven Years Later. *Places, 1,* 78–90.

Gallagher, N. (1986). Coming Home: The Making of a House. *Image* (April 27), 30–34, 50.

Grabow, S. (1983). *Christopher Alexander: The Search for a New Paradigm in Architecture*. Boston: Oriel Press.

Grange, J. (1977). On the Way Toward Foundational Ecology. *Soundings, 60,* 135–49.

Heidegger, M. (1971). Building Dwelling Thinking. In *Poetry, Language, Thought* (pp. 145–161). New York: Harper and Row.

Jackson, N. (1986). On the Edge of the Bay: JSW. *Architectural Review, 181,* 33–39.

Krakauer, J. (1985). A Clean, Well-Lighted Place. *New Age Journal, 2,* 40–45; 74–75.

Meadowcreek Notes, 7 (summer 1984), Fox, Arkansas: Meadowcreek Project.

——— . *8* (summer 1985), Fox, Arkansas: Meadowcreek Project.

Mulfinger, D. (1984). Shaping a Home of One's Own. *Architecture Minnesota, 10,* 42–43.

——— . (1987). Putting *A Pattern Language* to Work. *Fine Homebuilding, 38,* 49–53.

Norberg-Schulz, C. (1985). *The Concept of Dwelling*. New York: Rizzoli.

Polkinghorne, D. (1983). *Methodology for the Human Sciences*. Albany, New York: SUNY Press.

Relph, E. (1976). *Place and Placelessness.* London: Pion.

———. (1981). *Rational Landscapes and Humanistic Geography.* London: Croom Helm.

———. (1984). Seeing, Thinking, and Describing Landscapes. In T. Saarinen, D. Seamon, and J. Sell (Eds.), *Environmental Perception and Behavior.* Chicago: University of Chicago, pp. 209–224.

Retondo, P. (1984). An Uncommon Bench: A Small Building by Christopher Alexander and Associates. *CoEvolution Quarterly* (fall), pp. 78–85.

Seamon, D. (1982). The Phenomenological Contribution to Environmental Psychology. *Journal of Environmental Psychology, 2,* 119–140.

———. (1985). Heideggerian Thinking and Christopher Alexander's *Pattern Language,* paper presented at the annual meetings of the Environmental Design Research Association (EDRA), New York City, June.

———. (1987). Phenomenology and Environment-Behavior Research. In G. T. Moore and E. Zube (eds.), *Advances in Environment, Behavior and Design,* vol. 1 (pp 3–27). New York: Plenum.

———. and Mugerauer, R. (eds.). (1985). *Dwelling, Place and Environment: Towards a Phenomenology of Person and World.* New York: Columbia University Press.

Shipsky, J. (1984). Christopher Alexander: Theory and Practice. *Architecture, 74,* 54–63.

Sieverts, T. (1982). Image and Calculation in Urban Planning, *Daidalos* (4), 86–100.

Spense, R. (1986). Burgess Entrances. *Architectural Review, 181,* 40–43.

Spiegelberg, H. (1982). *The Phenomenological Movement: A Historical Introduction.* Dordrecht: Martinus Nijhoff.

Zimmerman, M. (1983). Toward a Heideggerian Ethos for Radical Environmentalism. *Environmental Ethics, 5,* 99–131.

———. (1985). The Role of Spiritual Discipline in Learning to Dwell on Earth. In D. Seamon and R. Mugerauer (eds.). *Dwelling, Place and Environment.* New York: Columbia University Press, pp. 247–256.

Contributors

Gary J. Coates is a Professor of Architecture at Kansas State University. He is an architect and editor of *Resettling America: Energy, Ecology and Community* (Andover, Massachusetts: Brick House Publishing, 1981). He is interested in Christopher Alexander's Pattern Language as one means for harmonizing formal and functional approaches to environmental design. Currently, he is writing a book on *The Architecture of Eric Asmussen.*

Kimberly Dovey is a Senior Lecturer and Associate Dean of Research at the Department of Architecture and Building at the University of Melbourne. He has a Ph.D. in Architecture from the University of California, Berkeley. His scholarly interests focus on a phenomenological approach to environmental design and place evaluation. His current research explores the relationship among phenomenology, postmodernism and social theory.

Karsten Harries is Professor of Philosophy at Yale University. He has written widely on art, aesthetics, and architecture. His books include *The Meaning of Modern Art* (Evanston, Illinois: Northwestern University Press, 1968) and *The Bavarian Rococo Church* (New Haven, Connecticut: Yale University Press, 1983).

Randolph T. Hester, Jr. is Professor and Chairman of the Department of Landscape Architecture at the University of California, Berkeley, and a principal in the firm, Community Development by Design. His research and writing use qualities of lifestyle and place to inspire landscape design, grassroots planning and community development. His books include *Planning Neighborhood Space with People* (New York: Van Nostrand Reinhold, 1984) *Community Design Primer* (Mendorino, California: Ridge Times, 1990), and *The*

Meaning of Gardens, edited with Mark Francis (Cambridge, Massachusetts: MIT Press, 1990). His built projects have won national and international honors that include the Virginia Dare Award, the National Trust for Historic Preservation Trust Award, the All-American City Award, and the American Society of Landscape Architects Honor and Merit Awards.

Catherine Howett is a Professor in the School of Environmental Design at the University of Georgia in Athens, Georgia. She was a 1984–1986 Fellow of the Bunting Institute of Radcliffe College, Harvard University, and received the 1988 Bradford Williams medal of the American Society of Landscape Architects. She is currently a Contributing Editor of *Landscape Architecture.* Her essays on the history and theory of nineteenth- and twentieth-century American landscape architecture have appeared frequently in such journals as *Landscape, Places,* and *Landscape Journal.*

Clare Cooper Marcus is a Professor in the Departments of Architecture and Landscape Architecture at the University of California, Berkeley. Trained in cultural geography and city planning, she has lectured and done consulting in the United States, Canada, Great Britain, Australia and China. Her areas of interest include medium-density housing, urban open space, children's environments, post-occupancy evaluation of designed settings, design guidelines, and the psychological meanings of home and garden. She has written *Easter Hill Village: Some Social Implications of Design* (New York: The Free Press, 1975), which received a National Endowment for the Arts Award for Exemplary Design Research. Most recently, she has written, with Wendy Sarkissian, *Housing as if People Mattered: Site Design Guidelines for Medium-Density Family Housing* (Berkeley: University of California Press, 1986); and, with Carolyn Francis, *People Places: Design Guidelines for Urban Open Space* (New York: Van Nostrand Reinhold, 1990).

Robert Mugerauer is an Associate Professor in the School of Architecture at the University of Texas at Austin. Educated in intellectual history and philosophical anthropology, he is interested in a hermeneutics of the ordinary landscape. He has published in philosophy, cultural geography, planning, architecture and literary theory and criticism. With David Seamon, he has edited *Dwelling, Place, and Environment: Toward a Phenomenology of Person and World* (New York: Columbia University Press, 1985). His most recent book is *Heidegger's Language and Thinking* (Atlantic Highlands, N.J.: Humanities Press, 1988).

Joan Nogué i Font is a Professor of Human Geography at the University of Girona (Catalonia, Spain). He has written *Una lectura geografico-humanista del paisatge de la Garrotxa* [*The Landscape of Garrotxa: A Humanistic Approach*] (Girona: University of Girona Press, 1985), *La percepcio del bosc* [*The Perception of Forest*] (Girona: Diputacio de Girona, 1986), and *Territorial Dimensions of Nationalism* (Barcelona: El Llamp, 1991). He has been a post-doctoral fellow in Geography at the University of Wisconsin, Madison, and is currently doing research on the history of geographical thought in Spain.

Edward Relph is a Professor of Geography and Chair of the Division of Social Sciences at Scarborough College in the University of Toronto. He is has written numerous articles on phenomenological geography and is the author of *Place and Placelessness* (London: Pion, 1976), *Rational Landscapes and Humanistic Geography* (London: Croom Helm, 1981) and *The Modern Urban Landscape* (Baltimore: Johns Hopkins Press, 1987).

Mark Riegner teaches in the Environmental Studies Program at Prescott College in Prescott, Arizona. He received his Ph.D. in ecology and evolution from the State University of New York at Stony Brook. He has published articles on ecology and animal morphology in, among other places, *Orion Nature Quarterly,* and is currently writing a book on wading birds of North American wetlands.

David Seamon is an Associate Professor of Architecture at Kansas State University. Trained as a geographer and environment-behavior researcher, he is interested in a phenomenological approach to environmental experience, place, and design as place making. He is author of *A Geography of the Lifeworld* (New York: St. Martin's, 1979) and is currently writing a book on longing, belonging and a phenomenological ecology.

He is editor of the *Environmental and Architectural Phenomenology Newsletter.*

Murray Silverstein lives in Berkeley, California and is a partner in Jacobson Silverstein Winslow Architects. He received his Bachelor of Architecture from the University of California, Berkeley, in 1967. His professional life has been a mix of practice, writing, teaching and research. His books include *A Pattern Language* and *The Oregon Experiment,* with co-authors at the Center for Environmental Structure in Berkeley. His recent articles include a study of Rudolf Schindler's King Road House in Los Angeles. Silverstein has taught in the Architecture Departments at the University of Washington and the University of California, Los Angeles and Berkeley. He recently wrote, with Max Jacobson and Barbara Winslow, *The Good House: Contrast as a Design Tool* (Newtown, Connecticut: Tauton Press, 1990).

Ronald Walkey practices architecture in Vancouver and is an Associate Professor in the School of Architecture at the University of British Columbia, where he teaches design and urban history. He worked at the Center for Environmental Structure in Berkeley, California, and has used Pattern Language as the basis for several innovative inner-city projects in Vancouver. He currently is Co-Director of the Urban Projects Workshop, a design atelier that facilitates place making and the implementation of incremental development in urban environments.

Index